Best wishes to Kate and Charles

Hope you enjoy reading it as
much as I enjoyed researching it.

Bob Thompson

HORSE GAMES

One man's search for the tribal
horse contests of Asia and Africa

Bob Thompson

Merlin Unwin Books

Typeset in 12 point Minion Pro by Merlin Unwin

Printed by Nutech Print Services

SUE

for accepting my travels without complaint,
looking after the sheep, the farm and my horses.
Without you, my expeditions would
have been impossible.

Contents

Acknowledgements

Vanessa, thank you for all your time, help and friendship.
Roger Field, thank you for your unwavering belief in *Horse Games*.

Always involved with horses in one way or another, Bob Thompson (right) in a hunter chase at Towcester, where he eventually came third.

CHAPTER ONE

Afghanistan: The King's Buzkashi

We make it with less than five minutes to spare. I have latched on to a French TV crew, here to film the buzkashi games in Afghanistan which are being held to celebrate the King's Birthday. A flustered guard at the entrance to the Royal Pavilion is checking press passes. I don't have one, but the crew pile me up with equipment and I'm waved through.

The best way to the press enclosure is through the Royal Pavilion and then on down the steps which the King will descend to present medals to the winners. The Pavilion floor is strewn with carpets, and at the front, overlooking the pitch, are some plush red armchairs, a large sofa and a low ornate gilt table. To the rear, under the languidly flapping awning, are three rows of straight-backed chairs for the lesser nobility. There is an uninterrupted view of the pitch, which is surrounded on three sides by cars, buses, lorries – anything a spectator can stand on to get a better view. Either side of the Pavilion are stands for lesser dignitaries and foreigners.

We go down the steps to the press enclosure. It is in a slight fold in the ground below the stone-walled front of the Royal Pavilion, cordoned off from the pitch by a thin red cord tied to some flimsy stakes. It is full of photographers and cine-camera crews, all waiting for the arrival of our own Princess Alexandra, who is the guest of Crown Prince Ahmed Shah, standing in for his father, King Zahir Shah.

Buzkashi (dragging the goat) is the adopted national game of Afghanistan. Every year, eight teams of twelve horsemen come to Kabul from the northern provinces to take part in a knock-out competition on the King's Birthday. The buz today is a beheaded calf weighing about 30 kilos. It has to be picked up, carried round a marker flag at the far end of the pitch, and brought back to be deposited in the team's scoring circle. There are two scoring circles, each marked with a pennant the colour of the team's jackets.

We are only thirty yards from the circles, and can clearly see the buz which has been placed on the ground between them, ready for the start of the first game. Each game lasts half an hour.

Drawn up in a line across the pitch are the eight teams from the Northern provinces who will compete in the championship. Only the best players, called chapendoz, represent their areas. In front of them are their team captains, in chapans (long striped coats) and turbans, and in front of them is a magnificently moustachioed army officer with immaculately polished brown boots.

Under a pale sky the excited chatter of the locals lining the pitch carries to the stands. Some members of the Royal Family and nobility have already taken their seats. In the distance there is the wail of sirens. The band strikes up and the soldiers guarding the Pavilion present arms. The moustachioed officer salutes and everyone in the stands gets to their feet as the Royal party arrives.

I take a couple of photographs before Princess Alexandra gets to her seat. All around me cameras click and cines whirr. Her outfit is very much Ascot, a blue and white check dress, but I think what she is about to see will be far more exciting. Once the Royal party are seated, the officer drops his salute and peels off to one side.

Drums roll and the line of horsemen advances to the edge of the scoring circles, where they halt. The team captains bow their heads to the Crown Prince, then all the teams wheel away except for the centre ones who form a loose circle round the buz. The two team captains

2

join the officer who is standing slightly to one side.

Red and blue are playing first. The two teams are dressed identically except for the colour of their quilted jackets, which are tied at the waist by a piece of cloth. They have quilted trousers tucked into heavy, calf-length boots, and a rolled goatskin hat held on with a piece of string tied under the chin. (Only chapendoz wear this kind of hat.)

The Crown Prince signals to the officer. He barks a command and pandemonium breaks loose round the buz. The riders push forward, their horses rearing, hooves thrashing the air above the carcass. A chapendoz on a smaller stocky horse pushes his way through the flailing hooves, leans down in an attempt to grab the buz, but fails to get a grip and his horse retreats. Several others try without success.

Suddenly a blue player, holding a leg of the buz with two hands, breaks free and rides straight towards the press pit. A team mate grabs his bridle to turn him as I join the panicky scramble back to the wall. The white stakes are sent flying as the red cord briefly wraps round one of the legs of the carcass. Somehow no-one is trampled, but a camera on a tripod disappears under the galloping hooves.

Feeling lucky to be in one piece, I resume my old position as the play moves up the pitch. It is difficult to see in the jumble of horses'

The King's Buzkashi: a panorama of the pitch with the foothills of the Hindu Kush in the background.

quarters and legs who is in possession. Only the scattered stakes and mangled tripod tell of the brief foray into the press pit and how close some of us came to being trampled.

A soldier runs out to retrieve the red cord.

'That was a bit close,' says a photographer next to me, his hands shaking as he replants his tripod.

Some of the photographers are already back behind their eyepieces searching for breathtaking images, but for me the play is already out of the range of my small telephoto lens, so I watch it through my father's Second World War field glasses.

'Who do you work for?' asks the photographer as he settles behind his camera.

'*Horse and Hound*'. I can't think of any other horse magazine off the top of my head, and I was doing a piece for them in Pakistan.

'Never heard of it. British?'

''Yes, and you?'

'*Time Life*. My mate in the stands is writing a piece about the King's Birthday Games, while I take the pictures.'

He looks me up and down.

'What is, what's the name? I see… *Horse and Hound*? You're doing something for them in Pakistan?'

I can tell by the tone of his voice he doesn't believe me.

Tremendous grip is needed to keep hold of the buz. The red cord (visible around the horse's legs and around the buz) was intended to keep the players out of the press area!

'Not having any luck,' I give him a rueful grin. 'I wanted to go to Gilgit in the Karakorams. They have an ancient form of mountain polo I wanted to see before it dies out, but they've closed the area because of the recent Indo-Pakistan war.'

At the far end of the pitch the play weaves backwards and forwards as first one team, then the other gains control of the buz.

'Then I tried to get into Manipur on the Indo-

At the King's Buzkashi: acrobatic riding, trying to pull the buz away from an opponent.

Burmese border where they play the forerunner of modern international polo, but they're not allowing foreigners in because of civil unrest.'

'Doesn't sound as if you had much luck.'

'At least I'm here now, and seeing this.' But I feel frustrated because I'm not seeing much of the game as the play is too far away to see what is happening. Even the cheering at the other end of the pitch does nothing to inform us which team has the buz.

'True,' he says adjusting his telephoto, 'good luck with whatever it is you are looking for.'

As the play comes back towards us a Red and a Blue each hold a leg of the buz and are leaning out, parallel to the ground, as they desperately try to wrest it from their opponent. Team-mates are leading their horses as they struggle, while others use their whips on their protagonists' mounts. Suddenly the Red sits up and lets go, and the horse of the Blue rider overbalances and crumples.

'Geez, did you see that?' asks *Time Life*.

'Yes.' But they are still too far away for my puny telephoto.

'I got the whole damned thing,' he says ecstatically. 'It'll make one hell of a spread.'

I glance at him. He is swiftly and smoothly loading another film, none of my flustered fumbling.

Suddenly they are much closer. A Blue on a small horse scoops up the buz at a canter. He lets his horse balance itself against the weight, before weaving through the other players. He is fast approaching the scoring circle when a Red rides him off and once again we have to cower against the wall.

In the chaos the carcass is dropped into the Red circle.

A trumpet blares and the crowds cheer. A soldier drags the buz to the start point and, at the command of the officer, play begins again.

They are halfway up the pitch when the trumpet sounds once more.

Play slowly subsides as the team captains ride among the players to say the game is over.

The Red who was carrying the buz gallops back down the pitch, one hand on the reins, the other gripping the carcass, which he has clamped between the saddle and his knee. He is holding a front leg and the calf's tail bounces on the baked brown grass. He does a wide loop between us and the scoring circles, then drops the buz exactly on the start point. The spectators roar their approval as he rides off past the Black and Beige teams on their way to the start.

Beige are clearly the better team, scoring two goals within a quarter of an hour. The battling is particularly fierce during the next start and two Black horses go down under the onslaught. In the ensuing chaos a Beige horse falls over one of the downed horses and the rider is catapulted into the centre of the mêlée.

A Black makes a break and the rest of the players stream after him. The two dismounted Black riders walk unsteadily over to their horses, but the Beige player lies motionless.

An ambulance, with a flashing yellow light and siren wailing, drives flat out over the rough ground towards the fallen player.

The whirr of cine cameras and click of stills ceases as the vehicle slides to a halt sending up a cloud of dust, obscuring the play at the far end of the pitch. After the briefest of checks, the unconscious player is rolled onto a stretcher.

The noise of photography begins again. A badly injured player will show the readers just how barbaric the game is. Cynically, I can't help thinking that if he dies, a photograph of him being carried off mortally

Riding over the dropped buz. The ones at the back are going slowly so that they can more easily pick up the buz.

injured will be worth far more than if he lives. Watching the ambulance race back over the bumps, I pray that he is unconscious, because the bouncing would make it an incredibly painful journey.

'Not again!' *Time Life*, picking up his camera, retreats to the comparative safety of the wall.

Two Beige horsemen, each holding a leg, are galloping flat out towards the scoring circles with the rest of the players strung out behind them.

Although the horsemen fill my lens, I stay put along with several other photographers. If I can just get one good shot of them dropping the buz – I don't bloody believe it! My camera won't wind on, I've run out of film.

The two players slow their horses and time their drop so that the carcass lands well within their scoring circle. The chasing group slows to a trot. White flecks of sweat spatter the horses' necks and their heaving flanks. One horse, which circles in front of me, has bloody foam coming from its mouth where the crude snaffle bit has cut it. They wait as the buz is dragged to the starting circle.

'Want a bet that Beige will score again in this game?' *Time Life* asks, as he repositions his camera.

I shake my head as I search my bag for an unused colour film. There aren't any. Damn. I carefully load a black and white film as the game starts again with undiminished ferocity. Each time the buz is picked up, it is torn from the rider's grasp. The end comes before they reach the turning flag. Most of the riders dismount and lead their tired horses off the field. A Black player walks back with the buz draped across his saddle. He drops it at the start, then jogs off the field as the next two teams come out.

The Beige team from Taloquan wins the final with a single goal in a hard-fought game, in which one player and two horses have to go off because of injury.

Time Life remarks he's got some good, though not great, pictures. I use up the rest of my film on the Prince presenting medals to the players.

The spectators, who stay to cheer the heroic horsemen, are held back until the Crown Prince's convoy departs with flashing lights and wailing siren.

It is cold in the back of the French TV crew's truck as it creeps through the traffic towards Kabul. It is two hours until sunset and the first snows tinge the tops of the surrounding mountains. The crew kindly drop me off at the Afghan Tour office, where the man behind the desk says there will be two days of games in the Kabuli stadium starting the day after tomorrow.

I ask where the players stay and if it is possible to talk to them.

He shakes his head and mumbles something about them not liking tourists. When I start to question him further he looks at his watch and scribbles something on a piece of paper, saying to hand it to a taxi driver, then shoos me out before locking the office door.

In the Horsemen's Tents

The following morning the taxi driver drops me off outside a factory. I check the address with him, but he insists that it is the place written on the piece of paper. I scour the area, but there is no sign of tents or horses anywhere. To make things more difficult, it is a holiday, so there is no one about, not even a security guard outside the high metal-sheeted gates. I can't even see anywhere that looks like a stadium, so decide to walk along the road until I meet someone.

I spot a man coming out of an alley and run to catch him before he disappears into one of the family compounds. He takes me round the back of the factory and points to a squat building about half a mile away across some playing fields. I stride over the sparse grass, enjoying the increasing heat of the sun.

There are some tourists about, but they are standing well back from the horses, and I can see why. Several horsemen carrying whips are keeping guard.

I look at the horses, most of which are covered in heavy felt rugs from their ears to their tails. A couple are being groomed, while some are picking at strands of hay on the ground in front of where they are tied.

I notice one horse on the end of the line keeps resting its near fore.

While the nearest guard is distracted by an American couple trying to give the horses sugar lumps, I saunter over to the horse resting its leg. Squatting beside it I run my thumb and forefinger down the tendon at the back of the leg. There is a slight swelling and some warmth around it.

Someone comes up behind me, but I don't look round, just run my hand down the off fore – beautifully cool. I look up to see an old man in a chapan standing behind me. I stand and face him, feeling very apprehensive.

'Leg not good,' I say in my bad Dari (the ancient Persian spoken in Afghanistan).

This was a turning point in my Afghani trip. Had I not spotted that the horse's leg needed attention, the rest would not have followed.

He pushes me out of the way and squats beside the horse. Carefully he runs his hand down the near fore until he comes to the swollen bit, then tests the off fore. Standing up he nods to me, then shouts for a groom. Once the horse is standing with its leg in a bucket of water, with the groom pouring more cold water over it, the baba (old man) unbelievably beckons me into his tent.

In a thrilled daze, I remember to take my boots off before entering and place them next to a row of sandals made from car tyres. The floor is covered with brightly coloured gilims strewn over a layer of rushes. The other occupants watch as I am guided to the bottom end of the baba's bed mat.

My host reclines on a pile of rolled bedclothes at the top end, next to the wall of the tent. The first thing he does is to apologise for there being no refreshment – it is Ramadan and they will not eat or drink until sunset.

The others gather round me, some squatting, some sitting, their strong Asiatic faces thrusting forward as they all question me at the same time. I try to answer them, at least those I think I can understand.

'American? Français?'

'Inglestan.'

'Are there horses there?'

'Yes.'

'Do they play buzkashi?'

'No.'

'Why not?'

'Because it's different there.'

'Is it far? How many days' ride?'

'Many weeks.'

'It is too far.'

The questions slow, and the baba asks if I saw the buzkashi yesterday. I explain where I was and how difficult it was to see exactly what was happening because the play was so far away. He moves to rest on his right arm so that he can watch the horses through the tent opening while we talk. He says tomorrow and the day after I will be able to get much closer in the stadium and also will be able to move around to watch from different places.

I ask how the chapendoz train themselves and the horses, but his reply is interrupted by more Westerners trying to give apples to the horses.

Two men grab their whips, which consist of a handle about 18 inches long attached to a plaited leather thong the same length and dash out to drive the tourists away.

To think that could so easily have been me.

The autumn sun flickers on the thin metal bands securing the thong to the handle and the bewildered visitors speedily retreat to their guide, whom they berate for not telling them the players didn't want them petting the horses.

The whips remind me of a question I have been meaning to ask. It is something which came up in a documentary on buzkashi, that neither fitted the way the game is played nor the demeanour of the players.

'Do you deliberately hit the other players with your whips?' I ask.

The baba leans forward, reaches under his bedroll, and pulls out his whip. Looking me straight in the eye he raises his whip, then turns towards me so that he is within striking distance.

'What will you do if I hit you?'

'Hit you back,' I reply with more assurance than I feel.

He puts his whip back under his bedroll. Then looks at me, smiles and shrugs.

'So there would be no buzkashi.'

'Tashakur,' I thank him. I knew I was right! I always said the players would be constantly fighting each other rather than playing, but the documentary-makers like purveying their ideas of the savagery of the game.

Doing my best with my laboured Dari, I ask about the training and feeding of the horses. My genial host does his best both to understand what I'm asking and to reply in the simplest way. A gust of wind blows some dust into the tent, and pushes out the hot air building up under the canvas. Outside the groom takes the horse's foot out of the bucket, stands and stretches.

My throat is parched and the baba, calm as ever, awaits my next question. He must be as thirsty as me, but has until this evening before he can drink anything and I feel it would be imposing on him to continue. I thank him for his hospitality and ask if I can return tomorrow with an interpreter.

He nods.

I rise, put my hand over my heart, bow slightly and thank him again before leaving.

'Did I see you come out of one of the team tents?'

I turn. The speaker is a woman in her late thirties, with curly blond hair, a patterned sweater and loose dark trousers.

'Yes.'

'I thought they didn't talk to tourists, it's just that I'm very interested in the horses.'

She is definitely not English. I try to place the accent. Yes. Scandinavian. I remember it from being on an army exercise in Norway.

She quick-fires so many questions that I'm only halfway through answering one before she is onto the next. I explain that my Dari isn't good enough to understand everything that I was told, but that I'm coming back tomorrow with an interpreter.

The barrage ceases and she apologises for not introducing herself. She says despite being in Kabul for several years she has never met anyone who has been invited into the tents before.

I don't quite catch her first name, but the second is Ungaro and she is the wife of the Italian chargé d'affaires. She and Carlo, her husband, live in Kabul and love riding. They share a horse which is stabled in the outskirts. She asks about me.

I say I've ridden since I was seven and have recently left the British Household Cavalry, and am here to find out all I can about buzkashi.

She gives me a lift back to my hotel in her chauffeur-driven embassy car. It is wonderful to meet a fellow enthusiast, especially one with good connections. She knows she would never be allowed into one of the tents because she is a woman, but asks if we can meet at the stadium so that I can tell her all I've learned while watching the buzkashi.

I agree and the following morning I go to the main Afghan Tour office to collect an interpreter. I telephoned first thing to arrange it, but when I get there nothing has been organised. They want to see I can pay in cash before contacting the interpreter. When they ask for half as much again as originally quoted on the telephone I demand to see the manager.

He apologises for the misunderstanding and orders a glass of tea for me while I wait for the interpreter, Abdullah, to arrive. He is a slim young man with a scraggly beard, wearing a western suit, with his shirt

Afghan farmers who have come down from the hills with their last few animals to get relief grain because of the drought.

Galloping flat out towards the press pit for a second time!

tails hanging down to just above his knees.

In the taxi on the way to the tents I ask if he knows anything about horses. He says, in passable English, that his uncle lives in the mountains and the only way to get to his house is by horse. He has only ridden a few times, but has seen the film *The Horsemen* and would like to find out more about buzkashi, because he could then explain it to the tourists.

I realise it might be difficult with the technical information, but I'll get far more with him than I would on my own.

When we arrive the baba I met yesterday is checking his team's horses. First they are trotted past him, then he checks them for sore backs and girth galls before running his hands over their legs. I pull my cheap, locally bought suede jacket round me to keep out the wind as we watch the inspection. There is no sun, just scudding clouds and a touch of moisture in the air.

'Salaam Aleikum,' I greet the baba with an inclination of my head and my hand over my heart. Without waiting I begin the ritual greeting – 'are you well, and your children, your family and your team and horses', while he makes similar enquiries.

I introduce Abdullah and see the lines of the baba's face turn to a scowl. Of course, how stupid of me! Abdullah is a Pathan and there is long-standing distrust between the Asiatic people of the north and the hook-nosed tribesmen of the south.

Luckily Abdullah gives a long formal greeting, while showing none of the arrogance for which his people are well known.

The baba invites us in. The tent is empty besides us. The horsemen are either exercising or tending to their horses.

He points to where we are to go, then sits on his bedroll facing us. What would I like to know?

Everything.

Abdullah glances at me.

I open my note book. Last night I wrote three pages of questions, but where to start? I look up, they are both waiting expectantly.

'How do you train your horses?'

'Do you mean how do we get the horses strong or how do we teach a young horse?' the baba asks.

'Teach a young horse,' and so the three-way discussion starts. I soon realise how long it is going to take, especially as Abdullah doesn't understand all the questions or answers, so that I have to keep clarifying various points.

Most of the best horses are from the union of a top buzkashi stallion and a racing mare by a buzkashi stallion. Mares are raced at special races and only those with the greatest speed and stamina are selected. They are mated every other year so that they get a chance to recover and are in the best condition to breed a strong foal.

'Is there any betting?'

Abdullah is shocked that I should ask such a question, as it is against their religion, and is taken aback when the baba shrugs his shoulders and says, 'Of course.'

Colts run free until their fifth winter when they are broken to the saddle and ridden on quietly till the spring, before being turned out for the summer. In their sixth winter they are got fit with long, slow exercise before being put into a game. If an animal is willing to fight for its place when being jostled and bumped by the other horses, it is kept in training. Otherwise they are sold or put to work on the owner's farm.

A chapendoz, who has come in and is sorting out his kit in the corner of the tent, butts in to say poorer people often buy the turned away horses in the hope they will become braver when they are fully mature. He has such a one.

The baba shakes his head and says it is rarely so.

They practise picking up a sack filled with straw and later one covered with a skin so that the horse gets used to the smell of a dead animal. Finally they slowly increase the weight of the buz until it weighs between 30 and 35 kilos.

'He says when a horse is running it is taught to turn away from the side the buz is being carried,' Abdullah tells me.

'Why?'

'Because otherwise the weight of the buz would unbalance it when galloping.'

The baba continues. In the seventh winter they are taught to walk into the melee on their hind legs. It is not until their eighth year that they take an active part in the game, but are counted as novices for several more years. The best horses are in their teens and go on into their early twenties. To me this is really old, because a lot of the competition horses I know in the UK are considered past it once well into their teens.

'Have you had a favourite horse?'

'Yes,' the old man pauses as he smiles to himself. 'I had a horse who bent his knees.'

Abdullah and I look blankly at each other.

'A horse that bends its knees is a gift from Allah, may He be praised,' he raises his hands out of his lap, palms uppermost. 'It makes it easy for the rider to pick up the buz, but it cannot be taught. It is born with it.'

We nod and I glance at my notes.

'How do you get a horse fit?'

Abdullah looks at me questioningly.

'How do you make a horse strong enough to take part in a game?' I venture.

'First walk and trot over long distances. Then we increase the speed. When a horse's mane is difficult to pull out it is strong enough. When it is ready we ride part of the time at a canter and part at a gallop. This way we can cover long distances. It makes it used to suddenly increasing speed and it is good for the breathing. To gallop too much on rough ground will injure the horse.'

This must be what we'd call interval training, like we did when training to row at the Henley Regatta. It builds up stamina, though I don't know of any racehorse trainers who use it in the UK.

16

Playing in the confines of the Kabuli football stadium. This is where in the Taliban era many people were publicly executed.

Time has slipped by and the tent is beginning to warm up. My throat is dry and for a second I feel sorry for Abdullah who is having to speak twice as much as the baba or me. Several of the occupants have entered quietly and are reclining on their bedrolls listening to the questioning.

'And the training of the players?'

Abdullah licks his lips, moistening them before translating again. Children start by picking up bags of straw while sitting on a donkey. At ten they are allowed to ride on the edge of the game to see what happens, learn the different moves and the unwritten rules. The baba says it is dangerous for someone who doesn't understand the game to take part. Accidents happen when someone who knows too little gets in the way.

Behind us there is a murmur of consent.

Young men in their late teens take part when they fully understand the moves. Players come into their prime in their late twenties and early thirties, when the combination of strength, skill, understanding and bravery are at their height. Those in their late teens to early twenties are often too rash, while those in their forties, many of whom have had several injuries, are no longer as bold as they once were.

The start of a game in the stadium. The buz is the black lump on the ground amongst the horses' hooves. Note the horse on the right, walking in on its hind legs.

A groom appears in the tent entrance and says something. The chapendoz stand up.

'It is time for them to get dressed,' says Abdullah.

I start to get up, but the baba signals for me to stay.

'He says you must see what they wear.'

I turn to watch.

First they pull over their shalwar kameez (Afghan pyjamas), a pair of padded trousers, which reach halfway down their calves. Next they wrap woollen bandages round their feet and calves. Over the bandages are pulled thickly woven socks and, finally, a pair of sturdy, calf-length leather boots. Their padded jackets are tied with a sash and their rolled goatskin hats with a piece of string under their chins. Finally they tuck their whips into their sashes and pull on leather mittens, which both help them keep a grip on the buz and protect the back of their hands.

We follow the baba out as he goes to watch his team mounting.

I look at my watch. Hell, I'm already late for Mrs Ungaro. I thank our host and ask if we can come back tomorrow. He nods, then goes to his horse, which is being held for him by a groom.

Abdullah asks for money – cheeky sod – I've already paid Afghan Tour. I tell him that if he meets me here at nine tomorrow morning, I will give him some extra.

He turns and walks away.

Mrs Ungaro is in the part of the stands reserved for foreigners, with her husband Carlo. He is shorter than me with a neatly trimmed beard and an engaging smile. Also with them is their driver, Mansoor, a clean-shaven Pathan. There are only a few people in our area, unlike the rest of the stadium, which is packed. Armed police stand on either side ready to keep back anyone who tries to clamber over the walls that pen us in.

I'm just in time, because the first two teams enter as I sit down.

The layout is the same as at Bagrami, the start and two scoring circles one end and the flag they have to go round at the other. The spectators quieten as the first two teams surround the buz and wait for the umpire's signal.

He raises his hand, then lowers it.

The spectators cheer as the horses surge forward on their hind legs. The play is much nearer than at Bagrami and I'm able to see a chapendoz, heel hooked round the high cantle of his saddle, stretching out to grasp a leg of the buz, while his team-mates try to protect him from the flailing hooves of the opposition.

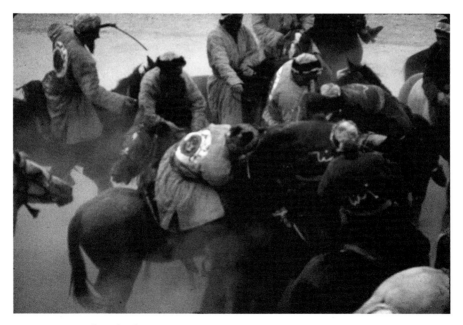

Scrummage for the buz.

As soon as he grips a leg he gives a shout, and a team mate next to him grabs the back of his coat, and heaves him up into the saddle.

To get closer to the action we run down the steps to the low wall that surrounds the pitch. Involuntarily we step back as the players gallop by. They seem much larger in their bulky clothes as they pass within touching distance. We can easily see the grimace on the face of the buz carrier as he desperately clings onto a leg.

'This is wonderful,' Mrs Ungaro says, 'I almost feel I'm part of the game.'

The players go round the flag and start down the far side of the pitch. There is a flurry of whips and the rider carrying the buz is turned away from the scoring circles, back into the middle of the pitch. The speed is restricted by the size of the stadium, but it means there is more tug-of-war with two, and once three, players all heaving at the buz at the same time. The horses are as involved as the chapendoz; with their teeth bared they fight their way out of a scrum, or lean to counteract the weight of the buz, while their rider, whip clenched between his teeth, clings onto a leg. There are several falls but all are able to remount and carry on.

During the third match it starts to rain; large cold drops that chill as soon as they hit the skin. None of our little party has waterproofs, so we hold Mansoor's shawl above our heads like a tent, but it isn't long before the water drips through soaking us. The pitch turns into a mud-bath with horses slipping and the buz becoming almost impossible to keep hold of. The last game is postponed. We make our way back to the Ungaros' car as the sky begins to clear. They insist I join them for tea.

At their house we take our muddy shoes off in the hall. I'm relieved I'm wearing one of the few pairs of socks I have without holes in them. I feel out of place in the drawing room in my worn travelling clothes, but Carlo waves me to a large sofa where Mrs Ungaro joins me. On my travels I'm used to white painted mud-brick walls and, if I'm lucky, a bare electric light bulb which gives a pale glow when the town generator is working. Here there is a large, deep pile carpet, high quality furniture and gilt-framed pictures. Above the figurines on the mantelpiece is a large portrait of a grey-haired Carlo.

'My father,' Carlos says, noticing me looking at it. 'He was the chargé d'affaires here during the war, and as a boy I lived in this house. He and a young Count who worked at the Embassy were both great

Anglophiles. They found it hard when Mussolini declared war.'

He breaks off as an Afghan servant brings in the tea.

'Green or black?' asks Mrs Ungaro.

'Green, please.'

I'm passed a cup on a saucer, the first I've seen in five months since leaving the UK. It's a joy to be holding a china handle, rather than gripping the rim of a glass between thumb and forefinger.

'Have you heard of the Fakir of Ipi?' asks Carlo.

I shake my head.

He tells me the Fakir was a religious leader who fought against the British on the North-West Frontier, keeping two divisions occupied before and during the Second World War. The Germans regularly sent him money through their Embassy in Kabul. Eventually the British heard about it and complained to the government. In a typically Afghan solution, 'bandits' ambushed and shot the German couriers.

I can't help but grin. 'Sorry, I just had a ridiculous image of the Germans in lederhosen goose-stepping through the passes.'

They burst into peals of laughter.

Carlo continues, 'The courier's job then fell – against his will – to the young Count, who was tall and dark like a Pashtun and spoke both Dari and Pashtu. He did it for three years without the British or anyone suspecting. He was my hero. All I knew was that he went on hunting trips and brought back exciting trophies like a Marco Polo sheep or a gazelle.

'I was much envied by the children from the other Embassies because he taught me to ride. He must have done it well, because I still love it.'

Mrs Ungaro reminds him they have a diplomatic drinks party to attend, and it is time to change. They organise for Mansoor to take me back to the Bost, my hotel, while they are getting changed. Could they give me a lift to the buzkashi tomorrow?

I decline because I'm meeting the interpreter.

The next morning I wait for over an hour before hitching a lift back to town. I am enquiring at the Afghan Tour boss's office where Abdulla his, when he comes in without knocking. He doesn't acknowledge me, but talks directly to his boss emphasising his speech with extravagant gestures.

His boss nods and Abdullah leaves.

I turn round to see my interpreter getting into a luxury mini-bus.

'He's got a job explaining buzkashi to some American tourists,' the boss says. 'He has organised a visit to the team you went to yesterday.'

'Do you have another interpreter?'

'No. Maybe he will be free tomorrow.'

'Tomorrow is no good,' I try to keep the anger out of my voice. 'Tomorrow they go back to the north.'

'You could hire a driver and interpreter from us,' he affords himself a smirk. 'I give you good rate.'

I storm out and catch a taxi. Back at the horse lines the interpreter is charging his clients for taking photographs of the horses.

The baba looks on with a smile, the ends of several Afghani notes sticking out of his waistcoat pocket.

I greet him and he takes me to the next tent and introduces me to the team captain. He too apologises for being unable to offer me refreshment. Everything here is more patched than in the baba's tent, and a couple of men are mending bridles.

I start by asking many of the questions I asked yesterday so that I can confirm what I learned. I am just asking about the feeding, when angry raised voices distract us. I follow the team captain to the tent entrance.

The American ladies are complaining about not being allowed into the tent.

The baba stands in front of his tent, arms folded, whip in hand. The interpreter pushes the Americans back, then confronts the baba.

There is a heated exchange. He turns to his clients who demand their money back. Everyone in the adjacent tents is now squatting or standing in their tent openings.

The baba glances round. It has become a matter of honour.

The interpreter returns with more money, but is greeted with a shake of the head. The interpreter's arrogance comes to the fore as he pulls himself up to his full height and says something.

There is a sharp intake of breath from the team captain standing next to me when he hears what the interpreter says.

The baba's eyes narrow.

The whip snakes out catching the interpreter across the cheek. An angry weal appears as he reels back.

The Americans retreat to their car, where they continue demanding a refund. I grin at the baba.

Hand-woven rug. The nosebag is for feed, but also to stop the tourists, in the background, from feeding sugar lumps, apples and anything else.

He inclines his head as he goes inside, honour satisfied.

I have no sympathy for the interpreter, after all it was only yesterday he learnt anything about buzkashi.

It is time for them to saddle up. The team leader says that if I ever go to Taloquan to look him up, and he will organise a game for me.

I meet the Ungaros in the stands, and she claps delightedly when I recite the happening by the tents. It is the last chance to see the game at close quarters, and Mrs Ungaro and I move round the stadium trying to get the best-angled pictures, Carlo stays to talk to Mr Tolon from the Turkish Embassy. There is some spectacular play, especially when two players, each holding a leg of the buz, gallop the length of the pitch leaning parallel to the ground.

Then, as we are returning to the foreigners' stand, a player from Maimana deliberately hits a player from Bakakshan.

Instantly the culprit is turned on by half a dozen players who belabour him with their whips.

To escape them he jumps the low wall surrounding the pitch and, somehow, his horse keeps its feet as it gallops through the stands, scattering the spectators in his way. He then comes back over the wall

Village buzkashi, trying to get a grip on the buz's leg.

and keeps going until he is through the stadium exit gate and heading for safety.

'You are interested in games on horseback?' Mr Tolon asks when we return to the stand.

'Yes.'

' Did you know we have a game in Turkey?'

'No.' He has my full attention.

'It's a real man's game.'

And this isn't? I think.

'What is it?' I ask.

'I don't know. It was banned in the nineteenth century by the Sultan because too many young nobles were being killed. I understand it is still played in a few villages in the eastern part of the country.'

'What's it called?'

'Cirit, I think. If you call on me at the Embassy I might have more information for you.'

This is totally fantastic. If there is another such game out there, it follows there must be many more. I could make it my life's work, finding and studying them before they die out.

'Come on,' Mrs Ungaro says, breaking into my reverie, tugging at my sleeve. 'I need to get some more pictures of the starting circle.'

'Thank you. I will definitely pay you a visit,' I say to Mr Tolon.

'Are you coming, Carlo?'

The three of us run to get to the start of the final game of the year in Kabul.

Mrs Ungaro points to the flailing hooves.

It amazes me that anyone is brave or able enough to lean down and pick up the buz in the mayhem, but the game is soon under way. The combination of cloud and early dusk make photography difficult. I switch from colour to black and white.

Then a shout and it is over. The buz lies, lonely, halfway down the pitch, while the spectators push and shove to get through the exits. A murmur of voices replaces the resounding cheers.

For me it has all gone too fast.

Of Death and Other Things

What a treat – a meal that isn't goat! Home cooked spaghetti with a delicious Bolognese sauce and plenty of Parmesan to sprinkle on top. I have to remind myself to make polite conversation between mouthfuls, not to stuff my face.

Carlo enquires what brought me to Afghanistan. I tell him about Nick's search for the lost city of Firuzkuh, and how the expedition collapsed before it had barely got started. Unable to get the necessary travel documents because of the famine in the interior, we agreed to try to get there without. Then, while I was laid up in Herat with dysentery, Nick set off with his girlfriend – a last minute addition to our number – only to be caught by the police and sent back under guard.

I got to Maimana, our jumping off point, the day after he got back. I helped patch up one of his horses, which had gone lame – I would certainly never have bought it as it had an enlarged hock. Once we had

Having broken free of the melee a player goes flat out towards the goal circle.

sold the horses he went for a long walk in Nuristan, while his girlfriend took the first flight back to the UK.

I went round the north of the country, visiting the horse bazaars.

'Not the safest place to wander round,' Carlo says.

I agree, and tell how I was arrested by the local police in Fayzabad, the capital of Badakhshan Province in the North East.

'What happened?' asks Mrs Ungaro.

'It was my second day. I'd been walking round the town asking the locals where and when the horse bazaar was. Two policemen came to the bungalow, the only place foreigners were allowed to stay, and asked me to go with them to the police station.' I twirl my fork dragging long tendrils of spaghetti through the sauce. 'There an officer took my passport and asked why I'd come to Faydzabad. "To see the horse bazaar." I told him. He asked me twice more. Then the big sergeant standing behind me hit me in the kidneys.'

I pause to ease another forkful into my mouth, sucking in the loose ends.

'There was more shock than pain,' I continue. 'I didn't realise they would rough up a chap for no reason. They kept asking why I'd come, and I kept giving the same answer. Nobody spoke English, and my Dari was not improved by wondering when the next blow would come. After what seemed an age, I was escorted back to the bungalow and told not to leave it. It was built on a rock in the middle of a fast-flowing river, and they posted a policeman with a rifle at the end of the causeway connecting it to the town.'

I pause for a drink.

'A couple of days later they handed back my passport and put me on a plane to Kabul. An Afghan Tour guide I met said the police probably thought I was a spy. They are only used to seeing climbers, shooting parties after the Marco Polo sheep, and the odd hippy. So they probably thought I was James Bond, with my short hair, dark glasses and polished shoes.'

'You were lucky,' says Mrs Ungaro.

'Very,' I agree, remembering having to sit down when I got back to the bungalow, because my knees were shaking so much. 'Lucky they couldn't read English, because my vaccination certificates, which I'd left in my passport, were stamped, "Combermere Barracks, Windsor". I've got rid of them since,' I add.

I refrain from telling the Ungaros that my maps are U2 spy plane maps, which were given to me by a Major at the Ministry of Defence in return for promising to let him know about the condition of the roads; not spying as such, just doing 'reconnaissance', like I did in the army.

'Officials here can be most awkward for no apparent reason,' Carlo says seriously.

'The same in Pakistan,' I say.

He raises his eyebrows.

'I was on a train to Quetta, and thought I'd take some pictures of the stunning scenery. I was just taking the lens cap off, when a man in uniform opposite me ordered me to put my camera away in case I photographed a bridge. "But we British built the bloody railway," I said to him.'

'I bet that endeared you to him,' Carlo comments.

'He produced his identity card, told me he was military police, and suggested we pursue the matter further at the next police station. Needless to say I put the camera away and hardly dared look out of the window for the rest of the journey.'

'You must remember that Pakistan has only just lost a war with India. With feelings still running high they are bound to be suspicious.' Carlo expertly winds up his last strands onto his fork.

Village Buzkashi. Not all the players are chapendoz, the player in blue on a black horse for instance. Spectators crowd on top of lorries and buses to get the best view.

'Would you like to come riding with us tomorrow?' Mrs Ungaro asks.

'I would love to. It's an age since I was last on a horse.'

'Mansoor will drive you back to the Bost this evening, and we'll pick you up at quarter to nine,' says Mrs Ungaro. 'Now tell Carlo how you came to leave the army...'

Back at the hotel the nightwatchman lets me in. Someone is sitting under the solitary tree in the small garden.

'Bob.'

I go over. It is Sharon, an American woman I have been living with since my return from Pakistan. She is in a deckchair, wrapped in a blanket.

'Hi,' I say, gently, taking her hand. 'What are you doing out here in the cold?'

'Waiting for you.'

There is a tremor in her voice I haven't heard before. She is always strong and independent, not given to being emotional.

'What's up?' I squat beside her chair.

'You remember the young American boys I was telling you about?'

'The ones with two horses and a chuck wagon going from Europe to India to raise money for charity?'

'They've been killed.'

She gives a sob and I put my arm round her. I remember her telling me what great guys they were after she met them at some money-raising function in Kabul.

'How?'

'Shot and robbed by bandits on the way to Jalalabad. They were only boys trying to help others. Jeez, I hate this country sometimes.'

We stay where we are for a few minutes, then I get cramp in my thigh and collapse on the coarse grass of the hotel lawn. It breaks the spell, and as I groan, rubbing my leg, she laughs through her tears. She stands up and pulls me to my feet.

I hobble after her.

'And so to bed. Didn't Shakespeare write that?'

'I expect so,' I say airily, trying to hide my ignorance about our famous playwright.

'Ignoramus,' she says, leaving me to limp up the stairs.

I wake to find Sharon sitting on the end of the bed with a shawl wrapped round her shoulders watching me.

'Come back to bed, you must be bloody frozen.'

She carries on observing me.

'Why did you come to Afghanistan?' she asks.

'I told you. To be a groom to Nick who was looking for the lost city of Firuzkuh, and to study Buzkashi and the horsemen who play it.'

'No-one who was an officer in the Queen's Household Cavalry becomes a groom,' she states. 'There has to be something else. This lost city thing... Who in their right mind travels thousands of miles, at their own expense, to join a half-baked expedition, where the organiser can't even get travel permits to the region he wants to visit?'

'Me.'

'I know, but it just doesn't make sense. There must be something else.' She gives a shiver.

'Come back to bed,' I throw back the blankets invitingly.

'Only if you tell me why you came here,' she says, looking straight into my eyes. 'I mean, you were offered a modelling job in New York weren't you?'

I nod.

'So why give up an opportunity like that to come to this dump?'

A back street in Kabul.

'Adventure.' I smile up at her. I wonder why everyone seems to think I've come here for another reason besides horses.

'And the story about why you left the army. It's... it's...'

'True. I rode across the back of the rifle ranges and my Corporal of Horse was shot off his horse by a stray bullet. My army career was finished.'

She stays silent, shivers again, then without a word curls up to me, resting her head on my shoulder. Her skin is all rough with goose-bumps. Her henna-dyed hair is spread over the pillow, and I study her face. In the early morning light there are thin wrinkles at the sides of her eyes and well-defined lines on her forehead. She's older than I'd thought, probably six to ten years older than me.

Lying back it occurs to me that this is the third time she has questioned me. Nicely, but persistent all the same. I wonder why.

'How much longer will you stay here?' I ask.

'Depends,' she says sleepily.

'On what?'

'Business.' She nibbles my ear to distract me.

She buys clothes and jewellery for different shops in the States, and has been here for at least four years. She has a network of buyers all over the country.

'Did you say you were riding with the Ungaros this morning?'

'Do you want to come?'

'Can't, I'm afraid. I'm meeting one of my buyers.'

'I must come with you one day. I'd love to see you at work.'

'Didn't you say you wanted a good story?'

'You know I do. I need a really juicy piece that will get published in the UK papers, then I might be able to become a freelance journalist.'

'I might,' she drawls, 'have just the thing.' She pauses keeping me in suspense. 'There's a rumour that some European guys are getting white girls hooked on local heroin and hiring them out to rich locals. Here, in Pakistan and down into India.'

'Any idea where to start looking?'

'Instant Dysentery.'

It's a place that sold strawberries and cream in the summer. Totally delicious, but...

'One good turn deserves another,' she says kissing me fiercely.

The stable where the Ungaros keep their horse is in a high-walled compound. We park outside, near a manège surrounded by rough wooden railings. A corpulent man in highly polished boots, army jacket and baggy, old fashioned breeches, is giving a riding lesson to some children on horses which are far too big for them. He shouts his instructions in poor English and ineffectually waves a long whip. The horses know they are out of its reach, and consequently pay no attention to the urging of their riders' short legs.

We walk into the compound where our horses are ready saddled. There are five wiry ponies between 14 and 15 hands.

'The grey is ours,' says Mrs Ungaro.

It is the largest, being about 15 hands, and has clearly been well looked after.

'Carlo is riding him today. He is a bit strong for me out of the school. The nearest bay is yours.'

'Who else is coming with us?' I ask.

'The groom. He'll be our guide and sort out any problems we have with the locals. Not that we have had any,' she adds hurriedly.

'The fifth horse?'

'That belongs to the Turkish Colonel giving the riding lesson. He only likes to ride in the school. His is the chestnut on the end.'

It is thinner than the rest, with prominent hip bones. If it can carry him, my stocky horse will certainly carry me. At home I race ride at 10st 9lb, but at the moment, thanks to a couple of bouts of dysentery, I'm under nine and a half.

Once I've adjusted my stirrups, we ride out of the compound and are soon cantering along a track between stubble fields.

The groom shouts at two women dressed in dark blue chadors to get out of the way.

They scurry to one side and turn their backs as we pass, despite the garment completely hiding their faces.

It is all I can do not to overtake Carlo, not because the pony is a hard puller, but because of the different style of riding. The reins are plaited together, about 2ft 6ins from the bit. One hand controls the bit for turning and stopping, while the other uses the long tail of the reins to hit the horse to make it speed up.

By the time we slow at the top of a slight rise I have adjusted, though still find the short, choppy stride uncomfortable compared to that of my thoroughbreds at home. We follow the track that weaves across a small plain before disappearing into a village of mud-walled compounds in the distance. The brown countryside merges into the far hills and finally into the overcast sky.

I ride up alongside Carlo and ask if he has heard about the killing of the two young Americans.

He says one survived by playing dead and is in hospital in Kabul. They were both hit in the opening salvo of gunfire. One of the bandits then came over and kicked one brother who cried out, and was shot at point blank range. The other saw what happened to his brother and played dead, even though he was kicked as well. A passing car came across the scene after the bandits had gone and brought him to Kabul.

I say how traumatic it must have been for the survivor, and wonder how he will cope with his brother's death.

'I agree,' Carlo says, 'I have had to arrange for secure transport to take a young Italian boy to a mental hospital in Italy.'

'How come?'

'He and two other freaks (Carlo always calls druggies 'freaks' rather than 'hippies'), were hitching from Kandahar to Kabul. Unable to get a lift, they camped near the road, instead of going on to the next village. They were probably high anyway.' He shrugs and stares into the distance.

Spectators enjoy a hard-fought game: note the buz beneath the right hand group of horses.

'What happened?' I ask, breaking a minute of silence.

'Oh, yes, sorry. The boy in the centre woke to find the head of his companion on the right had been placed on the body of his friend on the left. And vica versa.'

'You mean someone had decapitated them while he slept and swapped the heads over?' I ask incredulously.

He nods and a rueful smile cracks the corners of his mouth.

'I can almost guarantee the killer stayed to watch the expression on the boy's face when he woke. Afghan sense of humour!'

It is so terrible we both break out laughing. So grotesque that it's funny. And so, so Afghan.

'Race you to the village,' Carlo says, urging his horse into a canter.

My little bay gives chase, laying his ears flat back and taking a real hold. Carlo slows to negotiate an uneven patch of track and I take advantage of his caution to get ahead. My horse stumbles in a rut hidden by a layer of dust, but luckily finds another leg.

I pull up sharply on the edge of the village. Snarling dogs bar the way. They will attack people they think are stealing sheep, the same as they would a wolf approaching their flock. They are big and hairy with no ears or tails. These are cut off when they are puppies so that there is nothing for a wolf, or another dog when fighting in the ring, to get hold of. They would make short work of me if I were foolhardy enough to continue towards them.

I turn to warn the others and we walk and jog back slowly, cooling our sweating mounts.

***

Over the next few days I try to find out more about the pimping of the European girls. No one will talk to me about it. Some people look at me as though I'm crazy, while others simply turn away.

'Instant Dysentery' is a shadow of its former self, the throng of colourful hippies have gone south for the approaching winter like migrating birds. The giant chess board, which one had queue for, is deserted, the pieces scattered on the brown earth round it. The few seasoned travellers still there aren't interested in talking to me, and the one 'down and out' who starts to say something is stopped by his companions.

I revisit a refuge Mrs Ungaro took me to. It is for young travellers who went to India to find enlightenment, and instead found poverty, dirt and gurus who relieved them of most of their money. They are clothed, fed and introduced to Jesus. Then, when they are healed, they go back to their countries to convert their contemporaries.

One of the missionaries, a tall lady with her greying hair swept back into a bun, says she also has heard the same rumour, and is willing to help. She leaves me sitting under a tree in the courtyard while she makes some enquiries. She says it is better for her to ask because the young trust her.

An hour later she returns, her thin lips pressed together. One of her charges, while in Turkey, in Istanbul, had been approached by a westerner asking if she wanted an inexpensive minibus ride to Kathmandu. He told her how it was well over 2000 miles to Kabul and it would be much safer to go with a group.

She said she was travelling with someone and the man said to bring them along as well. When she and the boy she was travelling with met the man, he was quite angry and said it was women only. A couple of days later she saw him driving out of Istanbul in a yellow minibus with a huge yellow flower painted on the spare wheel cover. He was with another, older man and there were several girls in the back.

Flat out chasing a player with the buz.

Six weeks later she was surprised to see the minibus outside a hotel in Lahore. The man had told her the journey would take under a month, and yet they had only got as far as Pakistan. The missionary also says that one of the boys she knows told her that when he was in Iran a yellow minibus with a load of girls stopped at his hotel, but when he approached them to have a chat, he was warned off by a large man.

I thank the missionary and set off to find out what I can about the yellow bus. The chances of it being in Kabul are almost zero, but I still do the rounds of the less salubrious hotels, just in case. I draw a blank. No one has seen it.

The next day I call in at 'Instant Dysentery', but the manager tells me to leave before I can ask any questions.

'Mrs Ungaro left a message for you,' Sharon says, when I get back to the Bost. 'She says you are to have lunch with them tomorrow to meet a Monsieur Bouyer who will take you to Kunduz the next day.'

'But…'

'It's not good hanging round here, pissing people off with your questions. It's better you concentrate on your horses. At least that's why you insist you are here.'

'Who have I upset?'

'Come on,' she grabs my arm. 'Let's make the most of our last two nights together.'

The man with the raised whip deliberately hit another player and was driven out of the stadium.

***

'Welcome,' says Carlo as I'm shown into the drawing room. 'Paul – Monsieur Bouyer – won't be here for a bit. We asked you early so that we could tell you about him.'

'He is a remarkable man,' Mrs Ungaro says. 'I think you'll like him and he says you can stay with him while he is in Kunduz.'

'It's good you are leaving Kabul for a bit,' Carlo says. 'I understand your questions have upset someone.'

'So I've been told, but who?'

'It's all round Kabul that a mad English cavalry officer is trying to find out if white girls are being hooked on drugs and used for prostitution. It appears you are not popular.'

'But who? Why?'

'You must remember that not all countries are like the UK,' he says seriously. 'Everything is governed by baksheesh. No foreigner can do anything, legal or illegal, without the help of a powerful friend, especially where money is involved.'

'But...'

'Leave it,' Mrs Ungaro says with finality.

I am taken aback. Obviously I was closer than I knew. I am also fully aware how unwise it is to upset people here. Over a dozen foreigners have been killed since I arrived, mostly because they have upset someone in one way or another. I'm glad I have influential friends in the Ungaros, especially as the British Embassy have wanted me out of the country and refuse to have anything to do with me since my incarceration in Fayzabad. I stop speculating and concentrate on what Mrs Ungaro is telling me.

Paul Bouyer was 17 when the Germans invaded Belgium. Within two weeks he was on the run for killing one German soldier and wounding another. He was hidden by a friend of his father's in the cold store at the back of his butcher's shop, which he made his base. Paul was active in the Resistance all through the war, and when peace came he went to university.

The Ungaros first met him in the Congo where he was working for the UN education department. It was a difficult time with the civil war going on, mercenaries fighting for both sides, and atrocities being committed by both sides. When Paul heard nuns in an upcountry mission were in the path of one of the advancing armies, he led an expedition to save them. He got them away with a day to spare.

'He is a quiet man,' Carlos says. 'What the British call a gentle giant. I know you will like him, but don't be surprised by his eyes. He obsessively washes them out whenever he gets some dust in them. Now he has no immunity, so the whites are always bloodshot.'

A scrunch of tyres on the gravel outside announces his arrival.

He is well over six foot, with broad shoulders and half-closed eyes, which peer over half-moon glasses, giving him a slightly owlish look. He has fine, small hands and a gentle manner. Over lunch the conversation turns to why the Afghan population remains so steady when that of its neighbours is increasing rapidly.

'In one word,' says Mrs Ungaro, 'boys. Men can't get married until they can afford a wife. And this often isn't till they are in their thirties or early forties. In the meantime they make do with boys. To do it with other men is against the law. But not with boys. Rich men flaunt their teenage boy lovers. Eventually, when they do get married, quite a few can't manage anything, because they are so used to boys, or they don't know what to do. And the women...' She shakes her head. 'They are as bad as the men. I've yet to go to a dinner where one, if not both women beside me, don't try to stroke my thighs.'

'It's the Pashtuns in the south who are particularly bad,' Paul says. 'It's much less prevalent among the more Asiatic tribes in the north.'

'You know the old saying about Kandahar?' asks Carlo.

Paul shakes his head.

'*When a bird flies over Kandahar it only uses one wing, because it is covering its bottom with the other.*'

Everyone laughs and Mrs Ungaro claps.

'Have you noticed how they greet each other?' Paul asks me.

'Yes. At first it seemed over the top then, after an incident I had in the summer, I realised they were frisking each other.'

'What happened?' he asks.

I tell them about when I was travelling on top of a bus to Maimana. It was already crowded, with passengers sitting where they could on the luggage, when a large man, in a chapan as big as a tent, clambered up the ladder. He looked round, then came over and told me to move.

I refused, so he sat on my feet.

As the bus moved off there was a lot of squirming as he tried to get comfortable and I tried to extricate my feet. After about twenty minutes he produced a pistol from under his chapan, I think to frighten me. But I was fascinated because it was a sawn-off .303 Lee Enfield rifle with a rough pistol grip.

I asked if I could look at it and he was so surprised that, after only a brief hesitation, he handed it over. First I checked the safety catch was on – we had .303s in the Cadet Force at school – then I checked it for balance. It was quite unwieldy and would have needed two hands to fire it. But all the working parts were beautifully oiled and it was in superb condition.

The man nudged me and I saw he was now passing me a 9mm Browning pistol and a long, thin curved knife.

Not to be outdone, my fellow travellers produced knives and pistols from beneath their shirts and coats.

The big man moved off my feet so that I could go round the bus looking at them all.

Overbalancing. The ambulance is parked ready in the entrance.

When I got back to him I asked if the .303 pistol was difficult to hold still when firing.

He stood up, swaying with the movement of the bus, and worked the bolt, feeding a round into the breech. What would I like him to shoot at?

I pointed to a lone tree on the side of the road.

Gripping the gun firmly in both hands he aimed and fired.

The result was unexpected.

The bus driver slammed on the brakes and the big man and I fell on top of each other. As soon as the bus came to a halt the driver started shouting. Within seconds he was up the ladder. In the brief interval between the bus stopping and him appearing, the armoury had disappeared back under everyone's clothes. When he demanded to know what was going on all looks were aimed at me, and I was ordered off the roof and into the hot, smelly, squashed interior.

'I think,' says Paul, 'we will have plenty to talk about on our way to Kunduz.'

Kunduz

Two days later Paul drops me off at Kunduz market. I am the only person to arrive by car, the rest have come on foot, horseback, cart or horse-drawn ghari. When I was here in August, dust hung in the baking heat, but today the earth is tacky and the cool October air smells of damp animals and fresh dung.

I walk past a line of gharis, drawn up like a London taxi rank, before entering the market compound which is surrounded by a four foot high mud-brick wall. On my right is the ploughing pit, where two yoked oxen are pulling a wooden plough with half a dozen farmers watching. In the summer there were several queuing to demonstrate their animal's pulling power, and a fight had broken out because one vendor thought another had been showing off his ox for too long. Today there are only three, two hauling the plough through the mire, and the third waiting by the rim of the pit.

Remounting – note one rider trying to get on while the horse is not fully standing. The dense crowd watching the buzkashi from the terraces was the same all round the stadium.

There are a lot of fat-tailed sheep, mostly well grown young males, for which there is a brisk trade. Bargains are done with a slap of the hand, and the animal is led off.

I watch a fat man trying out a donkey. He sits astride it, hitting it with a stick while the owner looks on. Eventually the donkey gives up nibbling at some alfalfa shoots and walks towards the gate. Nothing will make it go faster but, when the fat man turns it round, it breaks into a canter heading back to the alfalfa. As soon as it gets there, it puts its head down. The rider fails to keep his balance, and slides unceremoniously down its neck, much to the amusement of the local farmers.

There are several horses being traded. One man has brought a chapendoz with him to try out the horses he is interested in. They look at a grey Turkoman horse, which could do with a good feed. As soon as the chapendoz puts his hand on the folded blanket acting as a saddle, the horse flinches. Despite the vendor's protests, he pulls back the blanket and finds a septic saddle sore. He shakes his head and his boss directs him to another. The vendor leads the grey behind a high wall, and I follow. I watch him fold the blanket forward and squeeze the sore until thick yellow pus comes out. He wipes this away with a dirty rag and keeps squeezing until no more comes out. He then pulls the blanket back in place and goes back to mingle with the other sellers, to try his luck with someone less discerning. I can't see anyone buying it until it has healed.

An Uzbek horse dealer recognises me and comes over. He has tried to sell me a horse twice in the summer, and I think he has the best horses in the market. We greet each other like old friends. 'How are you? Your sons? Your family? Is your father well? How are your horses?'

Once we are done his brown wrinkled face breaks into a smile.

'I have a horse you will like.' He takes hold of my sleeve. 'Big horse. Good for you.'

I go with him to a bunch of horses being held by a boy.

'Here my friend, did I not tell you?' he asks, taking off his turban and scratching his stubbly pate. I remember this habit from the summer, he always does it when trying to sell a horse.

I step up to the bay he indicates. It is a couple of inches smaller than the saddle-sore grey, but in first class condition, as witnessed by its shiny coat. The Uzbek never stops talking as I search its legs for lumps and bumps. There aren't any.

As always happens, a crowd of spectators gather when a Westerner shows any interest. A noisy babble ensues as the onlookers discuss the horse's merits. Luckily for me the man with the chapendoz pushes through, and starts to question the Uzbek, allowing me to escape.

I follow a buyer who has just bought a goat and is dragging it through a gap in the high wall. As I step up to the gap the smell of warm blood and the swarms of flies momentarily halt me.

The buyer hauls the struggling goat over to one of several gutters which criss-cross the area, and lays it on its side over the channel. This is an abattoir. There are several sheep and goats, some twitching, some still, necks stretched over the gutters, with young boys with bloody faces holding them down.

The buyer shouts and a boy comes over to sit on the goat's head. A mullah says a prayer, the goat's throat is cut, and the buyer goes back to the market.

The boy keeps the goat in position so that the blood runs into the channel, while fending off the flies. When the twitching lessens, he stands up and puts his foot on its head until it is still.

Once it's dead, he drags the carcass away from the gutter and cuts a hole in the back leg, just above the hock. He puts his mouth to the hole and starts blowing, separating the skin from the underlying tissue. Within minutes the belly skin starts to swell. Once it is taut the boy pulls out a knife from under his blood-encrusted shirt and splits the belly skin from top to bottom. He calls over a ghari and, with the help of the driver, loads the carcass onto the back. The lolling head and slashed throat provide a ghoulish spectacle as the ghari bumps away to a butcher's shop.

Looking round I see several carcasses are being skinned close to the meat stalls near the market entrance, while others are being taken into town. I get out my camera, but a mullah spots me, and I am escorted back to the animal bazaar.

I'm just in time to see the chapendoz cantering out of the entrance on the fine bay. He is riding bareback, seated well back, with his knees tucked in behind the horse's shoulder muscles. He turns at the far side of the gharis and comes back at the same speed.

A woman and child are on their way out as he comes through the entrance. The woman pulls her child into the folds of her chador and freezes. The chapendoz appears not to have noticed them, but the horse does and deftly swerves round them.

He nods when he reaches his boss, and the stubbly head has more frantic scratching until hands are slapped. I have no doubt it was a good price, but easily half, if not a third of what I'd be expected to pay.

I walk back to Paul's house and, like yesterday, enjoy a long hot shower before dinner. Mahomet, Paul's housekeeper, puts on a sulky face because I refuse a fourth helping.

Paul says we are taking Maryanne, the new American English teacher, with us to tomorrow's buzkashi game, which is at a village a few miles away.

I ask if there is any chance of riding, but he says they would charge me a fortune to hire a horse, and would keep me well away from the play. I will have a much better chance of getting some photographs if I go with him and Maryanne in his jeep.

Maryanne it turns out is incredibly annoying, and her good looks count for nothing because of her incessant chatter.

The game was meant to start at noon, but Paul says it will start when they're ready. The buz, this one a goat, is already in a slight hollow which acts as the starting and scoring circle. It's a local game, so no teams, it is each man for himself. The buz will be carried round a flag, which is about three kilometres away, and brought back. The person who drops it in the circle is the winner. It is nearly impossible for an outsider to tell who the players are and who are the spectators. Everyone is mounted and all dressed the same, except for the chapendoz, who are in their distinctive clothing.

Tired of Maryanne's unceasing questions, and not being able to see through the steamed up windows, I get out. The bitter wind chills me immediately. There is nothing between us and the treeless grasslands of the Central Asian Steppes to the north, across the Oxus River. The flat dun landscape is broken only by the walled compounds of the village houses which do nothing to break the wind as it eddies round them.

The horsemen sort themselves out. Those playing gather round the buz, while the rest pull back, blocking my view. All I can see are horses' quarters and the drapes of the chapans. Suddenly there is a lot of shouting, which means they've started.

Paul toots the horn and I run back and jump in. He moves forward until there is a gap for us to see through, but it quickly closes as the buz is picked up. It is difficult to see what is happening, because one minute the players are encircled by the spectators and the next someone has made a break. I notice in the outward run that most of the chapendoz hang on the flanks of the play, letting those less experienced battle it out. At one point the horse of a young man carrying the buz comes down, and both disappear under the hooves of the other players.

'Jeez, that man's going to get trampled,' Maryanne says in a panicky voice.

I'm relieved to see the horse get up and, although the rider appears to be in the thick of the play, he walks out unscathed.

Behind me I hear Maryanne give a sigh of relief.

Paul does a brilliant job of giving both of us the best chance to watch what is happening. He has to concentrate because there are two other vehicles, whose drivers are as intent as their passengers on seeing on the game, and they veer wildly across us from time to time, either to avoid the play or to try to get closer.

On the way back, the chapendoz now start to get involved. Only the strongest locals on the best horses manage to keep in the fray. Next moment it is over. It's impossible to tell who scored, but an older chapendoz with a grey beard is being congratulated.

'Did you enjoy it?' Paul asks.

'If I hadn't seen it in Kabul, I wouldn't have had a clue what was going on,' I reply.

'You mean you actually understood what was going on?' Maryanne asks.

'Yes. It might have looked chaotic because it was every man for himself, winner takes all, but there were tactics as well as brute strength and superb horsemanship. Didn't you see how in the last kilometre the less skilled were out-ridden by the chapendoz – those players in the funny hats. It was time for them to win through.'

She shakes her head.

'Even if you explained it a hundred times, I'm not sure I'd be any the wiser.'

'Maintenant, we must get back. I have some official guests coming to dinner and I am cooking it,' Paul says.

Unlike on the journey out, Maryanne is silent as Paul and I discuss what we have seen.

***

The chase is on

The next morning I say goodbye and thank Paul. He and his official guests are off on an inspection tour of the area. After booking into a hotel I take a ghari out of town to an old chapendoz's house, for an interview arranged for me by Mahomet, the housekeeper. He has warned me there is no one who speaks English as well as I speak Dari, so it will be slow work.

I'm met at the compound gate by Ali, one of the sons of the house, who is keen to practise his English. To one side of the compound is a single storey mud-brick house with a verandah. Where a stream runs close to the house, there are trees with the blooms of climbing roses adding colour to the autumn leaves. Several heavily rugged horses are tied to the railings in front of the stables. I follow Ali's example and remove my boots before entering the house. My host is a square-set old man with a wispy grey beard and heavily lined, Asiatic face, wearing a turban, the tail of which hangs over his striped chapan. He greets me and points to a cushion on the carpet next to where he was sitting. Ali sits next to me, and apologises on behalf of his father that there are no refreshments because it is still Ramadan.

There are nine other Asiatic men seated on the floor around the room, their backs to the wall. Although Ali's English is basic, it is enough to help me out when I get stuck.

I tell them I'm interested about how they train and look after their horses. I say that unlike the fast moving type of buzkashi, qarajai, which I've been watching, I've never seen the more static tudabarai, which is played at weddings and other celebrations.

They say it is a simpler game. A player has to get the buz clear of any other players, but it usually weighs 100lb or more, so a lot of strength is required. Also there are a lot more players, often over a hundred and a game can go on for a whole day. The person who lays on the game always gives generous prizes: a rifle, an ox, or a large cash prize. There is competition among the rich to give the biggest prizes.

It is slow going, talking in Dari and writing notes in English, but everyone is patient, making sure I understand. Much of what I'm told I heard previously in the tents, but other things are new. Like the practice of feeding blood cake to sick horses. Sheep's blood in the summer, and goat's in the winter, is mixed with crushed grain in a mash. If possible they add a sweetener to encourage the horse to eat. They continue to feed it until the horse is better. In winter, when it is cold, the horses are fed fat from the tail of the fat-tailed karakul sheep to give them energy.

I notice the men are doing hand exercises as we talk, and ask why.

Doing the exercises becomes a habit, I'm told. Strong hands are needed to keep hold of the buz. If a man can halve a quince with his fingers he is said to have strong hands.

I can't even dent one.

This is the time of year for local games. In January the inter-district team tournaments start. By then the horses are at their peak of fitness and the novices are well schooled. It takes five years to school a horse. Some horses play into their late twenties. Often young men are put on them to learn the skills.

'A good horse will make a bad rider good,' says my host, 'but a bad horse will make a good rider bad.'

My host says he has just bought a young horse for 90,000 Afghani (£450) – a huge amount back then – whilst a good hack would cost up to 10,000 Afghani. We go outside to look at it. He points it out, only its face and legs are visible, the rest hidden under felt rugs. He calls for the groom who removes the rugs. It is taller than I thought, about 15.2 hands, with a slightly heavy head, broad chest, good heart room, short cannon bones and strong quarters. He says a good horse in its prime will fetch over 200,000 afghani.

'For that,' he points to a grey tied to the railings, 'I would want well over that.'

Sadly he doesn't remove its rugs.

Back inside we are discussing the financial rewards when a local mullah comes in with his assistant.

I can see both are Pashtuns by their black beards, long faces and hooked noses. Despite my host's friendly greeting, the atmosphere in the room changes.

The mullah stares at me hawk-like, squatting against the wall opposite me. At his command, his assistant pushes himself between me and Ali.

I continue with my enquiries, finding out a chapendoz's retainer is between 75,000 and 100,000 Afghani a year. Like a professional jockey he often rides for more than one owner and can earn 20,000 Afghani (£100) a week at the height of the season. (A fully qualified Afghan engineer earns about £750 per annum.)

The mullah says something and his assistant translates.

'What are you doing here with these people?'

'I am talking to them about buzkashi and how they look after their horses.'

'Why are you here? These people are ignorant people. Are you talking about religion?'

'No. I am talking about horses.'

My host interrupts to explain.

The assistant looks at the mullah.

'What does a feringee want to know about horses?'

The mullah says something before I can reply.

'Are you Muslim?' the assistant asks.

'No, I'm a Christian.'

'What is Christian? Do you follow Muhammad?'

'I follow Jesus, one of your prophets.'

'Do you know the prophets?'

'Abraham, Moses?' I guess.

'Why are you not a Muslim? Is there something wrong with being a Muslim?'

Glancing round the room I see my host and the horsemen are clearly embarrassed and are looking down at their hands.

The mullah says something to his assistant, who whips out a knife and pushes the point into the flesh under my chin.

'Will you become a Muslim?'

Two things flash through my mind – how bloody dare they? And would they change their religion? – No.

'No!'

My host pulls the assistant's knife-hand away.

There is a fierce exchange between my host and the mullah, who gets up and leaves with his assistant. My host says something to his son who goes out and comes back with an apple, which he offers to me with both hands.

'My father says to eat it.'

'But it is Ramadan.'

'But you are not a Muslim. Eat please.'

I take it with trembling hands. Everyone watches as I bite into the apple and munch my way through it. What to do with the core and the pips? I eat the lot. When I have finished my host slaps me on the back and the talk goes back to horses, but the heart has gone out of the interview.

I smell cooking and get up to leave. It will soon be dusk and they will be breaking their fast. My host says it is too far for me to walk back, so Ali will ride with me and lead my horse back.

I go round the room shaking hands and thanking everyone while the horses are being saddled. I shake hands again with my host, and then Ali and I canter off down the dirt road in the late afternoon sun.

Near the town the road is lined with trees and the first dead leaves skitter in the chill wind. Everyone we pass is hurrying home, hungry for their meal at dusk. With only the briefest of goodbyes I hand my reins to Ali who canters off, making an unwary couple jump out of his way.

Back in my room my hand is shaking so much I can't write my diary. I try to convince myself nothing would have happened, but remember hearing about three French boys in Kandahar. They were invited into a mullah's house and given drugged tea. Two had their throats cut and the third was disembowelled in the courtyard. The Mullah and his compatriots defence was that they did nothing wrong because the boys were infidels, but they were still hanged. Situations flare up out here without warning.

After supper Maryanne calls by with some friends who are driving back to Kabul. Would I like a lift?

Yes. It is time to go home.

Return Home

Their old Russian jeep has a wonderful heater that has us stripping down to our shirts. Soon after we start the climb up to the Salang Tunnel there is a problem with gear changing. The Kunduz bus, which we overtook earlier, comes past us blowing its horn. We creep up the winding road, the clutch whirring more on every bend. It's clear we'll never make it to the pass through the tunnel, and pull up at a village garage. The mechanic, a boy of about twelve, listens to the noise and pronounces it 'kharab', broken.

We push the jeep onto a patch of oily hardcore.

There the mechanic is joined by a younger boy. Before long the gearbox is out and the transmission in pieces. We wait, sitting out of the wind with our backs against a wall, warmed by fleeting patches of sun. Three hours later the boys' boss, a lad in his mid-teens, tells us it is mended. We purr away from the village, but after a mile the vehicle starts to vibrate. We stop and the driver takes it out of four-wheel drive and finally we are off again. Near the tunnel it is snowing heavily and the road gets whiter. Somehow, despite having no four-wheel drive, we slither and slide our way to the top, wary of the huge drops which appear from time to time through the snowstorm.

Well after dark I am dropped off at the Bost and bump into Nick. He has just got back from another attempt, this time on foot, to find Firuzkuh, but still no luck. He too has decided it is time to go home, so we will travel together.

The next two days fly by. Saying goodbye to the Ungaros; failing to get hold of Mr Tolon from the Turkish Embassy to learn more about the Turkish horse game cirit (he has been on leave since the buzkashi games) and organising my luggage – my backpack plus two 50 kilogramme metal trunks, containing carpets, horse equipment, sheepskin coats and oddities I have picked up on my journeys.

When I say farewell to Sharon she gives me a long lingering kiss in front of her new paramour, before telling Nick, 'Look after Bob, he's so green'.

For a moment I'm hurt. I was really naïve when I came out, but now – I think of the mullah in Kunduz, and admit she is right. I haven't made a single trip without getting into some sort of scrape.

The bus journey is a nightmare: first there is an argument over my trunks and I have to pay the driver a large amount of baksheesh before he agrees to take them on the roof. Then there are three breakdowns before Kandahar, a flat tyre that takes an hour to change, and a long freezing night where the window in front of us is broken. In Herat the bus boy demands extra money before allowing me to take my trunks off the bus, despite my having paid the driver in Kabul.

Angry and tired, I go to sort it out with the driver. He is in a chai khana drinking tea with some of the Afghan passengers.

When I remonstrate with him, he gives a patronising smirk and says it is nothing to do with him. I remind him I paid for the trunks in Kabul, but he just shrugs and sips his tea.

Infuriated, I call him a 'son of a dog' and turn away.

He jumps up and hits me on the back of my head, knocking me to the ground.

The best way to travel, on top.

As I get up he grins at his triumph. Until I kick him in the stomach.

His expression turns to rage and his hand flies under his shirt. Both of us are fighting mad, but mercifully Nick grabs me and drags me outside, while the driver's friends restrain him.

'You bloody fool.' Nick is really angry. 'You could have got killed.'

'But the bastard is cheating me.' I'm not in a mood to see reason.

'Just pay!' he says.

One of the driver's friends comes out and shouts to the bus boy to give me my trunks because I have already paid the driver for them.

With bad grace he drops them off the roof onto the road. Luckily they dent rather than break open.

At the border, Customs look at the broad coloured bands of material I've sewn round each trunk, fetch some sealing wax, pour it on the join, and stamp it. They demand an inordinate amount of baksheesh. I've learnt my lesson, and pay up.

At the Iranian border the Customs spend an age finding a bigger stamp than the Afghan one, before waving us through to catch the bus to Mashad.

Again the trunks cause consternation to both me and the bus company because they take up so much space in the hold. After some hard negotiating, and a couple of back-handers, we are off to Tehran, where the trunks are put in the luggage van of the train to Istanbul.

Relieved to be rid of them, I watch the brown winter countryside slip by. At Lake Van, part of the area I plan to visit next year searching for the horse game, the snow comes down to the water's edge. On the steppe we pass small villages, smoke curling up from the chimneys of the flat-roofed houses. Shepherds, well-wrapped against the cold, tend their sheep, which scratch the thin covering of snow, searching for any fodder they can find. Nearer Istanbul, long queues of horses pulling carts piled with beet wait in lines by the factory gates.

In Istanbul bureaucracy takes over. There is no way my trunks will be allowed across the Bosporus without being escorted by a Customs official, and there are none to spare.

Eventually, with the promise of a large 'gift' and lunch at a top restaurant, the boss agrees to accompany both Nick, who has kindly stayed on to help, and me. We leave the trunks in the Sirkeci railway station Customs' warehouse, and take the rotund official to a restaurant Nick knows. There we argue over the amount of baksheesh, but as the trunks are now on the right side of the Bosporus, I can drive a hard bargain.

The following day I'm told there is no one 'high up' enough to sign the release papers for them to be sent on the train with me which is leaving in two hours. As the office is closing for the day a senior Customs official asks what the problem is.

'Are they going to be opened in Turkey?' he asks, looking at the various stamps and seals.

'No.'

He signs a piece of paper.

'They will have to go as freight, second class, to London. Now I am closing the office.'

Relieved, but sad to have missed Nick, whose train left earlier, I board the Paris train.

There are three Swiss in my compartment, a girl dozing with her head in her boyfriend's lap and a tall thin chap reading a book in the corner. Conversation has been minimal so far on the journey, so I decide to try a nightcap in the restaurant car before turning in. I take my sleeping bag out of its cover so that I won't disturb anyone when I come back.

The bar is packed, but I manage to squeeze in with three couples, one American, one Dutch and one French. They all have stories to tell of their travels through India, Pakistan, Iran and Afghanistan; near escapes, funny incidents, language problems and, of course, stomach upsets to a greater or lesser extent. I start to relax, glad that all these problems are now behind me.

We are so engrossed we don't notice the other passengers leave, until the large conductor and his mate come over to say that a Turk, sitting alone on the far side of the restaurant car, wondered if anyone would like to go for a drink in his first class compartment.

We turn to look at a fat, sallow-faced man who suggestively runs his tongue over his rubbery lips. There is a universal 'no'.

'Very wise,' says the conductor, 'he is not a nice man.'

The conductor and his mate try to join us, but their intrusion breaks up the party.

As we are leaving the conductor asks if anyone wants a couchette, there is an empty carriage of them. Two of the others already have them, and the Dutch couple are going back to their friends. I ask how much and I'm told 'Free'. The beds are not made up, but look far more comfortable than sleeping on the floor of my allotted compartment. They show me where to go, and after wrapping my coat round me I'm soon asleep.

I'm startled awake by something pressing down between my shoulderblades, and the light of a cigarette lighter being waved in front of my eyes. I struggle to get up, but am pinned down.

'We have come for payment.'

Now wide awake, I recognise the big conductor's voice. I try to get up, but he slaps me hard across the back of the head.

'Be still,' he growls. 'My friend doesn't fuck women, he fucks boys and he's going to fuck you.'

By the light of some street lights I see his mate already has his trousers round his knees, his erection swaying with the movement of the train. This is no time to lie back and think of England, it is time to fight. I try to get up, but he has me firmly pinned down and laughs. Wrapped in my coat, with a broad canvas money-belt underneath my trousers, which are held up by a strong belt, I feel confident I can put up a good fight.

The conductor raises his fist.

'Turn over.'

I force myself to go floppy, and offer no resistance as he rolls me onto my side. Suddenly I lash out, kicking wildly.

The mate, who is getting ready to undo my trousers, shuffles back out of range. The conductor, while holding me down with his right hand, tries to get my belt buckle undone with his left, but he can't. He says something to his mate, who gets both hands on the buckle.

As he fiddles to get it undone I kick out again.

He gives a gasp and the conductor curses and hits me hard on the head. I see flashing lights, but it's not stars from the blow, it's the lights of a town and the train is slowing. The conductor lifts my head by my hair.

'You stay!' he commands and slaps my face.

I lie still listening to his receding footsteps.

I glance at the mate who is still holding his groin. A lucky kick.

He makes no attempt to stop me as I get up and look along the corridor. I run back to my compartment. The Swiss are asleep. I roll my sleeping bag out on the floor and lie on top of it, feeling certain the conductor won't try anything with other foreign travellers around. Despite this my body is trembling uncontrollably. There is no point in reporting it. The police would probably lock me up 'for my own protection', and I've heard too many stories about Turkish gaols not to stay well clear. Eventually I sleep, only to wake with a start as the Bulgarian border guard enters to check our passports.

***

Standing in the bows of the ferry, the White Cliffs of Dover have never looked better. A night in London, then back home to my old farmhouse and my horses. At last there will be no more baksheesh, just straight-forward pricing. I know I am truly in the UK, because there is a train strike and we are being bussed to London.

About halfway, a passenger goes forward to have a word with the driver. Could he drop him and his friend at a junction about a mile ahead? The driver is adamant – he has been told no stops. The man pulls out his wallet and starts putting ten pound notes on the dashboard. The driver nods, pockets the money, and lets the two men off.

In London, my first stop is the Officers' Mess at Knightsbridge. I've lost the telephone number and address of the ex-army friend I'm meant to be staying with, but several officers will know it. I'm conscious of the contrast between my travelling clothes and their immaculate uniforms and highly polished riding boots.

A mess waiter brings me coffee as I explain where I've been, but only one or two know or care where Afghanistan is. Soon the conversation reverts to hunting, shooting and what parties are on this evening.

I slip out with the address and telephone number in my pocket and go to the stables to see my old army charger, Tigress. She whickers when I produce a sugar lump pocketed in the Mess. I rub her forehead, blow in her nose, and give her a final pat before leaving. Sadly, I realise she is part of a world to which I no longer belong.

CHAPTER TWO

Household Cavalry Summer 1971

How was I in a position to travel the world in search of the last vestiges of war games on horseback? I had once taken part in them myself and it had happened like this: I had always had horses and was thrilled when I was posted to The Life Guards Mounted Squadron, at Knightsbridge in London. Besides ceremonial duties there were chances to take part in a variety of horse-related activities, including a cavalry charge...

***

We emerge from the sparse pine trees onto a low ridge. The squadron wheels right, coming to a halt in two ranks on the forward edge. It is about to begin.

Below us a company of Foot Guards, dressed in 1880s uniform, marches across the flat valley floor behind their pipes and drums. There are spectator stands on the rising ground to the right where the Royal Family and dignitaries are seated.

The loudspeaker announces the enemy has been spotted and the Foot Guards form two ranks.

Tigress, my favourite charger, paws the ground impatiently, just as she did before the start of the Melton Cross Country Race. But this time we are waiting to do a cavalry charge as part of a 'tableau' for Her Majesty the Queen. Before any charge in times past, it must have been like this: horses snorting and stamping, the jingle of bridles, everybody tense and ready to go. It never occurred to me that I would ever be taking part in one.

Tigress's head comes up and her ears prick as the Royal Horse Artillery gallop forward to unlimber their guns at either end of the Foot Guards' line in the valley below. The crackle of rifle fire closely followed by the boom of artillery start the mock battle against an imaginary enemy. Tigress's ears flicker at the gunfire and she tosses her head.

I have placed the slower horses directly behind me – my privilege as the troop leader. Yesterday, during practice, I just escaped being speared by a trooper whose sword-point was a mere foot from my backside. The swords we carry now for ceremonial duties are 1912 cavalry issue, as used in anger in the First World War and they have lethal points. It occurs to me a cavalry officer's all-important élan was probably more to do with keeping ahead of the lances or sword-points of his own men rather than any desire to close first with the enemy.

The Foot Guards form a 'square' as the loudspeaker tells the spectators that the enemy cavalry is about to attack.

The shouted order to 'Draw Swords' breaks my reverie. I fumble reaching for the hilt of my sword. My steel cuirass restricts moving my arm across my body, and my thick leather gauntlet is difficult to feel through. I grip the hilt at my third attempt.

Tigress tenses as my sword rattles out of its scabbard.

I shorten my reins.

The troopers in the ranks behind me curse as their horses try to pull forward. The Squadron Corporal Major growls at them to rein back into line.

I watch the Squadron Leader. He nods his plumeless helmet and his trumpeter blows 'Walk March'.

A slight slackening of my reins lets Tigress know it's time to move.

Again I hear the Squadron Corporal Major's voice chiding the troopers to keep the lines straight as we advance down the gentle slope.

Ahead of us ripples of rifle smoke issue from the sides of the 'square' as the Foot Guards fire blank rounds at the imaginary cavalry who are said to be attacking them. I'd hate to have ridden for real against the hedge of bayonets and constant, withering fire. No way could a horse break in as long as the ranks stayed solid.

'Trot' is blown and the jangling of the bridles now masks the firing in the valley ahead. As we go into 'Canter' the loudspeaker announces to the audience that the imaginary enemy cavalry is retreating, and we are to chase them.

I have to haul on the reins to keep Tigress behind the Squadron Leader. I glance to my right. My troops' swords are in the correct 'Engage' position; elbow locked into the side, sword-blades parallel to the ground.

Three-quarters of the way to the Foot Guards' square, the trumpet blares 'Charge'.

Standing in my stirrups, sword arm extended from the shoulder, I kick on, screaming my war-cry like the rest of my troop. As we pass the square, the Guards wave their bearskins and cheer us on unheard, all other sound drowned out by the rolling thunder of galloping hooves.

Tigress stretches her neck, and her ears go back as she gallops flat out, determined to keep ahead of the horses behind her. The soldiers in my wake curse when mud flies into their faces as I go through a wet patch of ground. I use my legs to steer round a puddle. Head down, Tigress charges on. I keep a light hold on the reins in case she stumbles in the rougher going, and needs holding up.

Household Cavalry officers sometimes got a chance to be extras in films – here's me with a false moustache in a TV series about Queen Victoria.

The rough ground breaks up the formation of the cavalry charge, part of a 'tableau' the Household Division performed in front of Her Majesty the Queen.

A riderless horse appears alongside me. I learn later it stumbled in a rut and its rider came off. He was muddy but unhurt.

Well past the stands the trumpeter blows 'Recall'.

First the swords come up onto the shoulder, then everyone takes a pull on the reins. Some of the horses are blown and slow immediately, but others need a lot of heaving to stop. Sloping swords is essential because, in the chaos of pulling up, it is easy to stab someone by mistake.

As we form up for the ride back to camp, big canopied parachutes come through the clouds as the Guards SAS arrive to start a modern set-piece battle.

We set off past the Guards Parachute Company who are in open-topped vehicles, engines running, ready to dash in to assist the SAS. Further back are a company of Foot Guards in armoured personnel carriers. On the hill we have just vacated, a troop of wheeled Saladin and Ferret armoured cars from my regiment, The Life Guards, are already moving into position to give fire support.

The explosions start before we are clear. Tigress's ears flip backwards and forwards, and one or two of the most nervous horses skitter. To everyone's relief, the rumble of the modern day battle is swiftly left behind, replaced by the familiar jingle of bridles and of shod hooves on tarmac.

∗∗∗

A few days later, on troop exercise, we ride to an area well behind the rifle ranges at Pirbright in Surrey, to practise troop deployments on a piece of ground we rode over before the charge. Turning off the road we follow a narrow track through a hedge of brambles and scrub; the leaves are still covered in droplets from the early morning mist. Then we are out onto a flat area covered in heather. Beside the track is a notice board overgrown with brambles.

'Range area, sir,' says my senior Corporal of Horse.

'I've ridden here twice with the Squadron Leader, no need to worry.'

'What about the flag, sir?'

Three hundred yards away a tattered pale pink piece of cloth hangs limply against an off-white flagpole.

'Hardly flying, Corporal of Horse. It was the same when I came with the Squadron Leader.'

'Right, sir.'

The first flies of the day buzz round us, and high above in the cloudless sky a lark sings. I don't want the horses to get too worn out, because this afternoon is the inter-troop show jumping competition. After half an hour horses and men are hot, so I slow the troop to a walk. Suddenly a bird flies up from the heather, right under a horse's hooves. It shies. The rider, caught unawares, tumbles off, letting go of the reins as he lands in the heather. The horse bolts.

Leaving the junior Corporal of Horse in charge of the troop, the senior Corporal of Horse and I give chase. After a mile it's clear the runaway is making for camp and its lunchtime feed, so I leave the Corporal of Horse to follow it, and return to the troop by way of a sandy track running along the top of a ridge.

With one man dismounted I decide to use that track because it is the easiest way back. We do a steady jog to start with, but have to slow to a walk when the horseless trooper runs out of puff.

Next moment there is the unmistakable crack of a passing bullet. Seconds later two more go by.

As I am ordering the troop to dismount, my junior Corporal of

Horse gives a little cough and slips out of his saddle – like they do in Westerns. It takes me a second to realise what is happening. There was no firing when I came this way a few minutes ago. Bloody hell! First thing is to get the troop out of the line of fire before anyone else or a horse is shot. I order two troopers to stay with the wounded Corporal of Horse, and tell the rest to follow me to a clump of trees in a dip below the ridge.

***

Once I'm sure they are safe, I go back to the injured Corporal of Horse. More bullets smack past. For a second I wish I had a steel helmet instead of a soft khaki officer's cap. There is no sound of firing, just the angry noise of passing bullets. There's no way of knowing what height they are or where they are coming from.

The Corporal of Horse is half lying, half sitting, keeping just below the lip of the road. He lifts his shirt to show me where the bullet struck him. I am relieved to see no blood, just a purplish mark on his ribcage, like a nasty kick from a horse. He is bloody lucky, a couple of inches lower and it could have been a very different matter.

I collect his hat, which is still lying where he fell. There seem to be even more bullets coming by, so I order everybody with me to crawl on hands and knees until we are off the ridge.

My father was in the cavalry in Palestine during the Second World War, and it strikes me it must be a long time since a British cavalry unit on horses last came under fire and took a casualty. Thank God it's nothing worse, and none of the horses have been hit.

Once we are in the trees, there is nothing to do but wait for the firing to finish. Which does happen not for quite a while. Pine needles shower us as a machine gun opens up, but the bullets pass twenty feet above our heads. Everyone remains calm and looks after their own horse, stroking and reassuring them.

I ask the Corporal of Horse if he will be able to ride.

He nods.

Leaving him in charge, I walk with the dismounted trooper to the road, and tell him to return to camp and explain to the Squadron Leader what has happened. I am angry on the way back to the spinney. Someone on the ranges obviously isn't firing at the targets in the butts, but deliberately over them.

The troop is relaxed when I get back. The Corporal of Horse is now standing stroking his horse. Everyone seems more worried about their mounts than they are about themselves. The bursts of fire become more intermittent, then cease.

I check my watch. Nearly lunchtime. I wait five minutes, still no bullets. I order the troop to mount, and we gallop to the road.

Once we are safely on the tarmac, I ask the Corporal of Horse how he is feeling.

'Bit bruised, sir. But it could have been much worse. I'm fine, sir.'

'Do you have any complaint about what happened?'

'One of those things, sir.' He gives a grin. 'I'll probably be the last Life Guard ever to be shot off a horse.'

We are both laughing when the Squadron Leader, alerted by the trooper I sent back, arrives in his Land Rover.

'All well?' he asks.

'Yes,' I say, saluting.

'You OK, Corporal of Horse?' he asks.

'Nothing that won't mend, sir.'

'Good, get something to eat, we'll delay the show jumping by half an hour. Bob, I want a word as soon as you get to the mess.'

Apprehensive, I salute as he gets back into the Land Rover.

Now we are alone, my Squadron Leader is not pleased. His usually red face is nearer purple. My punishment is to be duty officer until we return to London in a week's time. He says I am lucky the Corporal of Horse is not making a complaint, because if he did, 'the shit would really hit the fan'.

Mid-afternoon the Squadron Leader is called away from the show jumping for an urgent telephone call.

Soon I am standing in front of his desk again. My junior Corporal of Horse has been to see the Medical Officer at the Guards Depot at Pirbright to ask for a check-up because he had been shot. The Commandant rang the Squadron Leader to inform him that he was writing to the Commanding Officer of the Household Cavalry Regiment demanding a Court of Enquiry.

'Sorry, Bob, it's out of my hands,' he says resignedly. 'I rang the Commanding Officer, but he's away on leave and the Second in Command says it is too serious for him to deal with, so he's referred it on up the line.'

The Court of Enquiry takes a long time to convene. Apparently the incident went right up to the Major General commanding London District, who sent it back down the line, saying it was a Regimental matter, and criticised all those senior officers who had passed the buck. Over a couple of days of questioning me and all my troop, the Enquiry hears that the range warning signs were hidden by undergrowth and the flagpole was too far away to ascertain if there was a flag. If there was, it certainly was not flying.

The Court of Enquiry arranges for a site visit, and my troop and I are shocked by what we find. A 20 yard wide strip, mown to a height of two inches, has been cut all the way along the range boundary with the road. Newly painted signs stand out like beacons above the grass. A new bright red flag flutters in the early autumn breeze from a brilliant white flagpole. How, we are asked, could anybody not have seen either the signs or the flag?

To a man, everyone sticks to their original statements. Six weeks later I am summoned to see the Lieutenant Colonel commanding the Household Cavalry at Horse Guards, where Wellington and many other generals once reigned supreme. Feeling rather like a condemned man, I dress in my immaculately pressed khaki service dress jacket, highly polished Sam Browne belt, sword, best boots and breeches. At Horse Guards, I am shown straight in.

Facing me is the Colonel, seated at his desk in front of a life-size portrait of a moustachioed general in a dark blue frock coat. To my left, behind a smaller desk, is the Regimental Adjutant, beneath another life-size portrait. To my right, high sash windows overlook Horse Guards parade. I salute and keep standing to attention. My sword rattles in its scabbard as my nerves briefly get the better of me.

The interview is short and blunt. The Court of Enquiry held me ninety nine per cent responsible for endangering my troop. Promotion will not be coming my way. There is no chance of my going to the French cavalry school at Samur, so it is time to start thinking about what else I am going to do with the rest of my life.

I salute, about turn and march out. As if by magic the door is opened by a clerk as I approach it. No doubt he was listening and relaying everything to the others.

'Bad luck, sir,' says the chief clerk, confirming my suspicions.

***

Hearing I will be leaving the army, my father insists I go for an inter-view with the company which has taken over the family malting busi-ness. It turns out neither of us is enamoured of the other, so I spend my terminal leave training and riding point-to-pointers. I have no idea what to do next, except I'd like to travel and study horses and horsemen in a country which has an equine culture.

An army friend telephones me. He knows someone who is going to the central area of Afghanistan to search for the lost city of Firuzkuh. The expedition will be on horseback, and he needs a horse-coper to buy, look after, and eventually sell the horses.

I meet Nick a few days later. He is a well-built, six footer with longish fair hair, just 'down' from Oxford. He knows Afghanistan well, having spent the previous three summers there. Last year he found what he thought could be part of a city wall and, despite his camera not working and thus having no pictures to prove it, a publisher has given him an advance to finance the expedition. There will be just the two of us so that we can travel light and move fast. He is worried someone will hear about the expedition and try to muscle in to take the credit. Finding the lost city would bring him huge archaeological acclaim.

What luck! Afghanistan, the home of horsemen and buzkashi.

Me on the left, escorting HRH The Prince of Wales to receive the Freedom of the City of London.

CHAPTER THREE

Turkey: Cirit at Erzurum

It is impossible to get comfortable. The lack of legroom, the lumpy bus-seat padding and snoring of the Turk next to me, make sleep impossible. Also we are weaving through the mountains, and since our driver fell asleep at the wheel earlier in the night – our shouting woke him before we went off the road – I have been unable to relax.

Having spent the spring training my horses, and riding in Hunter Chases and Point-to-Points, it is time to continue my search for horse games, first in Turkey, then in Iran.

I am on my way to Erzurum in Eastern Turkey, where it has been suggested to me that cirit, a Seljuk cavalry training game, banned by the Sultan in the nineteenth century for being too dangerous, is still played.

Shortly after dawn we pull in at the long-distance bus terminus in Sivas. Everyone gets off, including the weary driver and his mate who has been sleeping on a mat in the luggage hold.

When the passengers claim their bags I see two chickens tied together perched on top of my backpack. A boy of about twelve scrambles into the hold to retrieve the fowls. He eventually succeeds with much squawking and flapping of wings. I just hope that some their inevitable accompaniment of fleas haven't managed to find their way into my clothes.

After a good breakfast of goat cheese, honey and half a loaf of bread, washed down with sweet black tea, we are on our way again. The same man is next to me. He sneezes loudly. His snot hits the window and he watches it slide slowly down to the sill. Once there he scoops it up with his finger and smears it on the back of the seat in front.

After a few minutes he fishes out a crumpled packet of cigarettes and lights one. The flaring match seems to suck all the oxygen out of the air, making me gasp for breath. After a few puffs he starts to cough, then spits between his legs. I look for another seat, but they are all occupied.

***

'*Yok!*' (no) says the receptionist when I enquire if they have a room. This is the fourth hotel I've been to that doesn't take foreigners.

I continue my tramp up the hill away from Erzurum bus station. Despite it being June, there is still snow on the tops of the surrounding hills, and a cold drizzle settles on my Norfolk jacket like a damp skin.

I pause to watch a horse being shod on the side of the road. It is still in its shafts. The shoe is cut from a piece of car tyre, and nailed on with carpentry nails; the cabbie holds up the leg while the farrier squats behind the hoof to knock them in.

I walk on until I meet a fellow traveller who tells me where he is staying. I go there. My room is on the top floor. It has a small filthy window, a bed with unchanged sheets – I'll definitely use my sleeping bag – and a stinking communal bathroom, where someone has artistically made the soap look like a Second World War seamine, by sticking cut toenails into it.

The tourist office is closed, but sitting on the steps is a badly shaven young man in a ill-fitting suit. He is Mahomet, a student, and asks in English if he can help.

I tell him I want to find out about a horse game I was told is played in eastern Turkey. (In Kabul Mr Tolon, the Turkish diplomat, had told me of an ancient wargame on horseback still played somewhere in this area.)

'That will be cirit,' he says.

'What?'

'Cirit. A game on horses, where men throw javelins at each other. It is very old and was banned, but they still play it round Erzurum. Come! My uncle is in charge of the Erzurum Horse Sports Club, I will take you to him.'

I can't believe my luck as I follow him down a narrow cobbled street.

His uncle, Murat, is a large man with a drooping moustache, wearing a flat cap. His office is small and dark, despite a naked lightbulb hanging from the ceiling. On his desk cigarette butts overflow the ashtray. A smile appears as Mahomet explains what I want.

'He says he will be honoured to tell you everything he can. Today most people are only interested in football. The name of the game is taken from the blunt ended javelin which players throw at each other. A cirit is about a metre long and two to three centimetres in diameter.'

Mahomet translates as Murat tells me about the game. The Seljuk Turks played it in the eleventh century to improve the horsemanship of

Warming up before the game. No protective clothing. The severe bit has caused the mouth to bleed.

Forgiving – waving a cirit over an opponent rather than throwing it at him at close quarters.

their light cavalry, to entertain their troops and civilians, and to show what formidable riders they were. In the nineteenth century, after a series of wild games at court in which young nobles were killed, the Sultan banned it, but it continued to be played in the eastern provinces. Still today, if a player is killed, he is *sehid* – that is, he will go straight to heaven as if he was killed in battle.

Murat says the teams are still called *alay* (regiment), and the team captains, *kolbashi* (army captain). The pitch at Erzurum is about 170 yards long and 50 wide with a high bank on either side which mark the edge of the pitch and provide a grandstand for the spectators. There are five parallel lines across the pitch: the centre line, and at either end there are the team lines, behind which the players stand. Ten yards into the pitch from the team lines are the throwing lines, beyond which an opponent must not throw. The area in between is the opponent's "neutral zone".

I ask how points are scored. He explains that one point is scored for hitting an opponent, two for knocking him out of the saddle or catching a thrown javelin and one point for "forgiving" an opponent, that is, waving a cirit over him rather than throwing it at him at close quarters. Points are deducted for going outside the confines of the pitch; failing to throw when it is your turn; crossing the team line before the opponent has thrown and entering the "neutral zone".

Issindi, the Georgian version of cirit.

If a horse is hit by a javelin, the thrower is sent off for the rest of the game. This shows the high value the Turks place on their horses, because in neighbouring Georgia, in Issindi – their version of **çççç** – a point is scored for hitting a horse.

The horses are mainly Tschenerans, well-known for their manoeuvrability, endurance and intelligence. They are a cross between Turkomans and Iranian Arabs. Their training starts aged four. Over the next year they learn to accelerate quickly, turn 90 degrees or more at a gallop, and hold a course while their rider drops down its side, or under its neck, to avoid being hit by a cirit. They must also be able to stop quickly.

'You want tea?' Mahomet asks.

'Yes, please.'

He nods to Murat who shouts loudly. Immediately the door opens and a young boy puts his head round it. Murat gabbles something and the boy retreats.

While we are waiting they ask me if I have any horses at home and what sort of riding I do. Racing they understand, but not jump-racing or cross country jumping. Why risk injury to yourself or your horse by going over something when you can go round it?

I enquire if it would be possible for me to visit a village to see the training.

'The villages are far away,' says Mahomet, who seems reluctant to answer. I push him to say more but, as soon as he mentions it, Murat throws his head back and says *yok*.

'There is no transport. It would be too far.'

'What about a taxi?'

'The roads are too bad; also the people in the villages do not like foreigners. I would not go to a village where I was not known. They can be...' Mahomet searches for the word, 'not friendly to people from outside.'

Five minutes later the boy returns with three large glasses of black tea and some bakhlava. We sip our tea in silence, each taking pieces of sticky pastry from the plate. When they are finished, we lick the last of the honey off our fingers.

Murat says there is a big game at the weekend, which I should see. The Erzurum *alay* will have its full complement of twelve horsemen; at lesser games there are only six or eight in a team. First there will be a parade through the town to attract spectators before going to the cirit field.

***

The procession is led by pipes and drums. Behind them come the kolbashi carrying their alay flags, then the Erzurum horsemen, in high-collared white shirts, thin black waistcoats and baggy black jodhpurs. The referees, in a horse taxi, bring up the rear.

Mahomet and I walk behind the cavalcade. At a crossroads some football fans cheer the horsemen, but carry on to the football stadium.

'When the old men die, there will be no one to watch cirit,' Mahomet comments. 'All the young think about is football.'

At the cirit ground the opposition are unloading their horses from a lorry backed up to an embankment. The horses in the lorry stand nose to tail, their heads over the wooden sides.

The spectators watch from the embankments on both sides and dignitaries have a stand with seats by the centre line.

While Murat, who is the senior referee, tosses a coin for the visiting kolbashi to choose ends, Mahomet points to a table where the Erzurum players and their blue-shirted opponents are each signing a piece of paper.

'It is a declaration by the players that their families will not carry out a vendetta if they are badly injured or killed during the game. Each player has to swear there is no ill will between them and any of the opposition. If there is, they will not be allowed to play'. He points, 'That shaven-headed player is very strong and will have a rope tied round his upper arm to stop him throwing too hard.'

We move to the embankment to watch the horses being tested to see if they are well-schooled. The referees ride some and players ride others. They urge them into a gallop, then turn sharply, stand in the stirrups pretending to throw, and rein them in hard.

Mahomet says the younger horses are always ridden by the same riders because they respond better to a rider they know. Any horse judged not to be well-schooled is not allowed to take part.

The players go to their respective ends where they plant their flags.

The two junior referees go to the throwing lines, while Murat remains on the centre. The game starts when the first Erzurum player trots down the pitch.

'How do they choose who starts?' I ask Mahomet.

'It is always the youngest player. He must be over eighteen, and have satisfied his kolbashi he is good enough.'

'How do they know whose turn it is?'

Setting off after an opponent.

Then he throws, his cirit missing the target as his opponent leans away from his horse.

'They line up in order of throwing. Every player throws at his opposite number and when everyone has thrown they start again.'

The horse breaks into a slow canter as it nears the Blues' throwing line. The young player shouts a warning and feints a throw.

His over-eager Blue opponent surges forward over his team line, incurring a penalty point.

There are two more feints, but no one moves. Then he throws, his cirit missing as his target leans away from it.

The first Blue urges his horse into a gallop.

The young Erzurum player turns swiftly, and lying low on his horse's neck, gallops back to the safety of his own end.

The Blue throws from just past the centre line, but his javelin goes wide. He frantically hauls his mount round to escape the next Erzurum player, who enters the game as soon as the cirit leaves the Blue's hand.

The next Erzurum player closes fast as his Blue opponent completes his turn and pushes his horse on with hands and heels (spurs are not allowed).

The spectators cheer their players on as the gap closes. The Erzurum player is directly behind and on a faster horse, so there is no chance of the Blue dropping down one side to present a smaller target.

Three quarters of the way down the pitch the Erzurum player shouts a warning, gallops up alongside his opponent, and waves his cirit over his quarry, 'forgiving' him. He then turns using the full width of the pitch to maintain his speed.

His Blue pursuer can't get near him, and has to throw from the throwing line.

The last man in the Erzurum team is Shaven Head. His horse bounces on the spot as he watches his team-mate being run down by a faster Blue opponent and nearly knocked out of the saddle when the javelin hits him in the ribs.

The Erzurum spectators boo.

As soon as the Blue chaser throws, Shaven Head lets his horse go, charging straight up the side of the pitch to cut off his opponent's retreat while he is still turning.

The Blue horseman spots Shaven Head's tactics and brings his horse to a sudden halt so that Shaven Head overshoots and has to turn back.

Blue slips past him.

Despite being in a sharp turn, Shaven Head shouts a warning and throws. The cirit passes well behind its target and hits an unwary spectator on the head. Shaven Head slows his horse, and, knowing he is too far ahead for the next Blue to catch him, canters gently back to his place on the team line.

Meanwhile two ambulance men carry the unconscious spectator away on a stretcher. In the brief lull, designated boys run round collecting thrown cirits from the pitch, and hand them to the players before the game speeds up again.

At half time, while everyone watches a troupe of local men dancing to the pipes and drums, Mahomet and I get a closer look at the horses. They are between 15 and 16 hands, light-boned with fine faces, strong necks and a high head carriage. Several have bloody mouths from the riders' rough handling and I notice that the martingales are attached to the bits rather than the nose band.

Mahomet talks to a young groom who is keen to tell us all he can. Next year he will be eighteen. He has already passed the riding test and boasts of his ability to throw a cirit. He says it is a matter of being part of the horse and using its momentum to help you throw further.

He says there are no big games in winter, but most weekends there are practices in the villages. In early spring they do long rides,

Trying to catch a cirit at close quarters

galloping fast for short bursts then dropping back to a canter. With the spring grass and extra grain the exercise increases until the horses are "campaign fit" – interesting they still use a military expression.

The music stops and the players remount. It is time for me to find a good place for photographs. With the embankments covered in spectators I try the edge of the pitch, but am immediately warned off. I go to the Erzurum throwing line, but am photographing into the sun. While going round the back of the embankment to get to the Blue end, where the sun will be behind me, I miss the start of the second half.

I get some good shots when the riders are near, but miss a melée round the centre line in which eight horsemen are involved.

Murat shouts at the riders to go back to their own ends as soon as they have thrown. The pace immediately slows as they sort themselves out rather than risk penalty points for disrupting the play.

I have a fast black and white film in one camera, but the colour film is slower, and with clouds causing light changes, the camera settings constantly need altering. Luckily Mahomet explained most of the moves in the first half so, although I can't follow the game as closely as I'd like, I have a good idea what is going on.

At one point an Erzurum player drops down the side of his horse to get away from a Blue, but his foot slips out of the stirrup and he comes off. He lands on his feet and for a couple of strides keeps upright holding onto the mane of his galloping horse. Then he trips and rolls head over heels.

The Blue player waits for him to get to his feet before 'forgiving' him.

Another Erzurum player rides out as the fallen rider limps slowly along the edge of the pitch towards a cirit picker-up who has caught his horse.

In the closing minutes the speed of the game increases as the players take ever greater risks, leaving before their opponent has thrown and chasing right up to the throwing lines. Points and penalties mount as the spectators encourage their teams.

It seems no time before the pipes and drums start playing, announcing the end of the game. The players ride to the centreline while the referees confer. The band stops as Murat announces the penalties and points. Erzurum win by two and their supporters roar triumphantly. The music starts again and both teams dismount and dance, while the grooms lead the sweating horses away.

Murat explains the dancing shows there is no ill-will, and soon the teams and their senior supporters will go to a feast.

He says I am lucky because it was one of the best matches he has seen. There will not be another game here for at least six weeks as the team will be visiting other provinces.

Tomorrow I will set off for our Embassy in Iran to find out if the Royal Artillery are willing to pay me £50 to go on to Herat in Afghanistan, to photograph some British cannons I found in the moat of the fortress. I think they date from the siege of Herat in 1837-8.

The next morning I nearly miss my bus to Tehran waiting for Mahomet. Sad to leave without saying goodbye, I hang on at the hotel. In the end I have to take a horse taxi to the bus station.

He is waiting by the bus.

'I am so sorry, Mister Bob. I had a message from my aunt last night; my uncle was very ill and I had to get him to hospital. He has rheumatism of the brain.'

'What is that?'

'He gets very bad headaches, and forgets things.'

'I hope he gets better soon.'

'Inshallah,' he says with a sad smile.

CHAPTER FOUR

Iran: Azil Arabs

'Bob!' I look up to the gallery above the reception area in our Embassy in Tehran. Standing there is Major Arthur Gooch, my ex-Life Guards Squadron Leader from Hong Kong. I can't believe it. I have just asked to see the Military Attaché, and he must be it.

'Come on up.'

I bound up the stairs, and follow him into his office. I still can't quite believe it.

He says he has only been here a couple of weeks. He is living in a hotel with his wife Sarah and two daughters until their house is ready.

He is Assistant Military Attaché. His boss deals direct with the Shah over the sale of some Chieftain tanks because the corruption is so bad. Apparently their defence procurers have been over-ordering and getting cash instead of the extra equipment. We chat over coffee, catching up. He thinks there is someone in the Embassy who might have a useful address for me. He rings a couple of people.

'Mrs Mary Gharagozlou at the Royal Horse Society is your best bet. She is in charge of the breeding programme of Persian Arabs, recording the blood-lines, some of which go back hundreds of years.'

'Please.' I can't get over it, meeting Arthur, and now this.

'Be there tomorrow morning, nine thirty,' he says putting the phone down. 'Where are you staying?'

'Down by the station.'

'Bit hot there, isn't it?'

'Yes.'

'No air conditioning I suppose?'

'I've got a fan, like in Hong Kong.'

'But it wasn't 110 degrees there.'

'True.' We both laugh.

'How about dinner this evening?' he asks. 'Pick you up about eight. Sarah will be delighted to see an old face.'

'Fantastic. I look forward to it.'

Before I leave, I ask about the guns in Herat. Arthur tells me the Royal Artillery are not interested, so there is no need for me to go to Afghanistan.

***

The next morning I set off in good time to walk to the Royal Horse Society office. It is just after eight o'clock and already the heat bounces off the pavement. The dual carriageway is static with traffic and the fumes, trapped by the tall buildings on either side, sting my eyes. I walk slowly, keeping in the shade wherever I can, because I'm wearing my lightweight Norfolk tweed jacket to look smart when I meet Mrs Gharagozlou.

In Turkey, the combination of my jacket and short hair set me apart from other travellers and got me interviews with the very conservative horse faction, who would not want to have any dealings with long-haired westerners.

Mrs Gharagozlou, a tallish, attractive woman in her mid-forties, ushers me into her air-conditioned office. Within minutes we are both talking at the same time, gabbling questions while trying to provide answers. Her late husband, Majid Khan Bakhtiari, chief of the Bakhtiari tribe, introduced her to the Asil (pure) Persian Arab horses, about which she is as passionate as I am about finding horse games. After two hours she asks if I would like to go with her to the Royal Stud in the mountains behind Hamadan in three days' time. What luck!

I hadn't expected things to happen this quickly, so bring forward my plans to visit Isfahan. There I photograph the huge polo pitch, with its galleried palace on one side, from which the Shah Abbas the First watched the matches at the beginning of the seventeenth century. Apparently there could be as many as fifty players on each side and the games became miniature battles. Now the pitch is an enormous traffic island decorated with flower beds and only the stone goal posts remain to show its past use.

***

The traffic is light, and the bus gets me to the Royal Horse Society an hour early. While waiting I visit a stall across the road selling crushed fruit drinks. My favourite is melon. Large chunks of fruit, plus a spoonful of sugar and a pile of ice are whizzed up in a blender. The result is a pale green mush with small pieces of ice giving it a crunch. Delicious, but not without repercussions, as I found out later.

When the Society opens the receptionist gives me a message. Mary's Land Rover has broken down and we'll be leaving at eight tomorrow morning from her house in Tadjrish, a fashionable area in the north of the city where the rich live above the smog and heat.

I catch a bus back to the station. A hundred yards from the hotel a severe spasm of stomach cramp doubles me over. While I am stationary a man collapses on the opposite side of the road. A crowd builds as his violent twitches reduce to smaller ones, then he is still.

One of the remaining polo goal posts in Isfahan.

The traffic rushes past, and the crowd drifts away. A policeman walks by, ignoring the crumpled body.

I gingerly straighten up, clench my buttocks, and pray to get to the hotel before losing control of my bowels. It's lucky the journey's not today, so I can take plenty of blockers-up before tomorrow. I will avoid the melon drink from now on.

It is a long slow drive because Hussein, the driver, says the new Land Rover is 'running in' and only allowed to do 60kph. Even with the windows open we are hot and tired by the time we reach Hamadan. The stomach pills have worked and, without the slightest twinge, I watch the scenery as it changes from dry scrub, to wheat fields and then green foothills with high mountains in the background. The only blot is the brick kilns two kilometres out, whose tall crooked chimneys belch thick, black, crude oil smoke. The old town itself is being ripped apart, to make way for wide, automobile-friendly streets and modern houses.

On the journey Mary tells me Iran was ravaged by African horse sickness 15 years ago – a midge-borne disease with a high mortality rate. A huge number of horses died and mechanisation took over to fill the gap. Now horses are becoming fashionable again but, in the intervening years, the knowledge of horsemanship has been lost. She gives me an example:

A rich man bought an in-foal Arab mare. When it foaled he called in an ancient horseman to see it.

'See what a beautiful strong foal I have,' the owner said.

'Yes,' replied the old man.

'Also look at its long ears, it gets those from its father,' the owner said proudly.

'Yes,' said the old man, 'it's bound to. You have a mule.'

Mary says mules are common here. It is believed that if an Asil mare is mated to an inferior stallion, some of his genes will remain in her system. These will come out in any future foal, even if she is put to a top stallion. To get round this, they mate her with a donkey whose genes won't be carried forward – the end result, of course, being a mule.

Also there is a saying, "a good foal is a caught foal."

Many Asil mares stand up to foal. When they come close to foaling, they often throw themselves onto the ground several times, as if trying to move the foal. Then, as the foal starts to come, they stand up. Quite a few are injured if someone isn't there to catch the foal as it comes out.

A mare with her mule foal. Mares are only put to top stallions because it is believed that if she is put to an inferior stallion some of his genes will stay in her and be passed on to her next foal, but if she is put to a donkey no genes will be carried forward.

Once we have our provisions we drive through the hills to Mary's house. I watch a mare and foal grazing in part of the garden while an elderly couple lay out carpets on the grass for us to sit on. We drink tea in the twilight, the long shadows of the surrounding trees slowly merge together in the gathering night.

I wash in a stream and put on my jacket and tie for dinner. It is superb. Rice, chicken, naan, yogurt and melon, followed by the inevitable black tea.

Hussein, the driver, who is also an accountant, says goodnight and installs himself away from the fire, while Mary and I, wrapped in our sleeping bags beside the dying embers, talk Asil horses well into the starlit night.

Her late husband, Majid Khan, introduced her to them. He gave her a top stallion to ride. Twice she rode with Majid, but the third time she went on her own. The horse behaved well, picking its way carefully over the rock-strewn hillside, until it saw a movement off to one side and broke into a gallop without warning. There was nothing she could do to slow him, and she thought at any moment he would trip and they would both be badly injured. The horse paid no attention to her as he followed what she could now see was a gazelle. After a couple of miles the gazelle jinked, scrambled up a rock-face and disappeared. The stallion slowed, and responded to her commands as if nothing had happened.

Back at camp she told Majid Khan, who understood immediately what had happened. He and the other horse owners often went gazelle hunting. While the others watched, the chosen hunter, armed with a single shot rifle or bow with one arrow, would approach a gazelle at a walk. It was necessary to come in at 45 degrees. Too shallow an angle, and the gazelle would run straight and, being faster than a horse, would get away before the hunter could get a shot. Too wide an angle; it would spot the hunter too early and escape. This is what the stallion was trained for; he had seen the gazelle and chased it.

He said the horses had to pick their own way because, once a rider was close to his quarry, he needed both hands to fire the rifle or shoot the arrow. To him the sure-footedness was in the breeding. Only the best tribal horses were able to run fast in such conditions.

'He took me on two hunts when we were first married,' Mary says. 'We followed at a distance. It was very exciting.'

'Is there any chance of seeing a hunt?' I ask.

'No. There hasn't been a hunt since the African sickness came, and ..,' she pauses and lowers her voice, 'Majid was … killed.'

From her tone I know not to ask any questions. I've been told that she has had a tough time since his plane crashed. It happened when the Shah was trying to stop the nomadic tribes from migrating, and the Bakhtiaris' political influence was being curtailed.

The old couple wake us as they relight the fire. Once I have washed and shaved in the mountain stream we sit round for a breakfast of black tea, naan and jam, then it is time to get back in the Land Rover. First to Hamadan for more supplies, then up into the hills to the Royal Stud.

Nearing our destination the track disintegrates into a bog, with rocks. The people in the lower village resent a man in the upper village who has an old army truck he uses as a bus, so they have blocked the irrigation ditch. This floods the road, making it impassable except in a four-wheel drive. By the time we are on the last stretch to the Stud, one of the shock-absorbers has a pronounced squeak.

Mary with her driver and head groom leaving a nomad encampment. Note the woven hurdles which kept the children in and the dogs and sheep out.

The village where the Stud is located is built on the side of a hill and has a stream that weaves its way down, watering the different gardens.

Mary takes me to the stables, which are built on a rocky outcrop and catch the cooling winds. Outside the main door raked horse droppings dry in the sun, ready for bedding down this evening. Thick beams resting on the stone walls support the roof of packed earth on wattle. The light comes from the large double doors at either end, but despite it being cool, the stable-block smells of urine and there are a lot of flies buzzing round. A few horses in railed stalls eat alfalfa off the floor, but most of the spaces are empty. Mary says a lot of the horses are grazing in a nearby paddock and that these are the summer stables, away from the heat of the plains. In the autumn all the horses will go down to avoid the winter snow.

We walk up a steep path leading to a stone house with a slate roof in urgent need of repair. It looks out over the village to the hazy plain in the far distance. Carpets have been spread out for us. We sit outside eating cherries from the garden, while our baggage and supplies are brought up by two lads leading donkeys.

We return to the stables in the late afternoon to watch the horses being brought back. They are longer-legged than most Arab horses I have come across, but are well put together. Mary says she and Hassan will stay to sort out the stables, while a guide takes me for a ride through the mountains. I am given a bay mare with a longish-back called Atlas.

The guide, once we have set off, makes it clear that he does not want to take me anywhere. As soon as we are round the first corner he breaks into a fast canter trying to leave me behind, but he isn't a brilliant rider and it is easy to keep up on my sure-footed mare. After 20 minutes he says we can turn back, but I insist we go on further to a small village I glimpsed when we went over a rise.

Reluctantly he agrees and lets me pick our route. Near the village he takes a short-cut, but the going is rough. By galloping on the footpath I beat him and, to his clear annoyance, ride up the narrow street in front of him. By the time we get back I'm in love with Atlas. She is a wonderful ride on a long rein, and so responsive. The stables smell of disinfectant and all the beds are made up with what looks like peat, but is in fact the dried horse dung I saw earlier.

After supper by the fireside Mary tells me about a horse game that has been banned. In the past brides were stolen from other encampments or villages, so that there was no chance of inbreeding. Later, rather than stealing girls, the marriages were arranged, but to keep the tradition alive a game was devised. The males of the two families involved lined up in two rows, with the bridegroom at one end and the bride at the other. The bridegroom rode through his family lines before passing between the bride's lines. When he reached the bride, he took a scarf from her head and galloped back to his village.

The bride's relations gave chase to take the scarf from him before he got there, while his village menfolk did their best to defend him. A lot of the skirmishes were good-natured, but occasionally they turned into running battles. On these occasions people were killed or injured and the bride could be widowed before she was married.

'Once,' she says, 'a mother wove the scarf into her daughter's hair to prevent her future husband from claiming her.

'The bridegroom was a fine horseman and, unaware of what had happened and showing off, grabbed the scarf at a gallop. He broke the girl's neck and in the ensuing melée he and a couple of his relations were killed by her family.

'The story reached Tehran and pressure was put on the Shah to stop the "primitive" nomads from pursuing such barbaric practices in the twentieth century.'

'What happened if the scarf was taken by the bride's family?'

'Mostly the wedding went ahead, but sometimes the groom was considered unworthy and there was no marriage. But that happened very occasionally. Majid Khan knew of it happening only once.'

We ride out every day to various black tent encampments in the surrounding mountains. At each we dismount but only after the ferocious anti-wolf guard dogs have been taken away. They wouldn't hesitate to rip a stranger apart. We leave our shoes outside before entering the low black goat-hair tents. Women in long colourful dresses, wearing a type of turban and jangling silver bangles on their wrists, serve sour yoghurt mixed with water to cool us, then strong sweet black tea.

Woven hurdles round the open front and sides keep the small children in and the animals out. The men are away working in the towns or in the hills. The older children shepherd the sheep and goats, searching for grazing on the barren hills. I'm told that in spring the hills are green, but now it is mid-summer and everywhere is brown, except for beside the little rills that run down the narrow valleys.

At each place Mary disappears into the women's quarters to hear their problems, while Hassan and I wait in the guest area. She was once a government minister and knows exactly who to contact to try to help improve the nomads' lives.

After a while we mount up and move on.

Left: Azil Arab mare with white socks and blaze, which are common markings. Right: the Shah's top stallion.

A yearling Azil Arab

She knows not only where the encampments are, but also the different family clans the people belong to.

On my last evening we sit close to the fire talking as the burning wood explodes from time to time, throwing sparks towards the stars. We eat cherry rice because we have run out of meat.

She asks whether I would come back to train racehorses here. Some thoroughbreds are being imported and there are plans for a new racecourse.

'It is an interesting thought,' I say very tempted. 'But first I must find more horse games before they die out.'

'You remind me very much of Wilfred when I first met him.'

'Wilfred?' I query.

'Thesiger. You have something of his driven quality. I wish you well.'

To be compared to the great British explorer of Arabia is the biggest compliment I've ever been paid.

'Got a fag, mate?'

I am staying in Davood's house. He is a taxi driver who picked me up at the bus depot in Tabriz and insisted I stay at his house. I have spent the last ten days travelling up the west side of the country, in between Lake Rezaiyeh and the Turkish border, in a fruitless search for more horses. It isn't a route used by foreigners and the police in each new town regard me with the utmost suspicion. In Sanandaj, after being searched by a police officer who spent far too long inspecting my crotch, while not even looking in my shoulder bag, I was locked up with an armed guard and missed my bus. Eventually an unshaven man in a creased suit arrived and demanded my passport from my escort. He looked at it briefly and, to my relief, sent me on my way.

In Mahabad three plain clothes police came to my room asking for my passport. After 20 minutes they still couldn't write my name on their form, so I filled it in for them. They became most effusive when I said I was a tourist and ended up staying for tea and cakes, while I tried not to scratch.

I first picked up human fleas on the bus from Hamadan and then proceeded to get more on each journey. One pair of socks was so infested I left them behind in Rezaiyeh. But in the heat in Mahabad, as I entertained the three friendly SAVAK (secret police), I was being driven nearly demented.

Once the policemen had gone I stripped off but was unable to find the fleas, though there were lots of bites on my stomach.

Hassan, Davood's brother, opens some purple doors off the street. We pass through a covered porch before entering a paved courtyard dotted with trees. He leads me to the house opposite the entrance. We remove our shoes and he takes me into a room, the floor covered in gilims and carpets.

His mother, a scarf over her head and lower face, peeps round the door.

He orders tea and fried eggs, then leans back against the wall and talks to me in broken English.

His sister calls from behind the door that the tea is ready and he takes the tray from her. Several cups later the eggs arrive, floating in oil and with an enormous piece of naan to scoop them up.

Hassan breaks the yolks with a piece of naan, then stirs before signalling me to dip in.

When Davood gets back we go to a chai khana (tea house) to meet some of his friends. The conversation turns to politics, a subject on which I refuse to be drawn. Several Westerners have been arrested for defamatory remarks about the Shah. Often the people who put them on the spot are SAVAK (secret police) agents posing as students.

As we go back to Davood's house he thanks me for being discreet. If I had said the wrong thing he and his brother would have been arrested as well. One of the group is a known informer.

The next evening we go to the cinema to see *Wild Geese*, which I saw last year in Pakistan in English. The audiences couldn't be more diffcrent. In Pakistan the watchers cheered as the British mercenary heroes, led by Richard Burton, looked as if they were going to win. Then booed at the final act of betrayal. Here, despite it being in Farsi,

Horses are still the main transport in the mountain areas because of the steepness of the hills and the rocky terrain. Good gazelle country.

no one even murmurs, and many walk out once they realise what is going to happen.

I ask Davood what he thought about the film. Looking round to see who is near him, he says betrayal is so common in Iran that it made him feel sick when he saw it. Even your brother might be an informer. There is a lack of chat till we get to a tea house, where he suggests we find some prostitutes.

When I decline he says he knows where there are some hippie girls who will do it for a good meal.

'I'm married,' I lie.

He looks sceptical.

'Why isn't your wife with you?' he asks. 'Most Westerners travel with their wives.'

'She is expecting a baby.' I pull out a picture of my current girlfriend, which is passed round the table.

'She is very pretty,' Davood says, slapping me on the back. 'You're a lucky man.'

It is my last morning and I have just finished washing when Davood's mother taps me on the shoulder and, to my surprise, beckons me into the women's quarters. Here the floor coverings are more worn, the mattresses thinner, and the bed covers more faded than in the main living room. Davood, whose mattress I have been using, is asleep, sharing with his youngest brother. I sit by the plastic sheet spread in the centre of the room. Naan and chai are laid out for me and Davood.

At 5am the alarm goes off. Davood's mother shakes him. He looks at me blearily, then nods.

On the way to the bus station we are stopped by a policeman. He comes straight to me, demands my passport, then asks for porn magazines.

I say I haven't any. He glances at my backpack, shrugs and hands back my passport.

Davood says my jacket and tie made me look too official for the policeman to do anything. At the bus station Davood kisses me on both cheeks as he says goodbye.

It is stifling in the bus, but no one will open a window because of the dust. The countryside is back to boring brown as we trundle through the hills north of Tabriz. It is so unlike round Lake Rezaiyeh, where yellow fields of sunflowers intermingled with green grass paddocks and, in the far distance, hazy brown mountains met the clear blue sky. Water buffalo and cattle lazed in the shade unlike here, where sheep and goats wander constantly searching for a few stalks of dry grass. I let the curtain fall back across the window, cutting out the sun. I try to sleep; it's a long way to Ardebil.

***

'Eh mister, you speak English?'

'Yes,' I say wearily for what seems to be the hundredth time today. I know what is coming next.

'Hello, 'ow are you?'

'Fine, thank you. And you?'

My questioner bursts into giggles with his friends. I swear that is the last time I answer anyone again today.

'Hey mister, you speak English?'

I keep walking.

'Oi mate, you speak English?'

I look across the street to where the voice came from, but there is no Englishman there.

'Want a fag?'

It has to be an Englishman, nobody else speaks like that. A young Iranian man detaches himself from a group of youths and crosses the road.

'You English?'

'Yes,' I say, still dumbfounded.

'Thought you must be. No one else would wear a jacket and tie in a dump like this.'

'I'm Bob,' I say holding out my hand.

'Shaibet,' he says taking it. 'I'm doing engineering at Southampton University. I'm home for the summer holidays. What are you doing here?'

'Looking for games played on horseback.'

'You're wasting your time here. Tractors have taken over. All part of the Shah's agricultural reforms. You might see a few horses pulling carts, but the horse sickness killed off most of them. Look, I'm with some mates who don't speak English, so how about me showing you round tomorrow?'

'Great! I'm at the Hotel Sepide,' I point back down the street.

'O.K. Meet you there at ten.'

***

Although in a back street, Shaibet's house is quite grand. It is arranged round a courtyard with carefully tended flowerbeds and trees. In the guest room there are expensive carpets instead of gilims. We sit under the trees drinking chai, before he shows me round the town.

He is right. It is a dump. A huge modernisation programme is going on and it looks as if a bulldozer has been driven through the centre to make a new dual carriageway. On one side is what is left of the dome-roofed bazaar, which is still trading, and on the other stumps of mud-brick houses.

The next day we take a taxi to Sarein. The driver, a fat man, (whose enormous belly fully tests the strength of the cotton holding on his shirt buttons), has to use a starting handle to get the car going. Then, at the top of every hill, shoehorns himself out to refill the steaming radiator. All the while the grating of the rear axle vibrates through the back seat on which five of us are squashed. From the top of the last rise he coasts down to the village.

Although it is in the middle of nowhere, there are several hotels and a number of holiday chalets. Shaibet tells me the hot springs attract people from all over northern Iran. We walk past the high-walled swimming baths with hessian screens on top of the walls hiding the ladies' enclosure. Cars and minibuses jostle for parking amongst the stalls. Those nearest the baths sell soap, shampoo, towels, sarongs and swimming trunks, the others mainly food and fizzy drinks.

We walk to the largest public bath. Shaibet says his father sometimes hires one of the smaller ones for parties. We each buy a shampoo sachet.

Inside it is rather like a Roman bath must have been. The roofed sides have pegs on the walls for hanging clothes. Shaibet chooses some empty pegs while I look round. It is a large rock pool with grey water just over waist deep. At one end the men float, swim or stand chatting, while at the other they are washing, the white suds frothing down an open drain. The hot water burns my legs, even away from the thermal springs which bubble up through the gravel floor.

Shaibet laughs at the face I pull, and insists we stay in for ten minutes. It will give us an appetite. A lot of people come here because the water is supposed to make them hungry. Judging by the size of many

The hot water baths at Sarein.

of them, they could do with losing a few pounds, not putting more on. They parade round the edge proudly sticking out their paunches.

Shaibet and I agree to take turns watching our bags while the other washes their hair. He cuts a hole in his soap sachet on a protruding nail before getting in.

I take the opportunity to survey the scene. There is no standard dress. The better-off wear swimming trunks, while others wear sarongs or towels. In one corner, a group of grey-bearded men in patched long-johns sit on the side with their legs dangling in the water.

Shaibet comes back. I can't find his nail, so decide to tear open the sachet once I am in the washing area. I tug and squeeze, but the plastic is too strong. I resort to ripping it open with my teeth. The instant it punctures half the contents squirt into my mouth. Instinctively I wash my mouth out, and immediately regret it as the shampoo foams furiously. It takes several mouthfuls of filthy water to get rid of the froth.

'You have no idea how funny you looked,' Shaibet says laughing. 'You looked like a mad person.'

Mad is how I feel for the next two days cooped up within instant striking distance of the loo. I'm sure it's because of the water I washed my mouth out with that I am now twisted with stomach cramps.

Alexander's Wall

When I get back to Tehran I contact Arthur who insists I stay with him. He says I look thinner than when he last saw me and we both laugh as I explain why. He apologises that it will have to be a bed on the verandah. For me it will be wonderful after the small baking-hot brick room on the roof of my down-town hotel. Although they are in their house now, they are still waiting for the bonded warehouse to release all the boxes containing their personal goods so that they can finally be surrounded by their own things.

I ring Mary Gharagozlou. She wants me to meet Louise Firooz, who discovered Caspian Horses while looking for ponies for her children to ride.

Louise, an American married to an Iranian, lives in a large house in the countryside just outside Tehran. Over the inevitable black tea she tells me about the small horses she discovered seven years ago. They are like miniature thoroughbreds, which is why they are called horses rather than ponies, even though they average only 11.2 hands. They were being used for pulling carts and carrying loads in the steeply wooded hills south of the Caspian Sea. She found six stallions and seven mares and started a carefully controlled breeding programme. While she is telling me this a young goat canters in and leaps on and off the white leather sofas.

'Don't take any notice of him,' she says. 'He'll settle down in a minute. No!' she shouts fiercely. 'Don't poop on that chair!'

The goat takes no notice and, once it has finished, gallops round the room twice before munching on a large flower arrangement.

A servant comes in with a dustpan and brush, and sweeps up the offending pellets.

Louise takes us outside to some beautifully railed paddocks where the Caspians are kept. They are fine-limbed with neat heads – just as I was told: 'little thoroughbreds.'

She says they are kind; her children ride the stallions as well as the mares.

'They are the chariot horses on the friezes at Persepolis,' she says. 'Until now it was thought the ancient sculptors made the horses look small because they were less important than the soldiers.' Louise pauses. 'But now measurements have been done and the Caspians are in perfect proportion to the chariot horses on the friezes at Persepolis. That means they're one of, if not the, oldest breed of domesticated horse in existence.'

For a time we watch her children having a riding lesson from a German, who has been employed to instruct the top Iranian riders in dressage.

'Our old ways will soon be forgotten,' Mary says quietly as we take our leave. 'Everyone wants to compete with the West. We have, or had, a lot to offer. You, my dear friend, are too late...'

We drive in silence.

'I am taking you to the Shah's stables. You will see what I mean.'

We drive through some green well-irrigated paddocks to an arena where they are show jumping.

'They have discovered that, besides being wonderful long-distance horses, Turkomans are good jumpers.'

I look at the horses. They are much more like thoroughbreds than any Arabs I have seen.

'In the north these horses were once used for racing and raiding. They could cover over a hundred miles in a day without water. In the past they ate more or less the same as their riders: meat, dates, barley, raisins, and alfalfa. Now it is just alfalfa and grain.' She shakes her head, then brightens up. 'You must go to Gorgan, there are some good trainers there. They still do things the old-fashioned way.'

***

The bus to Gorgan tears along the Caspian beach, swerving to avoid parked cars. Out of the window I see women in black garb wallowing in the mud-coloured shallows, while men and boys in swimming trunks play in the deeper water.

'Westernisation ends at the outskirts of Tehran,' says Ali, the boy sitting next to me.

I make no comment.

'Why are you going to Gorgan?'

'To see some Turkoman horses and visit Alexander's Wall.'

A caravanserai. The animals stay in the centre while the people and goods stay in lock-ups under the arches. The water in the centre is used for both animals and humans.

'There are no horses,' he states. 'What is Alexander's Wall?'

'It is a wall built hundreds of years ago from the Caspian Sea to the mountains in the east. It was built to keep out raiders from the steppes.'

'I have never heard of it. Are you sure?'

'Yes, it is marked on a map I have.'

'I will ask my cousins. They will meet me off the bus.'

His cousins come with me to find a hotel. Five hotels offer them a room, but change their minds when told it is for me. Two say they are full and the eighth agrees to take me at twice the advertised rate.

Ali apologises. The boys are embarrassed by the racism shown by the hotel receptionists towards me, and insist on accompanying me everywhere. Despite Ali's comment that there are no horses, the cousins know of a stud five miles out of town.

We catch a minibus to a village, then walk a mile to a high-walled compound on a slight rise above the flat plain. The gates are open, so we walk in and ask a young boy to take us to the person in charge.

He points to a man in the centre of enclosure with five horses being ridden round him. He is wearing a long loose coat with a sash, with a knife hanging from it, a round sheepskin hat and short boots without heels. When we get closer I see he has Asiatic features, as do all the stable boys.

'He is Turkmene,' Ali says quietly.

I salaam with my hand over my heart.

The cousins explain I am interested in horses and he smiles, the lines round his eyes forming into a single crinkle. Taking my hand he leads me over to a lean-to stable where half a dozen horses are tied up, eating freshly cut alfalfa. I note their fine limbs and long necks. These are his milking mares. By the end of their first week foals are taught to drink from a bucket. They have their mother's milk for 90 days and are then swapped onto camel milk because, he maintains, it is better for their bones. They are also given grain and dates in season, but kept off green feed because it makes the teeth go soft. Sometimes they get raisins and, in winter, the fat from the tail of fat-tailed sheep, which helps keep them warm.

I go over to look at a foal. It is five months old and I'm told it will be racing in the New Year. So young! I'm stunned. I question the old man again. He tells me all horses race as yearlings. The fastest are kept and others are sold off to local farmers for pulling carts; nowadays most are sold to people for riding. What happens if a horse is a late developer? He shrugs; either they race well as yearlings, or go.

What about the horses circling? They all raced at a year old and are being got ready for the coming season, which will start when the weather gets cooler.

The jockeys?

On the yearlings the riders are small boys, under five stone. The more experienced ride the older horses. He says before the border with the Soviet Union was closed they were able to pick from a wide range of stallions and mares, but now breeding has to be more carefully organised. However, this year the government has arranged for four stallions from Turkmenistan to be imported to improve the stock.

I watch the circling boys. They have small saddles but, unlike Western jockeys, they ride long, with their feet thrust forward and knees tucked in behind the horse's shoulder muscles. The position is not unlike people riding bareback.

I point to several heavily rugged horses standing in the sun. Thick felt blankets stretch from their ears to over their tails and are held in

A track near Hamadan: a long and difficult journey lay ahead.

place with a surcingle round the chest just behind the withers.

The trainer says the rugs make the horses sweat to stop them from getting fat, while protecting them from the sun.

Before I can ask any more questions Ali says his cousins are bored and it is time to go.

Despite everyone's lack of interest, finding Alexander's Wall quickly becomes a fixation for me. I am desperate to see and walk along a piece of history which has largely been ignored.

Leaving Ali and his cousins, I go north east to a small town called Bandar-e-Kabus which, according to my contraband U2 spy plane map, isn't far from the Wall. On the bus I meet Walter, a German, on his way to meet Dieter, a fellow student who is researching the similarities between the Turkish and the Turkmene languages.

We book into the hotel Dieter recommended and he joins us later that evening. Walter insists in cooking with a primus stove in our bedroom. He is very particular about what he eats and bought 10 days' supply of food before leaving Tehran. The only local things he will consume are bread and tea. While Walter is doing the cooking, Dieter tells me he often crosses the Wall, because he is living a few miles north of it, but there isn't much to see; just a big ditch and a bank with some bricks on it. All I have to do is take a minibus.

We go to a pre-wedding party being held under a large awning on the edge of town. On the way an Iranian who calls himself Mac swoops on us. His English is good and he describes himself as a 'tourist hunter'. He claims there is nothing he doesn't know about the area and will be our guide. He persists on walking with us until we get to the party, where some young Turkomans welcome Dieter and turn Mac away.

All the men are in their finery, with sheepskin hats, ornate waistcoats over their shirts and baggy trousers tucked into soft leather boots. There is music and dancing with beer being served at the back of the shelter. Men dance singly, while women in bright shawls saunter in the background.

As it gets dark lanterns are lit and food is passed round. Walter tries to refuse, but Dieter says it would reflect badly on him if one of his friends didn't accept what was offered. We pour a small dish of sauce over the pilau rice, then scoop it up with naan. It is highly spiced and smells of saffron.

The next morning I leave early with Dieter. Walter was up half the night and says he is too ill to go anywhere.

The minibus bounces in and out of the dust-filled ruts, throwing us from side to side. The smell of unwashed livestock farmers increases as the interior warms up.

Dieter points ahead: I can see only scrub disappearing into the distance, but he says we are there. He shouts to the driver who stops with a jolt, throwing us into a heap. The bus-boy slides the door open, Dieter waves and I'm on my own.

The Wall is a scar across the flat landscape. On the north side – facing the enemy – there is a wide ditch from which earth has been scooped out and back to make a mound between six and twelve feet high on top of which the brick wall was once built. I walk along the top. There are broken red bricks everywhere and some bits of pottery. The countryside is in differing shades of brown, except for some green-tinged low hills back towards the town, where flocks of sheep and goats are grazing.

I set off heading west. Before long I come to the outline of what was probably a tower. Slowly I build a picture. The straight line of the outside facing the steppes, chain-mailed soldiers in the lookout towers resting on their spears and, on the hills behind them, sheep and goats and their families. Almost no change to today.

Walking on I come to a larger fort where some of the bricks are still in position. There are also shards of pottery. I scrabble in the debris looking for something more exciting, but find nothing. At first I don't notice the build-up of heat, but by mid-morning I can feel my arms burning and roll my sleeves down. I reach into my bag for my water. It isn't there. Suddenly I feel overwhelmingly thirsty. I check my watch. There is least an hour and a half of hard walking to the drop-off point.

When I reach the road I sit on a pile of bricks from the wall, marking the gap for the bus to drive through. The air is still, just the odd dust swirl. I never checked to see what time the bus returns, or if it does today. The only thing is to walk back to town.

I set off, remembering seeing a flock gathered round a water-trough. The distant green hills shimmer in the midday heat, but slowly get closer. I walk on, head down, making myself dream of life on the Wall rather than my thirst.

I look up and see the spring to my right with several sheep pushing to get at the low stone trough. They move away as I approach. The water is cold. I remember to swill it round my mouth before swallowing, as taught in the army. Cold water drunk too fast can cause stomach cramps. Soon I'm slurping handfuls of clear water. A large dog, no ears or tail, sniffs me. I'm too done in to be frightened.

It decides I'm no threat and moves away seeking the shade of a stunted tree. I scoop the water in my hat and have an impromptu shower. It is time to move on.

I have begun to get light-headed when to my relief a jeep pulls up. The driver tells me to get in. We stop at a chai khana on the edge of town, where he buys me a large tea, and then another. Halfway through the second, sweat seeps from every pore, and by the time I have finished my shirt and trousers are soaking.

I go to pay, but my Turkoman rescuer won't hear of it. Instead he orders a big bowl of salty tomato soup. He leaves me to my meal and joins a friend under a tree for a beer. They pour the beer into tumblers, then sprinkle salt onto the froth.

***

Back at the hotel Walter is talking of going back to Tehran and then flying to a hospital in Turkey where he can use his health insurance. I tell him his diarrhoea will pass in a couple of days and go to the public baths to clean off the dust and sweat.

When I get back Dieter is there to see how his friend is. I tell him about my escapade and he laughs when I say from now on I will stick to horses. He says he knows a Kirghiz family who have several, and is certain they would let me look round.

There are some heavily rugged horses staked out round three yurts. A girl is milking a mare into a bucket and two saddled horses are tied to a hitching rope. A grey-haired man with several children in patched clothes salaams Dieter.

'He says you can ride with him.'

I say I am honoured, but feel nervous. Riding an unknown horse is always a challenge, but not knowing what riding aids to give makes it a far greater one.

'What about you?' I ask.

'I'll have some tea and wait for your return,' he says with a grin.

The old man is surprisingly nimble as he swings into the saddle. An older boy holds my horse while I mount, then lets go.

Luckily the old man waits as I adjust the stirrup-leathers, which are far too short. I let them down as far as they will go, but they're still too short, making it difficult to sit on the padded wooden seat.

The old man trots a few paces then breaks into a slow canter. My grey takes off after him, and I'm fine as long as I stand in the stirrups. The horse has a smooth action and hardly pulls at all. Luckily my muscles are still strong from race riding, because we canter for the next half an hour over the baked, scrub-covered ground. I am soon sweating profusely, but my mount stays dry loping along. On the way back the old man speeds up making it an exciting ride as we swerve round the larger bushes.

'How was it?' Dieter asks.

'Fantastic,' I say watching the old man dismount. 'Absolutely bloody fantastic! Thank you so much for arranging it for me.'

Following the old man's example, I keep my left foot in the stirrup while swinging my right over the high cantle, then drop to the ground. The young man from earlier takes both horses away.

We join Dieter sitting on a carpet on the verandah in the shade. The old man sits beside me while a pretty girl pours the tea.

'He says would you prefer a beer?'

'No thanks, I don't drink alcohol.'

'Do you mind if he does?'

'Please go ahead.'

The son asks where we come from and gets very excited when he hears Dieter is from Germany. He goes into his yurt and comes out with a picture of Hitler.

'Hitler good?' he says.

'He's dead,' says Dieter.

'Yes, but he defeated the Russians.'

Dieter and I thank the old man and say it is time for us to depart. As we leave I see the young man piling rugs onto the horses while a boy draws water from the well for the sheep gathered round it.

***

It is wonderful to return to Arthur's to enjoy a few days respite before catching the train to Ankara in Turkey and resuming my search for Cirit.

In the intervening month the Customs shed had burnt down destroying all Arthur's furniture, and a beautiful doll's house made for his daughters by their gardener in Germany. Although the authorities

The palace built by Shah Abbas so that he could watch polo. Today the pitch is a big traffic island.

say it was an accident, it is widely believed it was done to hide the pilfering. Perhaps the doll's house has a new owner.

Sadly Mary is back in Hamadan, so I don't get a chance to thank her and say goodbye.

Back in Turkey I spend several months and travel hundreds of miles in the eastern, central and northern parts – the truly wild parts – but fail to find another game of Cirit. Most people have never heard of it, and those who have misdirect me. I return to Erzurum, but the team is in Konya, to which I make my way. When I get there I am told the team has moved on and I'm given the choice of several destinations.

With the coming of the first snows I decide to return home and come back next year. On that second trip the game again eludes me and I realise just how lucky I was to see it in Erzurum.

***

Today Cirit is played more extensively than when I was there. These days the Cirits are lighter and have rubber ends so that they do less damage. The games are more for tourists and general entertainment. Whether the players are sehid, I do not know.

CHAPTER FIVE

Pakistan: King of Games at Gilgit

Since my last trip ten years ago, I have married, had two children, Nick and Caroline, and have been running my farm on the mid-Wales border. We have three horses, seven hundred breeding ewes, twenty -five store cattle, a hundred and twenty acres of cereals, a workman and a huge overdraft.

Although I have been kept very busy, horse games have never been far from of my thoughts. I have deliberately developed the farm so that it can be run by one man during the less busy periods.

I want to see the ancient forms of polo played in Manipur in north-east India and in Gilgit, north-east Pakistan. Once lambing is over, I tell Sue I will be away for four to six weeks. In India I find out that Manipur is closed to foreigners because it is in a state of political turmoil, and there is no chance of it ending in the near future. Not wanting to waste time, I catch a train to Amritsar, cross the border to Lahore and go on to Rawlpindi, from where I plan to make my way to Gilgit.

***

The taxi swings into the drive of the 'Mrs Davies' Private Hotel,' Rawlpindi, and, despite not having been in Pakistan for eleven years now, I feel as if I've come home. The ancient doorman still wears a white turban with a starched fan-like end sticking out of the top, thigh-length white jacket and white jodhpurs, insists on carrying my backpack. In the reception I check the menu. It's just the same! Breakfast – cornflakes or porridge with hot milk, followed by poached, boiled or scrambled eggs, ending with toast and marmalade. Supper – Brown Windsor soup as the starter and trifle for pudding.

The bungalow rooms are a bit more dilapidated, but I'm pleased to see there are no rats or droppings in the wardrobe, as there were last time I was here. It is a bastion of the long-past Empire. I love it! Unlike my seedy hotel in Lahore where I was robbed.

***

It happened shortly after my arrival. I was talking to the hotel manager in my room when his assistant came in. The manager placed himself in between the table where my money-belt was and me. I hardly noticed the assistant slip away as the manager and I looked at a map, discussing the best way to get from Rawlpindi to Gilgit. Later I noticed a buckle on my money-belt was undone, and immediately checked the contents. Three £20 notes were missing. I checked again, only to confirm my fears. On my way to confront the manager, a hippy stopped me.

'You had some money stolen?' he asked.

'Yes.'

'Going to see the manager?'

I nod.

'Don't! It's part of a scam. They steal the money, the tourist reports it. The police come and find a packet of cannabis while checking your backpack. You're arrested, charged and sentenced. The police split the stolen money with the manager, and get an additional bounty from the American government for catching someone with drugs. It's the way it is here,' he gave a grin and shrugged his shoulders. 'You just have to be careful.'

Angry with myself for trusting the manager I went back to my room, relieved that I met the hippy in time to stop me falling into the manager's trap.

***

There are letters from Sue at the Poste Restante, the first I have had since leaving home. She has sent them here first rather than Delhi.

The day after I left home, one of the villagers was found dead in his house. He was lying on the floor on one side of his bed and his shotgun on the other. For a time murder was suspected and a road into the village was sealed off. After a lot of questioning, it was established that he had committed suicide rather than go to hospital. Sue wrote that until it was sorted out she slept with a loaded shotgun beside the bed. Now everything is progressing as normal, although spring is late and she has had to order another load of sheep feed because the grass isn't growing. She says she and the children are missing me and hope I will return soon.

It is difficult to relate to home, when it is so different here.

***

The manager at Mrs Davies' suggests I go to Gilgit via the new Karakoram Highway rather than fly. Late snow storms in the mountains along with low clouds are stopping flights to Gilgit. There is a long waiting list already.

I take his advice, and next morning I'm in the front seat of the Rawlpindi to Gilgit minibus, to get the best view. After Abatobad, where we stop for breakfast, the Highway – it is not so much a highway as a dirt road – begins. The plantations and grazing grounds give way to steep barren hillsides, into which the road has been blasted. There are no barriers, just a drop of over a thousand feet one side and a cliff face on the other. If the driver makes a mistake, that's it!

In some places the cliff face overhangs the road. Once we skid to a halt in front of a boulder in the middle of the road. The driver pulls over to the edge of the abyss and starts to inch past. When the outside wheels scatter the loose shale on the lip of the road all the men, including me, get out and walk, leaving the women in the back.

While weaving round hairpin corners the driver tells me about building the road. The area towards the Chinese border was very primitive and the first surveyors were shot by the locals as intruders. The surveyors had to be given army escorts while they worked out the route. The Chinese engineers blasted their way through the mountains, but the explosions weren't contained, so that whole rockfaces shattered and boulders, like the one we just passed, fall every day. Often there are landslides which block the road for several days at a time.

Despite the boulders, and apparently unconcerned at the chance of meeting another vehicle or a fresh rockfall, the driver keeps his foot to the floor round the blind bends. I glance at the speedometer, but it is broken. Once we meet a minibus coming the other way and, after some terror-inducing skidding, pass each other on the wrong sides of the road.

We stop for a pee break, but the women aren't allowed to get out. I walk to the edge of the road; far below there is the blue pencil line of a river. Looking down I feel my head start to spin and back away, before looking up at the sheer rockface towering thousands of feet above us.

Am I completely mad to have trusted my life to this unknown driver who calls upon his God every time we speed round a blind corner?

We are still in the mountains as darkness falls and the headlights keep shining into the void before swinging back onto the road. I begin to wish I was in the back, and unable to see out of the windscreen. It is totally black, no lights, no stars, just the two beams lighting the road.

The road goes downhill, so we go faster. The speed increases again as we come onto a tarmac road across an undulating plain.

Is seeing Gilgit polo worth this drive?

Once, when we hit an unmade-up piece of road, there is a groan from the back and the scent of warm urine floats through vehicle.

A man shouts angrily and a woman sobs. The last stop for the women was at Abatobad at nine this morning, and looking at my watch in the light of the dashboard I see it is eleven thirty at night. We arrive just after midnight, to be met by people with lanterns and torches – the town generator shuts down at midnight.

While I'm waiting for my backpack to be passed down from the roof, I compliment our speedy driver on delivering us safely.

He asks where I'm staying, and I say I'm not sure, I hadn't really expected to arrive so late. He suggests a hotel just along the road, then climbs onto a seat in the back and wraps a blanket round himself.

Ali Khan, one of the passengers, says he will fly back rather than risk another road trip. He tells me the driver will do the return journey starting at six tomorrow. Apparently Ali knows Gilgit well and will show me round tomorrow. I mention horses, but he's disappeared into the night.

Let other people play at other things,
the king of games is still the game of kings.

So reads the inscription above the archway into the polo stadium in Gilgit, which was paid for by the Aga Khan.

To get to the pitch we pick our way across the sodden, poached grass, taking care to avoid the cow pats. We walk towards a gap in the wall which runs each side of the pitch, which is about 250 yards long and 40 yards wide. A lean cow is grazing in the middle of the pitch, while its boy herder leans against the wall below the VIP stand. Ali Khan shouts at the boy, who runs to the cow and drives it off the pitch and out through the entrance.

'This is the famous Gilgit polo pitch,' Ali waves his hand in front of him. Even heavily-used football pitches in the UK in mid-winter aren't in such a bad state. Every cattle hoof-print is filled with water from last night's rain.

'You say there is a tournament happening soon?' I query.

My picture of polo is the Guards Polo Club at Smith's Lawn near Windsor with its immaculately mown grass.

'Yes, in three days' time.'

He says the farmers bring cattle here for a bit of free grazing. 'After all,' he points to the completely barren hills surrounding the valley, 'there isn't any grazing there.'

On the way back through town we pass a clothing shop called 'Harrods of Gilgit'. It has crossed polo sticks at either end of the name, and a sign in the window saying 'kwality clothes'. I idly wonder what its counterpart in Knightsbridge would make of it. Would they sue over the name if they knew?

Ali takes me to see Asif Khan, a slim 40-year-old with a large moustache in a white shalwar kameez (baggy Afghan/Pakistani pyjamas) who runs the polo here. We sit on deckchairs in his garden, sipping tea and eating sour cherries, in the dappled shade of a birch tree. I'm mildly concerned to see the water for the tea is taken from

Bouncing the ball off the wall. Riding off against a wall is allowed.

the irrigation stream which runs through the garden and also fills the garden pond in which our host washed the cherries.

Asif Khan tells me that Gilgit polo has been played here since at least the sixteenth century. It was not so much a game as a miniature battle between teams of six a side, played for the honour of one village or district against another. Most villages had a polo pitch on the maidan (village square), because it was the largest patch of level of ground in the area. There were walls on either side to stop the ball disappearing down the mountain slopes. Goals were scored by hitting the ball into a street at the end of the maidan. It was then the scorer's job to jump off and pick up the ball.

One of the few rules was that if a player, or horse, was badly injured and had to retire, his opposite number would also leave the pitch. He can remember one match where they ended up with one player on each side. The last player to be killed was three years ago. He was ridden off against the side wall and his horse stumbled throwing him head first against it.

'Blood came out of his ears,' Asif Khan says grimly.

Now the game is more subdued. There are goalposts, so no one needs to get off to pick up the ball, which was when a lot of the injuries occurred because, when trying to pick up the ball from amongst the hooves of other players' horses, the scorer could get trodden on. The sticks are still made with a willow handle slotted into an apple wood head. Unlike modern polo sticks, the handle is set at an angle to the head. That means a player can lean well out and still hit the ball squarely.

'I tried playing on an English saddle once and kept falling off,' Asif Khan grins at the memory. 'The local saddles have a high pommel and cantle, so you can hook your leg behind you when you lean out to play the ball at some distance from your horse.'

'Are there any special rules?' I ask.

'A player is allowed to catch the ball and score, if he passes between the goalposts with it in his hand. Players can do whatever is needed to prevent him scoring, short of hitting him with a polo stick,' he pauses. 'There is a story that one player caught the ball, only to find his way blocked by a large baker – a top player for the other team. The baker pulled the player off his horse and forced him to lie across his pommel. In his fright, the man continued to hold the ball, so allowing the baker to race to the other end and score, with the petrified man lying across his horse.' He strokes his moustache and grins. 'Of course it is only a story, but...'

'Ali mentioned a polo tournament?' I say, hoping it wouldn't be another non-event.

'Yes, the first match will be in three days. It will go on for four days. As I said, there aren't village teams anymore, but there are teams from the army, police and public works. It is still hard-fought. You must come. It starts at five in the afternoon. If you are in good time I will arrange a seat in the VIP stand.'

As we are leaving Asif Khan suggests we go to a stables and meet some of the players. I'm thrilled. Just one chance contact has opened lots of doors.

The following morning we visit Mr Soofi's stables where some of the Northern Light Infantry (NLI) horses are kept. There is a long central concrete manger shaded by trees, where the horses spend most of the day. Round the edge of the stable yard there are loose boxes where the horses go at night and when it is cold. When we get there, the horses have just been washed down after returning from exercise, and are being fed. They are given green Persian clover, wheat or barley chaff and whole maize.

The horses vary in size and shape. There are stocky Badakshan ponies, which an NLI rider tells me are the best (but are now hard to get due to the war in Afghanistan); fine Punjabi horses with their sharply curved ears; Balti ponies and an assortment of cross-breds. The NLI rider says they do long rides every morning to get the horses really fit. The game lasts for an hour with a ten minute break in the middle, and the same horses are used throughout.

Gilgit Polo

In the late afternoon I join the stream of men passing under the Aga Khan arch into the stadium. While they disperse onto the already crowded walls, I ascend the steps to the VIP stand, from which foreigners and local dignitaries view the game. Its front and sides are enclosed by chicken wire to keep us safe from a miss-hit ball.

Asif Khan greets me and takes me to a seat on the end of the second row, from which he says I will be able to get some good photographs. However, the sky is still overcast and I'm perched several feet higher than the players, so I decide pictures can wait until tomorrow. Opposite the stand, a pipe and drum band with several male dancers entertain the spectators as we wait for the Governor and his entourage to appear.

Police sirens announce his arrival and we stand to greet him.

He makes a short speech welcoming everyone to the tournament, and claps as the first two teams of six players, Green and Blue, line up facing each other either side of a ragged chalk line across the centre of the pitch. A door in the front of our VIP cage is opened. The Governor wishes the teams good luck, before tossing a new white polo ball between them.

They encircle it but, by the time the Governor sits down, the ball hasn't moved. It is stuck in the mud. Although the pitch has dried out – at least there is no longer any standing water – the ball has landed in a cow's hoof-print where it has now wedged.

The slashing of the polo sticks only serves to bury it more and change its colour to that of the mud. It is not a propitious start. After a couple of minutes the players pull back, and a Green hooks the ball out

The ball was stuck in the mud.

with the head of his polo stick. Play now starts, but the dampness of the pitch slows the ball despite some powerful hits. Rather than anyone getting a long run dribbling the ball, there is a constant scrummage of horsemen hitting at it whenever they get vaguely near.

A Green hits the ball onto a drier part of the pitch. He chases it, getting in a couple of good strokes before it hits a rough piece of ground and veers off towards the wall. Several Greens try to backhand it without success.

A Blue hauls his mount round as the ball bounces off the wall. He times it perfectly, knocking the ball well into the Green half. While the others are still turning, he swipes again, driving it towards Green's goal where a mass of spectators, six or seven deep, line the end of the pitch. He hits it forward again, but the crowd wait, no one wanting to be the first to retreat. As he brings his stick down for his final stroke, the spectators split, making a gap where they think the ball will go. It doesn't. It runs into a cow-pat and stops dead. The Blue rider overshoots and a Green backhands it towards the middle.

Another Green takes up the running, keeping close to the right hand wall so that the Blues can't get at the ball. He covers over half the pitch at a steady canter with the crowds on the walls cheering him on. One of the Blues gallops up so that he is in front of the Green's horse's shoulder and rides him off against the wall. The Green checks his horse to avoid it coming down against the wall, and the Blue backhands the ball towards the centre.

With the speed of play restricted by the condition of the pitch, it is 20 minutes before the first goal is scored. Another slashing at the ball session takes place ten yards in front of the Blue goal-mouth, filled with spectators all pushing forward to see what is happening. The crowd divides as a lucky hit knocks the ball between the posts.

The cry of 'GOAL' echoes off the surrounding hills.

A spectator hands the ball to the scorer, who holds the reins in his left hand, and the ball and his stick in his right. He gallops up to the halfway line, where he checks his horse, before throwing the ball forward. He takes a swipe and misses. The ball is swooped on by half a dozen players.

At half time the players dismount and hand their horses over to the grooms, who lead them round. A slim man entertains the spectators doing a folk dance to the band, the embroidered waistcoat over his shalwar kameez sparkles as a shaft of sunlight breaks through the clouds. Several of the players form a half-circle round him clapping in time to the music.

Goal!

Asif Khan comes over as I'm about to go down to get a closer look at the horses.

'What do you think, Mister Bob?'

'It is a game for brave players.' It is all I can think of to say without sounding critical.

He smiles.

'It is true. Did you notice how far they lean out? Impossible on an ordinary saddle. I think I told you, I fell off the only time I rode on an English saddle.'

'Yes.'

'It is a shame about the pitch. The tractor broke down. We have ordered a new part which will be here tomorrow morning, so we will roll it before the game. It will be much faster then.'

'The rain was bad luck.'

'Yes, we have so little every year, it is a shame we had it before the tournament. I came over to ask if you would like to ride tomorrow morning? You must be at Mr Soofi's at half past six. I will see you here at tomorrow's game?'

'Definitely, and thank you for arranging the riding.'

That's great! Besides trying out one of their horses, I will also get a chance to look at a different sort of hill farming.

He waves his hand as he goes back to re-join the Governor's party. I have missed my chance to go down to see the horses, because the players are already mounting up.

Except for their coloured shirts there is no uniformity in dress. A couple have polo hats, and one an old-fashioned riding hat, the rest are bareheaded. Only one pair of white breeches, otherwise it's local jodhpurs of varying hues. The footwear ranges from brown polo boots to army boots with puttees. Very different from the UK.

The ball is thrown in by the Governor. This time he tosses it over to the far side of the pitch where it is drier.

The overall view from where I'm seated is good, but I feel I'm missing the intricacies of the play and the atmosphere. The cries of 'goal' or 'out' are shouted with relish by the enthusiastic spectators on the walls, while the people around me remain silent. Tomorrow I will squash myself onto the walls.

The pace of the play speeds up and becomes rougher as the second half draws to a close. A Blue lifts his stick above his head ready to play the ball, but a Green hooks his polo stick and pulls hard. The head of the Green's stick flies off and the handle of the Blue's snaps as he makes his downward stroke. This was clearly a foul – Asif Khan said no hooking above shoulder height – but play continues. The ball is intercepted by other players, while the two antagonists gallop up the pitch to one of the gaps in the wall where their grooms pass them new sticks.

The Green's groom edges up the pitch inside the side wall, and when the play is some distance away, runs out to retrieve the head of his player's broken stick. The apple wood heads are valuable because they can be used again.

At the end of the game the players form a half-circle round the band with their arms resting on each other's shoulders and dance to the music. Many spectators join in, so that there are several lines of dancers.

The Governor leaves in a wail of sirens. The players remount and thread their way through the departing spectators, who crowd in on them trying to talk to their favourite riders.

On the way back I stop at a chai khana I've been to before. There is a saucepan containing a glutinous mixture of tea leaves in a pale brown liquid. More tea leaves are added with water and condensed milk, before being put on a stove and brought to the boil. The bubbling liquid is poured into a stained mug.

'You want steak?' the proprietor asks as I let my tea cool.

Normally there is a row of kebabs cooking over the charcoal burner on the pavement outside, but today there are thin slices of meat,

Hooking. Both sticks broke in this encounter.

which his assistant wraps in a piece of naan, before passing to the waiting customers.

'How much?'

Usually it is four kebabs plus a piece of naan for about fifty pence.

'Same as kebabs. A lorry load of sacred cows has come from India. Beef is cheap.' He explains there is a way of smuggling sacred cows over the border through the mountains. For a little bakseesh the authorities on both sides of the border look the other way. The trouble is there is no way of knowing when a shipment will arrive, and it has to be eaten fast because there are no storage facilities; so it is cheap while supplies last.

'I'll have one,' I say, then gingerly sip my tea. It is still too hot, and the sweet liquid burns my tongue. It's an acquired taste, but delicious if you like thick syrupy tea.

***

Asif Khan is waiting for me when I get to Mr Soofi's stables. The Northern Light Infantry first and second teams are already out practising. He has arranged for us to have a couple of reserve mounts.

Inside the compound grooms are holding our horses ready. Mine is a thin, slightly built cross-bred grey about 15hh. He is so slight I feel as if my knees will meet. He carries his head high, and I wonder if he has a sore mouth because his head comes up at the slightest touch of the reins.

We ride along a rutted track between small terraced fields of unripe green barley. Already there are women working in a long line, easing their way through the crop pulling weeds, which they put into baskets on their backs. Asif Khan explains that the weeds are fed to the stunted cattle I have seen tethered on bare patches of land.

He tells me that in the old days most of the women and children, plus some men, went to the high pastures in the mountains with the cattle, goats and sheep and lived there from spring until autumn. Although there is hardly any rain, the almost permanent mist round the mountain tops kept the short grass growing. However, with modern medicine lowering the child mortality rate there were more mouths to feed. So more stock were kept, and now many of the high pastures have been ruined by overgrazing.

Some women carrying full baskets of weeds stand to one side as we ride past. Although not veiled, the ends of their dresses are looped over their lowered heads to shade their faces. Once past them the footpath widens and we lob into a gentle canter. My horse has a smooth action and is responsive when ridden one-handed, but confused if I use two, perhaps because of his polo training.

I am relieved he is nimble, because several large stones from the terrace walls have fallen onto the track, but he has no problem avoiding them. The track goes up a slight incline and broadens where the bare mountainside meets the cultivated land.

Asif Khan pulls up at a culvert and, with only a light touch of the reins, my horse throws his head up to avoid the bit before coming to a standstill.

'There!' Asif Khan points along the mountainside, but I cannot see what he is pointing at. 'It is the irrigation ditch that comes all the way from a glacier much higher up. It is maintained every year and provides water for part of the town.'

I follow the line of the ditch as it slowly climbs ever higher, until it disappears round a spur. I look down at the narrow grey stream babbling under the road. The work needed to keep it flowing is mind-boggling.

'At one time it served the whole town. Soon we will have pumps that will provide water from the Gilgit River, then this will not be needed anymore. I thought you would be interested.'

'Thank you.'

Below us, as our horses pick their way down a narrow path littered with stones, I get an overall view of the town. On the far side of the river is a narrow green belt of trees and barley fields with a few houses, before the barren hillside climbs steeply to its jagged peak. A single, six foot wide suspension bridge connects the two sides of the town. A jeep on it inches forward following two pack horses loaded with large bundles of alfalfa. This side of the river there is a wide plain petering out at both ends where the mountains close in. As we descend, apricot trees and low mud-brick houses with small courtyards block our view.

We ride down to the river and along the road back to Mr. Soofi's, where I ask the groom about the horse being shy of the bit. Asif Khan translates. He tells me that it was hit on the jaw by a ball in a practice game and its mouth is still sore, even though the swelling has gone.

'Does he eat?' I ask, patting the thin neck.

'They water all his food, making it into a sort of porridge, and chop his alfalfa very small. He was a top polo pony, but now...' he shrugs.

I gently stroke the grey's forehead. Almost certainly he has at least one cracked tooth, and once infection sets in – there are no horse dentists here.

***

There is a livelier atmosphere around the pitch than there was in the VIP stand yesterday. The spectators on the walls 'ooh' and 'ahh' at every strike of the ball, and cheer at a long pass or groan when it is intercepted. The play is faster today because the pitch has dried out and has been well rolled.

I stand in a gap with the grooms who are holding spare polo sticks. I involuntarily step back as the ball is dribbled past me; the rider keeps bouncing it off the wall. A player's stick breaks. A groom pushes past me and runs across the pitch to meet the player. There is a brief discussion while the player chooses one of the sticks, then he rejoins the game. The groom starts back, sees the players galloping towards him and hesitates, before desperately looking round to see which wall is nearest. He turns to run when a long drive is hit. The ball passes within feet of him.

Playing across an opponent's horse.

Attempting to hook after missing the ball.

The spectators near me fall silent. The groom, still indecisive, looks back towards us. The men near me shout conflicting advice. He remains frozen as the leading players reach him. He is obscured by the galloping horses. Those round me groan, shake their heads and look away.

I'm transfixed, like the poor chap in the middle of the pitch. When they have passed he is still standing, rooted to the spot. A second groom runs onto the pitch shouting at the first one, who comes out of his trance and runs shakily towards us. Everyone slaps him on the back saying how lucky he is. Being a groom is more dangerous than I realised.

At half time I walk onto the pitch with some other spectators to watch the same man as yesterday dancing. People clap in time to the music as he twirls while doing intricate hand movements.

Looking at the horses being led round, I see they all have standing martingales attached to the bit, rather than to the nose-band. Several horses have the reins tied short in a knot so that the riders do not need to keep adjusting the length. The saddles have high pommels and cantles, and are rendered less slippery with a variety of woven covers kept in place kept in place by a surcingle.

For the second half I manage to squeeze onto the wall, and am rewarded with a new perspective, which comes with the danger of being pushed onto the pitch by those at the back straining to see.

In front of me a battle develops between two players from the army and the police. The army player is hitting the ball on his off side towards the goal, when the policeman rides up on his near side, leans across the back of the smaller army horse, and tries to play the ball. The polo sticks tangle and the policeman's breaks, but the army player has over-ridden the ball and those behind take on the play.

The player who most impresses me is a moustachioed army player, who, after scoring a goal, scores a second from the halfway line, when he throws the ball forward and hits it between the posts. His attempt to repeat the process is unsuccessful. He completely misses the ball, but the spectators still give him a rousing cheer.

For the next day's game I go to a goal mouth. The spectators here are younger men, who take great delight in playing 'chicken', – seeing who will be the first to fall back as the players approach. I am nearly run down when the first goal is scored, because those behind wouldn't move. The ball misses me by a couple of feet as I struggle to get out of the way. Some of those around me scramble to get the ball. A fight breaks out as two of them grab it at the same time. A third dashes in – I wrongly assume to separate them – grabs the ball from them and runs back to hand it to the goal scorer. For the rest of the half I stand next to the large multi-coloured goalpost, behind which I can shelter if necessary.

The final match is the Northern Light Infantry 1st team against the Police. The walls are more densely packed than they have been before, and there are masses of spectators at either end. I decide to return to the VIP stand, and am ushered to the section set aside for foreigners. The game is faster than any other I have seen here, with long drives, hard riding off and full use of the walls, which are the unique part of Gilgit polo.

While watching, I fall into conversation with an Australian. I learn he is desperate to get away from Gilgit. He has been on a walking holiday in Hunza and is worried about catching a flight from Karachi in five days' time. Because of the low cloud-base, several flights from Gilgit have been cancelled, and he is anxious about making his connection. He has decided to take the minibus to Rawlpindi tomorrow, but so far hasn't found anyone who wants to buy his flight ticket.

I ask when it is for.

Five days' time.

I'm due to go to Gulmit, to meet Shah Khan, a horseman friend of Asif Khan. I can't see any reason for me not being back in time. The only thing is, I'm short of money and won't be able to get any more until I get back to Rawlpindi.

I offer him half the price.

He declines.

I tell him about my lack of funds and point out half is better than nothing.

He agrees. All I have to do is say I'm John Robinson and hope they don't ask for my passport.

Shah Khan

The minibus pulls up on the old Gulmit polo pitch, which is now a lorry and bus park. Gulmit is the last town in Pakistan before the Khunjarab Pass and China. There are few people about. I'm told most of them have gone to the high pastures. Tethered, stunted cattle and sheep pick at small piles of freshly picked weeds. Every patch of fertile ground is used, and where it is too small to grow wheat, there are apricot trees.

The only place to stay is the tourist lodge, a rectangular building with two main rooms, a dining/sitting room with a large table and a dozen straight-backed wooden chairs, and a dormitory with military style metal-framed bunks. There is a small kitchen which serves breakfast and evening meal.

I enquire about Shah Khan. The receptionist says he left this morning for Gilgit. Damn! Our buses must have passed each other.

Another wasted journey.

***

On my arrival back in Gilgit there is a message from Asif Khan asking me to dinner the following evening. It will be a good way to end my time here.

There are more people than I expected; among them are four Europeans, including a woman in her late thirties wearing a head

Start of play: a dignitary throws in the ball (see arrow) from the safety of the screened-off VIP stand.

scarf and baggy local dress. There are several local men, including Shah Khan – a distinguished looking man with swept back greying hair, with whom I easily fall into conversation.

He tells me his father, a local mir (chieftain), wanted him brought up in the traditional way: riding, shooting, playing polo and learning how to govern. However, the elders insisted he also needed a modern education, so he was sent to boarding school in Abatobad. He was in the army for a time, before ending up as a wing commander in the air force. He fought with the Gilgit Scouts when they drove the Indians out of Free Kashmir – the part of Kashmir which was occupied by Pakistani tribesmen – and held the passes over the winter of 1947, until the UN fixed the ceasefire line.

'I remember firing mortars on a small garrison who were playing polo on little Ladakhi ponies,' he pauses in recollection. 'I felt bad about it, but I don't think any horses or men were injured, and by the time we got down to the camp the soldiers had withdrawn.'

I say he must have seen a lot of changes here in the last twenty-five years. He agrees, but says that since the coming of the Highway, change has speeded up considerably.

Children – boys and girls – now have to go to school, so they no longer go to the high pastures to tend the livestock. The brightest ones leave the area seeking jobs in towns. The men who remain prefer to earn money working on the road rather than farming, which is harder and much less lucrative. As a result terrace walls are falling down and the irrigation ditches are collapsing.

He thinks it will not be long before the whole way of life in the area will be altered for ever. Apricots will be the crop of the future. They require less tending and yield a higher income. Also an apricot drying plant will provide work for some locals, while the Highway means the product can easily be transported to the rest of Pakistan and beyond. In the end the local people who stay will be better off.

'But what you want to hear about is the polo,' he swings his arm as if playing. 'Not what I think about what will happen in the future.'

'Aren't they entwined?' I ask.

'I suppose so,' he says, then swallows a third of the liquid in his tumbler. 'In the old days, the only way to escape being a peasant farmer was to be in the local Mir's army. To do that you needed to be a good horseman and play polo. In those days all travel was on horseback, so there were a lot of horses about. It was possible for even the poorest person to borrow a horse and have a go.' He drains his glass, which is promptly refilled.

The view from the VIP stand at the start of a game.

'Hunza pani,' he says. 'Have you tried it?'

'No. Since I had a horse racing accident resulting in brain damage, the doctors said I must never drink alcohol again.'

'But it's only slightly alcoholic.'

'Not what I've heard from some climbers who have tried it!'

We both laugh.

'Back to your horses,' he says, taking a sip before continuing. 'You were in the cavalry?'

'Yes.'

'Did you ever shoot from a horse?'

'No.' I refrain from telling him I got a soldier shot off one.

'We used to have a shooting competition before the big polo tournaments. A sheep's bladder was tied to the top of a pole halfway along the pitch. The horsemen started at the goal line, galloped down the pitch, and were only allowed to shoot after passing their rifle under the horse's neck.'

'Didn't that mean they were past the target before they could shoot?'

'Exactly! It was actually being kind to the horsemen, because it is much easier hitting a target going away from it, than approaching it. I don't know why, but it is.' He takes another draught. 'The shooting has died out now. The last time I saw it, the young men were using shotguns, and missing – no passing the gun under the horse's neck either.'

I enquire about other sports on horseback, but he doesn't know of any, and asks if there is anything more I would like to know about the local polo. Off-hand I can't think of anything. I have learned so much from Asif Khan.

Shah Khan says I should meet Ismail Khan in Rawlpindi, his commander when they liberated Free Kashmir. He is a great horseman, and was Minister of Protocol under President Bhutto, but has since fallen from grace.

He takes me over to meet the European in local dress, an English midwife called Jane.

'She will be interested that you were in Afghanistan before the Russians, when it was very different from now,' he says, before going to look for some paper to write down Ismail Khan's telephone number.

Jane tells me she works in the refugee camps.

'They must welcome you as someone who can really help the women,' I say. 'I remember how welcome Western doctors were when I was there ten years ago.'

'Not anymore,' she says shaking her head. 'There are factions taking over some of the camps, and they kill any of the maliks (local chieftains) who don't side with them.'

'But I thought there was one common enemy – the Russians?'

'It is much more complicated. There are hundreds of fighters afraid to go to Afghanistan, because when they are away another faction might take over the camp and their families will be left to starve. As a Western woman I am banned from some of the camps which have been taken over by religious groups.'

'Do you stay in the camps?'

'Sometimes, though more often I go out from our base in Peshawar.'

A sudden thought occurs to me.

'Would you be able to introduce me to someone who could take me into Afghanistan?'

'I'm not at all sure...'

'Please.' I flash her my best smile. 'I would love to find out what has happened to the people I knew.'

'Well,' she looks me straight in the eye. Hers are dark like her hair. 'If you're serious, come to Peshawar next week and we can talk more. No promises.'

'Bob! Ismail Khan's telephone number,' Shah Khan interrupts us. 'Let me introduce you to these three travel agents. They are interested in Gilgit polo.'

He says their names, but I'm still thinking about going to Afghanistan, and what a whizz it will be. Sue might not be too pleased, but what an opportunity. Perhaps I might even get a pop at a Russian.

Their names don't register, but I catch their countries. The plump couple are from from Germany, and the sleek suited chap from Italy. They planned to see the last two days of the polo, but low cloud and a landslide delayed them. Luckily it is a recce trip, so there are no dissatisfied customers in tow.

They want to organise riding holidays, and to include seeing polo up here, down-country and in India.

I ask if they've seen Ladakhi polo.

The Italian vehemently denies there is any polo there, and it is only when both Asif Khan and Shah Khan assure him that there is, he grudgingly backs down. He admits he has never been to Ladakh.

So much for tourist guides!

Karma

'Jolly good, look forward to meeting you here at my house, nine-thirty tomorrow morning.'

I can't believe my luck. I'm meeting Ishmail Khan tomorrow and he has a horse he wants me to try out.

When I get back to Mrs Davies' from Gilgit, I ring the Embassy who also suggest I contact Ismail Khan. With theirs and Shah Khan's introductions he agrees to see me.

I think it best not to mention to the Embassy about trying to get into Afghanistan, it would be bound to cause a storm. However, they are pleased with me telling them about the hotel/police scam in Lahore. They have managed to get several young people released.

I enquire at the Habib Bank near Mrs. Davies' about the transfer of £500 to them from my NatWest account in the UK. They say they don't deal with foreign exchange, but their new branch in the centre of town does. I go there, but am told that if the money was sent to the branch near Mrs Davies', that is where it will be. After spending a fruitless afternoon going from one bank to the other it is clear the money will not be forthcoming now, or in the foreseeable future.

I cash my last traveller's cheque. I have enough left to last another week. I will have to drastically alter my plans. No question of going to Afghanistan – perhaps that's for the best. Certainly Sue will think so. Once I have found out all I can from Ismail Khan, I will go to Karachi and take the first flight home.

The next morning I am shown into Ismail Khan's drawing room, where he stands up to greet me. He is wearing an immaculate white shirt with long sleeves, a striped tie (regimental?), dark grey trousers with razor-sharp creases and highly polished shoes. There are a couple of large sofas and several armchairs with deep cushions.

On the walls are military and horse pictures, a couple of which are by Snaffles. But what really catches my eye is the carpet. It is beige, but has hoof prints sewn into it.

'How is my friend Shah Khan?' He asks. 'I haven't seen him since his last whisky run.'

'Whisky run?'

'Did he not tell you?' He lets out a belly laugh and then continues. 'He and his friends in Gilgit take it in turn to come to 'Pindi and obtain a dozen bottles of whisky from different embassies.'

'I thought alcohol was banned, and you could go to prison for making or possessing it?'

'You're quite right, but a blind eye is turned provided you don't flaunt it openly. The President knows I drink, but chooses to ignore it. G and T?'

'Tea, please.'

'Nothing stronger?'

'No thanks.' I tell him about my racing accident.

'Do you mind if I do?' he enquires going over to a table, and fixing himself a gin and tonic. 'What would you like to know?' He has an Oxford accent.

He says he is waiting for a telephone call to let him know when we can go to look at the new polo pony he wants to buy for his son, who is at university in America studying economics and computing. The horse is being looked after on an army base, and anything to do with the Forces always requires delicate handling when foreigners are involved.

I mention seeing The President's Body Guard in Delhi and ask about the possibility of seeing the Pakistani one. He says to do so will first involve someone from the British Embassy contacting the security services. Anyway, they are not riding at the moment as a lot of the horses are laid up, after being worked too hard in the heat. He says most of the horses in Pakistan, except for those in the hills, are now bred by the army.

He shows me a film he took of Buzkashi in Kabul. His telephoto was no better than mine, so a lot of the play is indistinct.

Just after eleven thirty the telephone goes. It is the horse trainer who says I will not be allowed onto the camp. Ismail Khan can go, but not me. He apologises profusely and insists I stay to lunch, even though it is curry, which he dislikes.

Spectators scatter as the play approaches the goal area. In the foreground a young boy runs with his pretend polo stick.

Over lunch I learn horses have been the great love of his life, and that he taught polo to the Turks when he was Military Attaché in Ankara. A great Anglophile, he has many friends in England and hopes to retire there. Everything about him is from the era of the Raj, no shalwar kameez, just Western clothing. He feels his country is going backwards, becoming mired in fundamentalism. When I leave I say I hope he will call on me when he comes to the UK.

After changing my flight home, I go to the station. I have enough money for a ticket to Karachi and one night in a reasonable hotel, but the man in the ticket office says there are no tickets available for four days. I plead my father is gravely ill. After pocketing some baksheesh, he looks again at his charts, and hands me a third class ticket for a train already in the station.

I buy a couple of bottles of water and board the train. There are knowing smiles among the other passengers when I ask for directions to my seat. I see why – the wooden slatted seat is next to the loo. Besides the smell, I will have to move my legs every time someone comes past. I'm still sorting stowing my luggage when the train jerks into motion.

We pass shanties built next to the tracks, their occupants dressed in much-patched clothing. Children run alongside holding out their hands for money as the train picks up speed. Houses and hovels give way to irrigated fields and villages with walled compounds.

It is baking hot. The only breeze comes from the torn canvas where our carriage and the next are coupled together. While we are moving it is fine, but waiting in the stations, it soon becomes uncomfortable.

On other trains out here I have travelled first class. At each station there are people to take your order for food and drink, which is passed through the window at the next station. In third class this doesn't happen. Families sit round a plastic cloth spread out on the floor, light their primus stove, and heat up their food.

As night falls the family nearest me kindly ask me to join them. I am famished. It is a long time since my cornflakes with hot milk, scrambled eggs, toast and marmalade at Mrs Davies', and I've finished my two bottles of water. The meal is naan with a hot vegetable curry. The sweet tea accompanying it heightens the heat of the chillies, so that my mouth feels on fire.

Back at my seat I take some clothes from my rucksack to pad the wooden slats, and pull on my thickest sweater and Norfolk jacket, because the cold desert air blows straight through the gap in the canvas. I am so lucky to have had a hot meal to keep me going till morning.

In the morning I wash and shave in the thin trickle of water from the tap in the loo, and then look for breakfast. But there isn't any. The kind family from last night have gone and the newcomers eye me with suspicion. I'm desperate for drinking water, but daren't leave my baggage unattended, and anyway, the way to other carriages is sealed off because a missing footplate below the gaping hole in the canvas makes it unsafe.

Mid-morning the train has been stationary for over an hour and the heat is making me feel lightheaded. I stand and take a couple of steps, then have to grab onto a bunkbed for support. A hand rests on my arm as I turn to go back to my seat. It is a man from further down the carriage with a tin mug of tea for me. After I have drunk it, he insists I join his family. I glance at my pack, but he shakes his head and says 'OK.'

I sit with him watching his children playing, deliberately not looking in the direction of the women whose faces are shaded by shawls; all but one. She is a plump grey-haired lady with a ready smile and a little English. She tells me she worked as an assistant amah for an English family, until they went home.

When we reach the edge of Karachi everyone bustles around packing everything away into bundles. I thank the family, and after a lot of handshaking and well-wishing, return to my backpack.

The receptionist at my chosen hotel is not interested in my custom. I insist the manager is called and eventually he agrees to my having a room, provided I pay upfront. In my bedroom I see why. My smart pale blue shirt and light trousers are splodged with soot and my face is streaked black.

***

Sue picks me up from Hereford station, and we go straight to where the children are at a birthday party. Nicholas and Caroline are thrilled to see me, but the atmosphere amongst the grown-ups is sombre. My brother's daughter has collapsed and been rushed to hospital. Tragically she has an inoperable brain stem tumour and dies thirty-six hours later.

I thank God my money didn't come through. If it had, I could easily have been in Afghanistan; out of touch for months and unable to give my family any support.

CHAPTER SIX

Ethiopia: Addis Ababa

My one-man plan for running the farm worked well, except the 'one man' was me, and I was never able to get away for long enough to do another trip. When produce prices fell I decided to sell off all the land not adjacent to the farm buildings and clear my debts. I would much rather follow my horse quest than go back to 'working for the bank.'

With Nick and Caroline at university and Tom (our youngest) at boarding school, Sue agrees to look after the sheep and horses while I go off. So, after sixteen years, I am back searching for horse games.

I am excited, if slightly nervous, to be travelling on my own in

Ethiopia, a country I know little about. I have heard that polo players in Kenya once got their ponies from Somalia, Ethiopia and Sudan. I can't go to Somalia because of the civil war (also I've been told that most of the ponies have been eaten), and it would not be prudent to go to Sudan, because Tony Blair supported the recent American bombing. That leaves me with Ethiopia as the safest of the three, even though it is recovering from a horrific civil conflict and is at war with Eritrea.

***

On the flight I chat to Amy, who is going to Addis Ababa to carry out a road mortality survey. She tells me Ethiopia has one of the highest number of road traffic deaths in the world. Just what I need to hear when planning to travel mainly by bus. I thought of staying at a hotel near the centre, but she says the Meridian, where she is booked in, has the internet, so I decide to lodge there until I get my bearings.

On my first morning in Addis I go to the British Embassy to see the Military Attaché. It has been a practice that has served me well in the past. Often they are not too busy, and know people who have horses.

At the Embassy gates one of the Ethiopian police guards in the gatehouse says there is no Military Attaché listed in his telephone pamphlet.

'What is his name?' he asks me.

'I have no idea. If you could let me have a look at the names.'

He closes the cover.

'I cannot help you.'

'Please,' I grovel. 'Please, is there anything under Military?'

Reluctantly he reopens the pamphlet.

'There is a Military Liaison Officer, a Colonel Richard Illingworth.'

'Yes, that will be him. Please will you telephone him and say Bob Thompson,' I say my name slowly, 'would like to see him.'

'Like Bob Marley?' The policeman asks with a grin.

'Yes. Tell him I was an officer in The Life Guards. I want to talk to him about horses.'

'Horses? What are horses?' His English isn't up to it.

As if rising to the trot, I bounce up and down, click my tongue, and I give a little neigh. He speaks hurriedly into the mouth-piece, and with a sigh of relief hands me the phone. Colonel Illingworth says he will be with me shortly.

On the way to his house, Richard Illingworth asks how long I was in the army. I tell him I did seven years finishing in 1972. I mention my travels in Afghanistan and studying Buzkashi, as well as all the other countries I have visited looking for horse games.

'Here we are,' he says turning up a gravel path. There are flowerbeds, a riot of colour contrasting with the dull brown of the surrounding grass. Off to one side is a vegetable garden with everything planted in neat rows. 'As you can see, Carrie, my wife, is a keen gardener.'

Over coffee he tells me that, as a cavalry officer himself, he is interested in most things equine, and will help, where he can, with my research. I ask if there are any traditional horse games in Ethiopia? He's not heard of any, but says we will go to the National Stud and enquire.

He is not busy at the moment, because the Ethiopians are about to launch an attack on the Eritreans, and that will ruin the work he has been doing for the last three months. He had been organising the delivery of a fleet of Land Rovers as part of an aid package, but the British Government has said that if the Ethiopians respond to Eritrean incursions, the delivery will be cancelled. He says the Ethiopians will take no notice because, once hostilities have cooled down, the Land Rovers will be sent anyway.

At the National Stud most of the horses live in a huge shed erected by British army engineers after the Second World War. We are shown round by the manager. The shed has concrete block walls and is penned off into numerous stables with walls and metal rails. Most of the light comes from the gap between the top of the walls and the roof, and it takes time for my eyes to adjust.

The manager explains that during the time of Haile Selassie (the last emperor of Ethiopia, deposed in1974) stallions were imported from Europe to improve the local horses. The Emperor was particularly keen on Lipizzaners, because their progeny from local mares produced strong, versatile offspring. Those days are long gone, and now there is no breeding programme.

I point to a particularly pathetic foal.

'It is from a water trough accident,' says the manager. 'We have too few grooms for all the horses. Sometimes the stallions are let out to drink before the mares have been taken away, then they get served by accident. Occasionally brother with sister, or mother.' He shrugs. 'These things happen.'

'What do you feed them?' Richard asks.

'When there is enough money, barley, molasses and hay. When there isn't, just hay, even for the ones being ridden.'

It occurs to me that rather than wasting valuable feed on the malformed and runts, it would be better to put them down. The manager is shocked. They respect horses far too much to do that.

There is a clang as the first stable door is opened, followed by some excited neighing as the rest of the horses wait to be let out. We step back into an empty stable as the concrete passageway fills with horses making their way to the water troughs outside.

In the army, when we watered the horses, one trooper led two horses at a time to similar water troughs, but here it is a mad rush.

A groom has to beat off a particularly runty young horse which tries to mount one of the better mares.

The manager says that on Saturday there will be polo at the old racecourse at Janmeda; perhaps one the local horsemen will know something. He has heard there was once a horse game using spears, but he doesn't know what or where, and asking too many questions, about anything, can still get one into trouble.

In the afternoon I plan to walk from my hotel to the city centre. Halfway there a car pulls up alongside me and the driver tells me to get in.

I refuse.

He says he is an antiques merchant and has spotted that a couple of ruffians are following me.

I turn round. Two men in ragged clothes are only a few feet behind me. I dive in through the open passenger door.

Driving along the shopkeeper tells me he has sold a lot of goods in London, and even stayed at the Savoy. When I get to his shop I can believe it, the jewellery and carvings are of the highest quality. After a cup of tea and a promise to return when I am buying presents before going home, he suggests I go to the Ministry of Tourism, which should be able to give me information about horse games.

After an hour's wait at the Ministry of Tourism, a clerk suggests I go to the Ministry of Sport.

They tell me I should go to the Ethiopian Horse Sports Federation, and give me a telephone number and address, but no one answers the telephone and three taxi drivers do not know where the place is.

Back in the Meridian bar I fall in with someone who, before the civil war, saw horsemen trying to spear each other as he drove past a wedding feast. It was in the heart of the Oromo region, to the south, near Goba. When he asked his guide about it, he was told the Oromo were the Cossacks of the Ethiopian plains, and what he had seen was part of their traditional game, but that was all he knew.

Goba! Now I've got a place to start.

I have to go to the British Council to use the internet – the one in the hotel has been dismantled and the room turned into another bedroom. On the way I check out how to get to Goba; bus will take at least 3 days, and hiring of a four-by-four at £100 a day plus fuel is out of my league. It is quicker and cheaper to fly.

Near the British Council there are the old, twisted stumps of traffic meters from before the civil war. Now young boys control the parking, collect the fees and squeeze as many cars as possible into their allotted area.

There must have been a certain grandeur about the streets of Italian-style houses with balconies and shuttered windows, but now the facades are in desperate need of paint and a lot of the shutters need rehanging.

Walking back I am joined by several students who want to practise their English. Some of them are fluent, and just need to build up confidence. Most of them come from the north and are studying agriculture; as a farmer I am keen to listen to their ideas. They all want to have tractors instead a wooden plough and oxen. I ask what would happen to the ploughmen and oxen if a single tractor did all the work. They are not interested, and think all their problems would be solved by using machinery and fertilisers.

At Meskel Square I turn up the dual carriageway leading to the Meridian.

'Where is your hotel?' they ask.

'On the road to the airport.'

'Why are you not staying at the Ghion or the Hilton?'

'Because they cost too much.'

'Will you take us to the Ghion for beer?'

'No, I am going back to my hotel.'

There is a brief pause.

'You give us money!'

'What? No!' How could I have allowed myself to get into this position?

'Yes, you give us money now!'

'Why?'

'Because we talk to you.'

'But I gave you an English conversation lesson. You should pay me.'

Three of the five shrug and walk away; another glares at me, and then decides to join the others.

'Give me money!' demands the last one.

'Fuck off!' I shout. I am really pissed off now. 'Who the fuck do you think you are?'

He takes a pace back.

'Money,' he whines, holding out his hand.

'Fuck off,' I say again, and start walking towards the Meridian.

When I look back over my shoulder he has joined his mates and they are all slouching away across the square. I am willing to give money to genuine down-and-out beggars, but these young men were well-dressed with new trainers.

***

On Sunday I go to Janmeda, the site of the old racecourse. The polo is chaotic; most of the riders and all of the horses seem to have little idea of what they are supposed to be doing.

The ground is uneven, and to complicate matters, a football from a nearby game keeps coming onto the pitch. It is retrieved by children oblivious to the galloping horses bearing down on them.

There is an old white-haired Ethiopian rider who trails just behind the play, making sure he never gets involved. During a break I ask him about the Oromo spearing game, but he has never heard of it. I talk to the other players, all of whom are westerners, a mixture of NGOs and Embassy staff, but nobody knows anything. On my way back across the old racecourse I spot the Ethiopian Horse Sports Federation office; it is closed.

Getting to Goba

The plane skims over a long camel train as we come in to land. Just before touching down, the land below us changes from desert scrub to a tarmac runway.

'Goba?' I ask the steward who is ordering everyone off the plane.

'Dire Dawa,' he says.

The flight was supposed to go straight to Goba. We watch as our luggage is taken out of the hold, and replaced by bundles of twigs covered in green leaves.

'Khat,' says an Ethiopian, as our luggage is loaded into the fuselage. 'People chew the leaves. It is prized for its amphetamine-like qualities. It is more profitable to grow than coffee. It is said,' he continues, 'that the khat plane to Mogadishu has never been shot at.'

The next time we land, the plane touches down on a grass airstrip. Bushes flash past the wing-tips as the brakes are applied. As soon as we come to a halt the steward taps me on the shoulder.

'Goba,' he says, handing me my backpack.

A boy pushing a wheelbarrow runs across the brown grass towards the plane. Behind him is a mud hut with tin roof and a policeman/ soldier sitting on the verandah, a Kalashnikov on his lap. No one else gets off. The boy chucks my backpack into his wheelbarrow, and waves at me to follow. Behind me the revs increase and I turn to watch the plane just clear the bushes at the end of the runway.

The boy tips my pack onto the ground and holds out his hand. I give him some birr (Ethiopian currency) — clearly not enough from the expression on his face. He squats beside the man with the gun who looks up, and points wearily to a footpath, before allowing his head to droop onto his chest once more.

I follow the path through the bushes until I come to a red and white pole barring the way. I duck under it and approach the first of three horse-drawn taxi drivers

'Goba?' I ask the nearest. He shakes his head.

'Goba?' I ask the second.

'Robé,' he answers.

'Goba?' I ask the third.

'Robé. Hotel?'

I nod and he signals for me to wait while he stows my pack, then offers a hand up onto the passenger seat. The fragile trap tips and twists with every movement. Once I am seated, he calls for the horse to start, but it remains stationary. He taps it with a long thin stick; its ears flick backwards. He gets down, grabs the bridle and starts to drag the horse. Eventually it breaks into a trot with the driver running alongside. After fifty yards he lets go, and scrambles up beside me. The horse maintains its steady trot and the grey-stubbled driver grins at me with a set of chipped front teeth.

Robé is a new town laid out on a grid pattern. There is a hardcore main road for motor vehicles, with dirt tracks on either side for horses and pedestrians. The tinkling of the bell attached to our horse's neck warns pedestrians to get out of our way, because the unshod hooves make no noise. The driver points to two hotels on opposite sides of the road. The one I choose has a guard on the gate; the other, I am pretty certain, is a brothel. It has music blaring and girls in bright dresses lounging on the verandah.

Booking in I learn that Goba is 20 km away, and Robé is the new provincial capital, hence the new airport. After leaving my bags in one of the bungalows in the hotel's overgrown garden, I take a horse taxi to the market. Everywhere there are crowds, colour and the heavy smell of spices. The yellows, oranges and browns of the powdered spices compete with the brightly coloured dresses of the women, the different hues of green of the vegetables contrast with the baskets of deep red chillies. With my poor Amharic (the official language of Ethiopia), I find out from the taxi driver that each family has a plot marked out with stones.

On the far side of the market is the cattle stockade, also areas for sheep and goats and one for selling horses. Rather like a car park, there is a horse park where horse-holders look after a dozen or more horses each. Some horses are held and some tied to a rail. Stallions and mares are kept separate with a small wall dividing them.

The horses for sale are all local, 13 to 14 hands high, but in varying condition. Those in good condition have had their hooves trimmed, while some of the thinner ones have long feet and larger saddle sores. Patches of white hair show where the sores have healed.

Several boys in shorts and torn shirts ask me for money; when I don't give them any they keep following me and shouting.

I escape from them by going into the cattle stockade. One beast stands out. Unlike the runty black cattle and the plough oxen, it is in show condition, its dun-coloured coat has a sheen and it is well-muscled. This is a bullock specially reared for kitfo, Ethiopian steak tartar. In fact the meat is seldom minced, but served in slices or small chunks, as a delicacy at a feast. I have been advised to avoid it, because foreigners not only get bad stomachs, but worms and other parasites as well. The owner beckons me over to inspect the beast. I oblige him, but move on when he starts mentioning money.

Outside the stockade the boys surround me again. I try to lose them by walking through the stalls, but the jostling pack keeps hounding me. I lose my way in the maze of alleys between the stalls, and end up at the horse park.

The children lose interest in me as a stallion, which has escaped its holder, tries to mount a mare. The holder of the mares does his best to calm his charges, as they lash out at the intruder. The stallion holder somehow grabs the reins of his horse, while dodging the flying hooves, and leads it away through a gap in the separating wall.

The man at the entrance to the horse park allows me through, but keeps the children back, waving a long whip. The horse-holders make it is clear they don't want me too close, but I manage to look at the saddles and bridles. The bits have long sides, and the piece which goes in the mouth is raised in the centre with a circular ring attached to it. They are taken out when the horses are not being ridden and hung from the pommel.

Some of the horses are tied to a rail with a thin rope attached to their head-collars, but most are hobbled with a rope that runs from their head-collars to just above the hock. On closer inspection it is possible to see that all the horses, to a greater or lesser degree, have scarring above the hock where the ropes have badly chafed the skin and in some cases ridged the tendon. I wonder if in time it causes the horse to move as if it has stringhalt.

The saddles have a long seat with high pommels and cantles. The wooden frame is covered with leather. There is a lot of padding on top of the saddle for the rider, but often only a thin pad underneath, which probably accounts for the large number of saddle sores. Some saddles have a decorative saddle-cloth on which different animals are embroidered. The most popular is an Ethiopian lion.

The boys have disappeared when I get back to the market. The stalls of the better-off traders have gaily coloured pieces of material tied to stakes to give them shelter from the sun; those less well-off sit in the open, their wares piled round them. The poorest have only a few items for sale, whereas others take up part of the roadways as well as their stalls. Some of the stall-holders beckon me across, but there is nothing that I need at the moment, so I browse, smile and move on. The boys approach me as I climb onto a taxi, but the driver waves his whip at them.

That night my sleep is broken by a scream. I cock my head and listen, but all is quiet, even the crickets are silent. Perhaps it was a bad dream. It comes again. A scream of pure terror and pain, the like of which I have never heard before. It must have been like this in the civil war, prisoners being tortured in the dead of night.

The screaming is coming from a bungalow not far away. As I open my bungalow door it comes again. The cry of agony makes me shudder.

The two night guards pound past me, one waves me back inside. I hear the snick of their rifles being cocked. Another scream, then whimpering.

A saddle-cloth decorated with an Ethiopian lion.

I force open the bathroom window. It jams after a couple of inches, but enough to get a squint. The guards hammer on the door with their fists, shouting at the occupants. There is another scream, not so blood-curdling, but the crying is louder.

The guards shout again. One of them fires his rifle in the air. Almost immediately the door opens and they rush in. All I can hear are muffled shouts.

A woman, supported by one of the guards, walks slowly along the path towards reception. Behind comes a tall, well-built man in a white shirt. He is arguing with the guard who keeps pushing him in the back with the muzzle of his Kalashnikov. In the morning nobody mentions anything, and when I ask about the shot, the receptionist says it must have been a car backfiring.

The bus for Goba left at 05.30, so with a ticket for tomorrow, there is time for a stroll. The countryside is flat, any hills are screened by copious stands of eucalyptus trees. Some barley has been cut and other plots are almost ready to harvest. The grains are smaller and thinner than we grow at home. There are several herds of small cattle being looked after by children who keep them out of the standing corn; a couple of girls have bags over their shoulders into which they are putting dried cowpats.

I come to a village. Cactus hedges separate the plots and keep the goats and hens off the wide, rutted dirt street. A young man with glasses plucks up courage to speak to me. He is a biology student in Robé, and hopes to become a doctor. He should be at school – his lessons between midday and 4pm – but there is no school today because the teachers are discussing the war with Eritrea. He hopes he will not be called up to fight.

I remember being told by students in Addis that they had run away from the north, where there was conscription for all young men.

He takes me to his house. The walls are mud and straw finish over a matting screen attached to a framework of poles. The tin roof overhangs by eighteen inches to keep the rainwater away from the walls. He introduces me to a wizened old lady with birdlike hands – his mother. He has a younger sister and brother who are both students, and a student from a distant village lodges with them.

There is also a younger woman in a beautiful blue shawl with a baby on her hip and three young naked children clinging to her skirt. I am not introduced, and I refrain from asking who she is.

We sit on log stools in the shade. The village was built fifteen years ago by the Marxist Derg government when the farms in the area were formed into a collective. Every household has a plot of land which it can cultivate. The rest of the land belongs to the government, but is farmed by a collective which is run by the elected members of the kabelle (local council).

I ask about horse games, but most of the horses starved to death in the great famine, and those that survived are now used for transport. His father, when he was drunk, once talked about an Oromo game on horseback from when Haile Salassie was emperor, but he never mentioned it again. During the time of the Derg, one wrong word could cost a whole family their lives.

He escorts me to the edge of the village, keeping back a pack of children demanding money. We shake hands. It is such a relief not to be asked for money, but it doesn't last for long. A young man tries to sell me a baboon which he has on the end of a short rope. Despite it biting him twice, he insists it is friendly and would make a good pet.

Goba

'My father had 20 horses before the famine, but they all died,' says the student teacher showing me round the best hotel in Goba.

'Do they still play a game here with sticks or spears?'

'Faras Gugse?'

'I don't know. All I was told Goba was the best place to see a game on horseback.'

'It was, but it is no longer played, except sometimes at Christmas.' He pushes open a door which squeaks as it is forced over the floorboards. 'This room good for you?'

It smells of stale sweat and smoke and on the bed are some crumpled blankets on a well-used sheet. I go over to the window. It looks out onto a garden with tables in it. I try the latch; it's stiff, but finally I get it open. A breeze from the hills wafts in, stirring the dust on the windowsill.

'It has own bathroom,' he says pushing aside a plastic curtain.

I look inside. There is a cracked wash basin with an intricate spider's web of bare wires three feet above it.

'And hot water,' he points to an ancient immersion heater.

I notice he does not put his hand through the wires to get to the switch to turn it on. More wires disappear into the shower controls. The loo actually has a seat and some attempt has been made to clean it.

'Best hotel in Goba.'

'Would it be possible to meet your father?' I ask.

'He is at work.'

'This evening?'

He hesitates.

'Of course I will pay you to interpret.'

His face lights up.

'You take the room?'

'I want new sheets and blankets.'

'Yes, and I bring mosquito net. What time you want my father?'

'In the bar after I have eaten. There is a market today?'

'Yes, big market.'

But it is not. Once it must have been, but now two of the terraces, where there were once stalls, are overgrown. Only a few marker stones show where they once were. Even in the market place there are empty plots. The livestock numbers are well down on Robé, and there are no horses.

Back at the hotel I ask if I can join a well-dressed man eating his lunch with a soldier with a sub-machine gun standing behind him. He is thrilled to have someone to talk to. He is a lawyer from Addis and speaks immaculate English. He is here working for the Commercial Bank of Ethiopia, but because he is an Amhara (one of the ruling northern tribes), he is in permanent danger of being attacked. The Oromo don't like outsiders, particularly from the tribes who overran them and have since tried to impose their culture on them. He is certain that without an escort he would have been killed the day he arrived.

I ask about the famine. He says much of it was brought on by traditional farming and fixed ideas. Most villagers are in thrall to their local chiefs who don't like change. The same seed has been used year after year, some of it getting less productive after each harvest, but they will not exchange it with other villages. The same with their livestock;

they seldom get new breeding stock, so the animals get smaller and less productive. He fears it will take years to modernise and there will be many small famines.

I ask about Gugse. He has seen it played near Addis at Christmas and says his father no longer goes to watch, because it is nothing like it used to be.

It is a game between two teams, the size of which depends on the team captains – normally ten to fifteen players. Two men play at a time. One has a long stick like a spear and the other a shield. Points are scored for hitting the man with the shield on the body. The spear is normally used with a stabbing movement, but sometimes it is thrown if the player can't get close enough to his opponent. The pitch is usually about 600 metres long. The spearman can attack his opponent in the middle 400 metres. When they get to the end of the pitch they swap roles for the return run.

I am excited by the sudden turn in events. I have got a good outline of how the game is played, and this evening I will be able to find out a lot more intricate details from the father of the student teacher.

Waiting for the student teacher's father in the hotel bar I study the odd assortment of pictures. There are several of Christ with his disciples, a banner saying "Happy Easter" in English and Amharic, a Father Christmas picture with blue and gold tinsel round it, and a

Crowds line either side of the Gugse pitch.

Tall horsemen on local ponies. An evenly matched pair, note the round shield and the stick in the left hand of the chaser.

huge faded mural of a balcony overlooking a calm sea with cliffs in the background. Southern Italy perhaps? I check my watch, half past nine. I hope he comes soon because I have to be up before five to catch the five thirty bus. I sip my third glass of black tea.

'I'm sorry Mister Bob, my father is unable to come.'

'I hope he is not ill, or did he have another meeting?'

He hesitates.

'He does not like foreigners.'

So much for my informative evening! Time to try elsewhere.

***

On the minibus from Shashamene to Awassa I ask a teacher crammed next to me – there are five of us on a seat for three - about three large Claas combine harvesters I saw on the side of the road with grass growing out of their engines.

'End of war celebrations,' he says.

'I don't understand.'

'When you defeat an enemy you break everything that was his. Did you see the telephone lines?'

'I saw the poles for them, but there were no lines.'

'Of course. They were all pulled down when Mengistu was defeated. The same with the combines. They belonged to the Derg.'

'But the machinery was given to Ethiopia to help grow more food.'

'They belonged to the Derg,' he says again.

The minibus driver takes risks as the passenger next to him passes him more Khat. Our side of the road has more potholes than the other, so he drives straight at the oncoming traffic, braking at the last moment as we swerve back onto the correct side. He handles the vehicle with amazing dexterity considering it is grossly overloaded with a pile of luggage on the roof, and six or seven passengers in each row.

'The horses I see wandering about, do they belong to anyone?'

'No, they are old and waiting to die. Some are sick, some are injured. Some are killed by a lorry or a bus. The rest die.'

'Do you not shoot them instead of waiting for them to die?'

'No, we have too much respect for horses to do that,' he looks really shocked.

'Do Ethiopians eat horses?'

'No! The Cuban soldiers ate horses, donkeys and mules, but we respect horses, we would never eat them.'

'But during the famine?'

'No, not even then. In the famine, if a cow was hit by a bus it would feed the people from the community, either the Christian or Muslim, not both. It depended on the religion of the first person to say a prayer over it. We are very strict about what we eat.'

The evening air rushes through the driver's window. It is luxury after the long journey in the "express" bus from Goba with all its windows shut to keep out the dust. Not that there would have been much draught; it took ten hours to cover a hundred and twenty miles. I can see why relief grain takes so long to get to where it is needed.

At breakfast, I meet a missionary lady who has been trying for the last twelve years, without success, to get the local tribes west of Awassa to use condoms. This year she returned to find them very much in use. She says it was nothing to do with HIV or birth control, but a condom salesman. He promised the chiefs a cut of his profit if they ordered their people to use them.

'I only wish we had thought of that,' she says with a grin.

I ask if she has heard of any horse games amongst the tribes she visits every summer, but she hasn't. The only person she knew connected with horses was an American horse welfare lady who tried to improve the lot of the taxi horses in Awassa. She got a boy to carry water to them, while they were waiting for a fare. It meant paying him and a small amount for each bucket of water. While the taxi drivers agreed that the horses which were given water at midday were healthier, could go faster and longer than those that went without, they ceased the watering as soon as she stopped paying.

While talking to the missionary I try to refrain from scratching. When I got here last night I stripped off my shirt to find I had twenty-three flea bites all round my left shoulder. At least I hope they are fleas and not lice, because a good washing generally gets rid of the former, but the latter are much harder to remove if they get into the seams.

On a patch of higher ground there is a small herd of abandoned horses. They are all appallingly thin. Several paw at the bare ground searching for something to eat, while others stand on the edge of the mire, nibbling waterlogged weeds. There is one horse, a bay, which has collapsed in the mud and is struggling to keep his head above the water.

I slide down the bank to try to get to him, but the mud greedily sucks at the first foot I put in the water, and I have to haul myself back to safety. Worn out, the bay lowers its head, the water bubbles and he comes up again. I can't do anything. Tears stream down my cheeks. How can these bloody people call dying like this respect?

I turn away and walk on along the causeway. There are a lot of birds round the lake, but even a brightly coloured kingfisher with a fish in its beak fails to lift me. Wandering into town I find myself outside the Awassa Agricultural College, and decide to find out more about the farming in the region. The guards on the gate stop me and tell me to use the foreigners' entrance which is the far side of the compound.

When I get there the high gates are chained and padlocked. I trudge back to the main entrance, but they will not let me through or telephone anyone in the compound. Thoroughly choked off I buy a bus ticket for Addis at six tomorrow morning.

Twenty minutes out of Awassa the bus hits a car and dents its bumper. The bus driver is keen to get on, but the car driver insists we wait for the police and the bus cannot be moved until they arrive. The conductor starts to hand the money back to the passengers, telling us to go back to the terminus and book another bus. The second bus of the day speeds past us, the driver waves and blows his horn, but makes no attempt to stop.

A parade of Gugse players. Unfortunately the game was cancelled because some young players got drunk in their village and one was killed. The priests said there would be more injuries and possibly deaths with families looking to avenge the death.

While I am waiting for the conductor to get my backpack from the hold, a student says he will come back with me and help me sort out a new ticket. Just then a rather decrepit looking bus pulls up to see if anyone wants to go to Addis. The student runs over and keeps me a place. I had paid sixty birr for the Express bus, but this is only eighteen. However we do have to sit with my backpack on our laps, and there are three on our seat rather than two.

The rule of the road is never give way once you start overtaking, even if something bigger is coming towards you. Our driver relies on the vehicle he is overtaking to slow down at the last second, so that he can pull in front of it just before he collides with the oncoming one. Scattered along both sides of the road are burnt out buses, lorries, and cars: proof that not every driver does slow down at the last instant.

Back in Addis I ask Amy how her research is going. Apparently she has collated all the information she needs.

'Did you do any long journeys?' I ask.

'You must be joking,' she says, looking at me as if I'm mad. 'I wouldn't dream of going outside Addis, it's far too dangerous.'

Sersie

After supper I chat to the barman. He has been told off by the manager for being rude to some 'broad noses'. Many Ethiopians regard anyone coming from south of Addis as lesser beings. He points out the offending group, three men and two women sitting at the far end of the bar.

'Boy!' calls the largest of the two women, whose ample buttocks envelope the top of her bar stool.

The barman gives me a nod, and strolls over as slowly as he dare. The large woman orders the drinks. Hardly has the barman got back to me than she calls for refills all round. They chat in English, I move to a table near them. To my surprise the large lady is holding forth about the size of penises.

'One man I know has one of 15 centimetres.'

'Extended of course,' says one of the men.

'No, no!' She laughs and he looks uncomfortable.

'I know a man who is 20 centimetres,' says the other woman.

'It has to be extended,' says another of the men.

She nods.

'The biggest man I have come across was 25 centimetres,' says the large lady. 'Only partly extended,' she adds with a look that challenges anyone to query her assertions.

One of the men orders another round avoiding looking at her. I glance up at the barman who smiles and shrugs his shoulders.

***

Richard and I laugh about my encounter on the way to the National Stud to meet Adāna, their top rider. He is exercising a white horse in a small arena marked out with broken rails; in the centre there is a jump, a bar resting on top of two upended 40 gallon barrels.

'This is my best jumping horse,' he calls to us. 'I will show you.'

He trots round, then slows to a walk as he turns into the jump. As soon as the horse sees the jump it starts to pull, but he keeps it walking. A few strides out he relaxes his hold. Instantly the horse breaks into a canter, takes two strides and sails over the obstacle. As soon as it lands Adāna hauls on the reins, but the horse, mouth gaping wide, makes two circuits of the ring before he gets it back to a walk.

'It is very strong,' he says unnecessarily.

'He goes well for you,' I compliment him.

He smiles.

'Do you know anything about Faras Gugse?' I ask.

'It is an Oromo game. I have only seen it a few times.' He gets off, handing the reins to a groom. 'Tomorrow there is a market in Sersie; a village forty kilometres from Addis. Colonel Illingworth,' he says turning to Richard, 'would you be able to take us there? We would need to leave about eight in the morning.'

'I'll look forward to it.'

Adāna shows us the way as we follow a rough track across a rolling green plain intersected by deep narrow streams. He directs Richard to the fords and occasional bridge. Though the plain is devoid of trees, Ethiopian Pines line the tops of the surrounding hills. The track is supposed to have been firmed up with hard core, but the locals pilfer the piles of stone to build new houses; so it is still a dirt track.

Approaching Sersie, we join a stream of people with goats, horses, donkeys, chickens, sheep, and cattle. Some are riding, but most walk, many carrying large loads, even young children are not empty-handed. We park on the edge of the village. In front of us anyone with anything to trade is setting up their stall.

The first cattle are already being killed and butchered just outside the stockade. Men hold the beasts while their throats are cut and, as soon as they are dead, the skinners get to work. Within minutes the first joints hang in front of a butcher's stall, while the rest of the body is still being dismembered.

We have to push through the throng to look at the stalls. Richard haggles over a finely woven basket, but Adāna says he will buy it later for him. The price Richard thought was good is three times what it would be for a local.

The smell of damp clothes and animals, fresh dung and wood smoke combine, giving the market a unique character. Many of the locals wear scarves and coloured woolly hats. Others have material wrapped round their heads like turbans. A few stare at us, but most take no notice.

Adāna takes me towards the horse bazaar area, but then leads me away from the cluster of milling horsemen, explaining that we'll get the best view of the races from just over halfway along the course. They race in pairs and the fastest horses make the best prices in the market after the racing is over.

'Perhaps there will even be one fast enough for Gugse,' he says.

I pull my coat round me; there is a cool wind and the sky is overcast with the threat of a shower. We wait while the horsemen have heated discussions. No one wants to start and lose the first match.

Richard joins us and asks what is happening. Just as I am telling him, a pair split from the others, and without any signal, start galloping in our direction. People on their way to the market run out of the way, while spectators whoop and cheer as the riders speed by. At a single post they pull their horses up. The smaller horse, a skinny grey, was about a length ahead when it passed us and looks as if it maintained that lead to the end of the 600 metre dash.

'That was fast,' Adāna says. 'Few of the others will want to race either horse. The racing is like Gugse, but there one man carries a spear, and the other a shield. If you have a fast horse, the person chasing you will not be able to get near enough to hit you when you are carrying the shield. But when you have the spear and a fast horse, you will hit him many times.'

There are several more races, but the grey does not appear again, and the bay easily wins its only other one. After the races buyers move among the vendors making offers. The rider of the grey squats a short distance from his hobbled horse, which is contentedly grazing the coarse grass. He seems untroubled that no one is interested.

'He's not selling,' Adāna says, after speaking to the man. 'He goes to the markets to show how fast his horse is, so that people will want to use it for breeding with their mares.'

The main market is in full swing with most of the stalls now set up, and the tea and coffee sellers doing a brisk trade. Lured by the smell of roasting coffee beans, we go to a stall. First the beans are baked on a flat piece of tin held over a small fire. The seller, holding onto the wooden handle, shakes the tin backwards and forwards to get an even roasting. When all the beans are dark brown, he waves the tin under the customers' noses before tipping them into a clay pot. He hangs a kettle over the fire and crushes the beans to a powder using a flat-ended stick. Once the kettle is boiling he takes off the lid and adds the crushed beans. After it has brewed for several minutes, he washes out some china mugs in a bucket of dirty water before pouring the coffee. It smells delicious and Adāna takes a cup, but Richard and I decline.

***

Richard suggests I contact David and Susan, a charming couple who live in the outskirts of Addis; both are keen riders and have four horses and an 85-year-old groom. They are sure he will have lots of stories about Gugse. But when we talk to him, he says he became a groom in Addis at the age of 12, and remembers nothing of consequence. They suggest we have a ride.

We are all on 13.2 hands high Ethiopian ponies, which are lightly built, tough and sure-footed, and have no difficulty carrying us safely along the steep narrow paths which wind through the eucalyptus woods that cover the lower slopes of the hills that surround the capital. It is great being back on a horse, even if my feet feel they are almost touching the ground.

The rain which has threatened all morning holds off till we get back, then there is a cloudburst. Water streams down the gullies on the hillsides and quickly washes away all the debris everyone has thrown in the large concrete monsoon ditches.

Over lunch I tell David about the combines I saw on the way to Awassa. He says he had the same sort of thing in Kenya. For several years he encouraged farmers to terrace their land, so they could be self-sufficient and not rely on hand-outs. They started with a single terrace; the next year there more, until by the end of five years a large area was terraced and they were selling their surplus. When he visited them after independence the terraces had fallen down, and the people were short of food.

'What happened?' he asked the local chief.

'We pulled them down,' he answered.

'Why?'

'Because they were part of our colonial past.'

A little further up the hill from David's is a large house occupied by a minister in the present government. It used to belong to a noble who was killed at the beginning of the revolution. At the end of the nineteenth century the noble's grandfather brought forty thousand slaves from central Africa to work on the new estates he had been given by King Menelik the Second, for helping him subdue the Oromo. Half the slaves died on the journey, and those who survived helped build the house before going to work on the land.

I ask David about some elephants marked on my map to the east of Harer. The edge of the Ogaden Desert just doesn't seem the right place for them, especially with the amount of food and water they need. He looks at my map.

'They weren't African elephants,' he says, 'they were Indian. They came here with the British, when the Indian Army sent a force to free the British Consul who was made a prisoner by Tewodros the Second. The elephants hauled the big guns, but once the campaign was over, it was thought they were too expensive to ship back, so they were left behind.'

'Are still there?'

He shakes his head.

'The Cubans used them for target practice for their tanks, and as far as I know there are none left. It was a terrible war,' he adds quietly. 'Terrible, yet many of the ministers from that time are still in power. Men who ordered people shot for being capitalists are now encouraging capitalism. The smaller charities, like us, are being side-lined for the bigger ones. Everyone wants money and modernisation,' he shakes his head.

The next afternoon Richard calls round for a drink. David rang him this morning in a panic because some government thugs, who said they spoke no English, marched into the Farm Africa offices, and demanded everyone leave within ten minutes. When Richard arrived the leader of the thugs waved a piece of paper in his face, and told him to get out. Richard refused and put his business card in the leader's top pocket.

'What do you mean by putting your card in my top pocket?' the man asked.

'So you do speak English,' Richard said.

After giving the leader a good telling off, he rang various ministries, and organised for Farm Africa not to have to move out for three days. He thinks someone must have upset a high up official.

The General's House

The party for the Queen's birthday is in full swing by the time I get there. Richard spots me and introduces me to a bunch of people including Sue Kitson, an American lady. She is a keen horsewoman and suggests I go for a hack with her tomorrow morning; but I am already riding with Sarah Sherlock, a doctor's wife, so we settle for the following day.

'Thanks for the introduction,' I say to Richard, when I see him later in the evening.

'Are you going for a ride with Sue?'

'Yes. Why?'

'You'll see,' he says, and roars with laughter, 'I should have warned you, sorry.' He turns to an African in military uniform and starts to make polite conversation.

The next morning Dr Sherlock picks me up. Before dropping me off at his home he has to go to the electricity company to pay his bill. It's his fourth attempt. The other three times they have been closed; if he doesn't pay on time the supply is cut off and a fine is imposed. This time he is in luck.

He is taking over a clinic for young women who've become incontinent through having babies too young. Often they are turned out of their house and made to live in a shed by their families. He is also trying to control HIV Aids. The government has declared the country is free of it, but it is rife amongst high school and university students living away from home. There is such a stigma attached to it that people with it commit suicide, knowing their friends and relatives will shun them – so he just treats them for pneumonia. The belief that having sex with a virgin will cure it has led to the rape of many young girls.

His house is a huge round hut with a central pole supporting the roof. Side rooms lead off the large, central sitting room. As one of the children is ill, the groom, Beniam, will accompany me instead of Sarah. He speaks English, is a good horseman, and will take me to see the Italian General's house.

He is waiting for me, holding two horses, a grey of 14.2 hands high, which will be mine and a bay over 15 hands. We are soon riding along a well-used track between fields of cracked black earth. It looks like dried peat, and the cracks are wider than a horse's hoof.

'Have you ever seen Gugse?' I ask.

'I have played it, Mister Bob. It is an easy game to learn, would you like to play it?'

'Yes.'

'We must stay on the track because the horses might break legs in the fields. It gets wider soon, so we will play there.'

He explains we start off side by side. Then, after a hundred yards, he will try to stab me with his riding whip; because I have no shield I will have to use my stick to ward him off. We trot along until the track widens; we pull up side by side.

'Are you ready, Mister Bob?'

'Yes.'

'We will start fighting where the long grass stops,' he points to the place with his stick, 'and we will finish where that track crosses ours.'

I nod, gathering up my reins ready to start. If I can keep well ahead of him, he won't be able to spear me.

'Go!' he shouts, hitting his horse on the flank with his whip.

Despite my best efforts, it soon becomes clear the grey is no match for the bay; also I am far heavier. As we approach the mark he drops back slightly so that he is just behind my left shoulder. I put my stick into my left hand and half turn towards him, ready to parry his first attack. He drops back a little then, as soon as I look forward, he speeds up and gets in a couple of sharp jabs before I can ward him off.

The combination of trying to keep to the track and protecting myself isn't working, so I pull over to the left, forcing him to slow rather than risk being forced into the field. This proves a good tactic, and for the remainder of the course I concentrate on swerving from side to side. I'm lucky to have been on the track, if I had been on open ground he could have kept scoring points. I realise just how vital speed is.

'That was good, yes? Mister Bob.'

'It was exciting.'

'On the way back, you will be attacking,' he gives a big grin. 'Over there is the General's house.'

On a small rise above the level plain and surrounded by trees is a large bungalow with a verandah round it. On closer inspection the green paint is peeling and faded and one of the shutters hangs at an awkward angle. We dismount and tie the horses to the verandah railings.

'We must ask the kabele if we can look round,' he says, in not much more than a whisper.

My leather-soled shoes resound on the wooden steps. There is no sound but us. No birds despite the trees. A gust of wind rustles the leaves; they sound intensely loud. The door grates along the floor as Beniam pushes it open. Sitting behind a table, are three members of the local kabele. Beniam approaches them respectfully. Only a short time ago they had the power of life and death over the villagers. Today, even though it is a democracy, few would dare vote against their wishes.

Beniam asks permission to show me round.

The only light comes from the gaps in the shutters. No photographs I am told, and do not to open the shutters. It smells musty; dust particles dance in the beams of light that come through holes in the ancient slats. Still cowed, Beniam leads me into the first of the rooms. My footsteps echo as I enter.

There are dark stains on the floor and drawings on the walls. I make a closer inspection. All the pictures are of torture and death. The man holding the rifle and bayoneting someone has two eyes, while his victim has one. Always it is the same. Those being beaten, shot, knifed,

Warding off the spearman with a shield.

throttled or electrocuted are the baddies with one eye, those inflicting the punishments have two. In Ethiopian art the good have two eyes and the bad one. To add to the horror, pools of blood are drawn beside the victims and their mouths are twisted in agony.

In the next room it is the same, except the broken shutter lets in more light so that the pictures can be clearly seen. Some are in pencil while others are coloured – which somehow makes them more horrific. Beniam says nothing, just glances uncomfortably towards the door now and again. The ghoulish atmosphere from the recent past is still present, but its other past, as a stylish villa with undoubtedly the best Italian furniture and decor, has long gone. We go into another room, but the kabele decide it is time for us to leave, and we are ushered out from the grim interior into the warm sunlight.

I pause briefly at the top of the steps to admire the view across the plain to the distant hills, but Beniam has already untied my reins and is holding them out to me. We ride in silence, tongues stilled by what we have seen.

At the crossroads where we pulled up before, I squeeze my horse into a gallop. My plan is to be in front when we pass the marker so that I can spear Beniam as he goes by, but before we are there he gallops past me, grinning. Periodically he slows, allowing me to catch up, then just as I am nearly in range he accelerates away.

'This would make a good Gugse horse,' Beniam says patting his sweating bay. 'I think he would be fast enough, but yours!' He laughs.

On the ride back he tells me how it is played. There are two teams, one village against another, and the team captains decide how many on each side. Two riders, one from each team play at a time. They try to put horses of equal speed together, so that it is good for the spectators as well as the players. Retired players along the track count the hits. Today few people have the traditional hippopotamus-hide shields, so have to defend themselves with their spear-sticks.

In the past Gugse was used to settle land disputes. The tribes were nomadic and rather than fight and kill each other over a piece of land, they selected their best horsemen to play Gugse, with the winning team getting the pasture. It was played with shields and proper spears. It meant there were no pitched battles, and necessitated the breeding of fast responsive horses. Occasionally four or more played at one time, but normally they were in pairs.

A depiction of Gugse in the first half of the 20th century.

Back at the Sherlocks' I find a picture of Gugse in a book. It is being played in front of a pavilion where people are lounging while the players do battle. Everyone is dressed in white, which means it was being played as entertainment, at a religious festival or wedding. Dr Sherlock says today it is sometimes played at Timkat (Epiphany) and Christmas.

I am here at the wrong time of year. It is a risk I run every time I travel. With nothing written down, there is no way of finding out when a game is played until I actually find it. I'll just have to come back for Timkat.

I ask Sarah about some paintings of the Ethiopian countryside hanging in the hall. She says she is the artist, but hasn't been able paint for some time. Wherever she sets up her easel, local children appear and demand money. When she refuses to give them any they throw mud and stones at her until she leaves.

Back at the hotel there is a message from Sue Kitson, she will pick me up at seven tomorrow.

The Horsemen of Addis

Driving to the stables we stop at traffic lights where a child runs out and taps on the window. Sue takes some money from her bag and hands it to her.

'She is my little beggar girl,' Sue says. 'Every morning she waits for me at these lights. What I give helps keep her family alive. It is very hard for those with nothing.'

The stables are next to the old racecourse, and her two grooms are waiting with four saddled horses. Dereji, the younger of the two, hands me the reins of a chestnut Ethiopian Pony cross Thoroughbred.

As soon as we are mounted Sue sets off at a brisk trot, the horses' unshod hooves slapping on the tarmac. She leads the way with the grooms just behind her, while I bring up the rear, unused to such a flat-out trot, even on my shod horses at home.

We turn onto an unmade track which leads up through the eucalyptus trees, which cloak the base of the hills surrounding Addis. The first women wood-carriers of the day pass us, bent almost double under huge bundles of firewood they carry into the city. We slow to a walk as the gradient increases. We pass through a coppiced area, from which much of the city's fuel comes, before following a track through the trunks of tall trees. Soon we have to dismount and lead the horses up a steep rock-strewn path.

I have developed a chest infection over the last few days, and soon my lungs are heaving as I struggle to keep up. Sue takes pity on me, saying that many people have problems at this time of year, with the smog and lack of movement of the air. We climb for another quarter of an hour before coming out on a grassy plateau.

No sooner are we all mounted than Sue sets off at a fast canter. My chestnut has no difficulty keeping up, though I am still getting used to his narrowness and how low he holds his head. I slow up to go round the edge of a football pitch, on which an early morning game is being played, but Sue, followed by her grooms, gallops straight through, scattering the players. I catch them up as they rein in on the edge of the plateau. Below the tree-clad slopes, the tops of the tallest buildings poke through the smog. Occasionally a murmur of wind thins it enough to see the red tail-lights of cars.

'There is a much better view from over there,' Sue points to a distant headland above the far corner of the city. 'I'll show you.'

With that we ride back through the football match. This time the players see us coming and split apart so that we can gallop through the middle. We steady to a canter going up a rise, before speeding up again on the well-nibbled grassland. Two mounted teenagers try to sell us their horses. When they won't take no for an answer, Sue dashes off at a gallop along a path about two feet wide with deep ruts on either side. The boys wisely turn away. It is a hair-raising experience on a horse I don't know, and I'm relieved when we eventually slow up.

'I will get Gebadi and Dereji to canter past you,' Sue says, 'and you can tell me what you think of their riding.'

She takes me to the top of a slight slope, then waves to the grooms. They come at a nice hack canter, sitting in the saddle, going with their horses, but their hands look as if they are glued to the withers. They are stiff shouldered and straight armed with no give. I say how nicely they ride, but mention their hands.

'It has taken me ages to get their hands down,' Sue says testily.

'If they raised them a bit they could relax their elbows and shoulders.'

She shrugs, says something to the two men, and canters off.

We canter along more narrow tracks through woodland, before coming to the headland she pointed out earlier. The view is stunning. Addis is laid out below us. The smog has gone, and although the air is not crystal clear, it is still possible to see the street patterns and the landmarks. Sue passes me a bottle of water and I realise how thirsty I am. After a long swig I look at my watch; it is midday.

'I had no idea we had been riding so long,' I say to Sue.

She pulls back her sleeve to look at her watch.

'Oh my God, I'm meant to be at a meeting at two thirty. Quick, mount up, we must go.'

There are no gentle canters and trots on the return ride; we are flat out, except where it is too steep and we have to walk. In one place the horses have to clamber down some steps. At the bottom, we gallop on the tarmac, or the side of the road where possible. One unfortunate man, peeing into a storm drain, has no option but to leap across it as Sue makes no attempt to avoid him.

It is ten past two when we get back. Sue flings her reins to Gebadi and runs to her four-by-four. She waves her hand, acknowledging my thanks, unaware that I am so saddle-sore that I can hardly get off. Thin trousers are not the best things for hard riding.

Dereji takes the chestnut from me and washes him down.

After saying goodbye, I hobble across to the Ethiopian Horse Association to see what they know about Gugse. They are not interested in old-fashioned riding. They say they are a modern organisation. There is a show-jumping competition the day after tomorrow, and I would be welcome to come.

Back at the hotel I confirm with Ethiopian Air that I will be flying home in three days, and then ring Richard to say goodbye. He insists I come to supper after the show jumping to tell him all about it.

Just as I come off the phone the hotel proprietor asks me into her office. Is it true that I am a farmer in the UK?

Yes.

Would I be willing to run her family's big coffee plantation?

I don't know anything about coffee.

That doesn't matter; she just wants my managerial skills. It would

Evenly matched antagonists.

be a good salary. What about my family and my own farm?

She says I could be here for six months and home for six months. I decline.

The proprietor tries again, but I am adamant. I thank her for the offer, and leave thinking what an interesting opportunity it would be, but not at the expense of my family.

The show jumping is preceded by three races. The 1000m for the pure bred, local horses; the 1500m for the cross-breds, and the 2000m for pure, foreign horses. These races are a far cry from the time of Haile Selassie when, like the Queen at Ascot, he would arrive at Janmeda in an open carriage, and drive slowly up the course. Now it is more like "flapping", races with crowds everywhere and anxious officials striving to keep the course clear as the races enter their final stages. Adāna wins the cross bred race, but the crowds are too thick for me to get a chance to congratulate him.

The first jumping class is the two foot high class for novice adults and children. The jumps are the usual selection of painted fillers, boards, a wall and several rails, though the latter are only 2 inches diameter. The crowd cheers everything; falls, refusals, knock downs. The only thing they don't cheer is the winner, a boy of twelve who gets a clear round.

Next are the intermediates with a three foot course. Some of the riders have old fashioned skull caps while others have modern crash hats. Clothing varies from jacket, breeches and leather boots, to short sleeved shirts, jeans and trainers. Dress does not hold any indication as to who will get a clear round, there are an equal number of mistakes from everyone. The crowd loves "heroic riding" – going as fast as possible. The person who gets the greatest ovation is a chap who gallops flat out into the ring waving his hat, completes two circuits without attempting a jump, gallops back through the collecting ring before eventually pulling up a quarter of the way down the racecourse.

I meet Dereji and ask him about the raised scarring on the backs of a couple of horses.

'Saddle sores,' he says.

'But the scarring?'

'Hot iron. If a horse has a bad saddle sore which won't heal, they use a hot iron to burn it. Once the skin had healed it will be much stronger. Mrs Kitson gets very angry when she sees it.'

I wince at the thought of the agony a horse must go through. There are no drugs here, so nothing to kill the pain.

While we are talking, Adāna enters the ring on a bay horse.

'You know this man, Mister Bob?'

'Yes.'

'He is very good rider, perhaps he will win.'

'I hope so.'

There are four of them in the jump off and he comes second. I try to get to him, but he is straight off the bay and onto the white horse we saw him practising on at the National Stud. A groom holds it, while he gets on and rides it round the collecting ring.

'This is the high jump competition,' Dereji informs me. 'Only a few jumps, but very high.'

There are three jumps: a set of rails about two foot six, another set a foot higher and a wall four feet high.

The crowd quietens down, eagerly awaiting the battle between the top horses and riders. There are eight competitors. A suited official from the Ethiopian Horse Association introduces each of them as they come into the ring. There are four policemen and three army officers, all in smart uniforms with highly polished boots, and Adāna in a short sleeved shirt and tie.

The first rider is from the army. He is on an agile local cross-bred. Dereji tells me this officer has been to America, where he had a lot of riding tuition. It certainly shows. He does a faultless clear round, sailing over the wall with a lot of room to spare.

The next rider's horse dives through the second rails, knocking the top one down with its chest and the bottom one with its hind feet. Somehow the horse stays upright, but the rider shoots over its head landing on his back. A steward catches the horse and offers him a leg up, but he limps off, while his groom leads the horse.

The next two each knock a block out of the wall.

Then it is Adāna; his feet are thrust forward and the reins gripped in his balled fists, as his horse surges into the ring. He repeats what we saw at the Stud, walking then letting the horse go for the last couple of strides. Using all his strength he manages to get it back under control between each fence. He, like the first competitor, sails over the wall.

The jump off is between the officer, a policeman and Adāna. The first two jumps stay the same, and a layer of blocks is added to the wall. The policeman knocks a block out of the wall, so it is just the two, who both go clear. In the next round both have a block out but, to my amazement, another set of blocks are added to the wall.

'Why?' I ask Dereji.

'They always do.'

'They should have made them jump again at the same height.'

He smiles as if I don't know anything.

Despite no clear rounds, the wall is raised twice more, and it becomes a demolition derby.

A steward announces the wall will be left out, so only the first and second jumps will be jumped. Without the wall the crowd lose interest and drift away. There is hardly anyone to cheer when Adāna wins. The prize-giving is like a country show in the UK, with the smartly dressed wife of a local dignitary handing out the rosettes and cups.

On my way back I call in at the stables to see the chestnut. He is in his stall munching some hay. Dereji shows me where they keep the tack, which is all beautifully cleaned and hung on hooks and saddle racks at the far end of a narrow room with a barred window. His neatly made bed is beside the door. He says he sleeps here every night to look after the horses and stop thieves from taking the tack. I look at my watch, it is time to change before going out to supper. I thank Dereji for his help and catch a taxi back to the hotel.

When Richard picks me up I notice he is constantly looking in his mirror.

'Is someone following you?'

'I'm not sure,' he says. 'I've checked several times, and no one seems to be. Yet, I've had two small accidents. Both times and within a couple of minutes, someone has appeared and said, "You go home Colonel, I'll sort this out".' He shrugs. 'I'm completely baffled.'

'Are there a lot of secret police here?'

'There used to be, probably still are, and it's easy to keep tabs on a white person. I don't suppose I'll ever know if I'm being followed.'

Over dinner Carrie tells me about the problems of gardening here. The monkeys take most of the tomatoes before they are ripe. The lettuces have to be fenced against tortoises, but the jackals dig up the fences along with the rest of the garden to get at the meat and bone meal fertiliser. The porcupines get through the broken fences and eat the carrots and any other root vegetables. Finally a leopard has eaten most of the cats in the embassy compound, so the birds descend in droves onto the peas and beans.

'Oh for the slugs and snails of the UK!' she says with feeling.

They are interested to hear about the General's house, and have a laugh over my saddle sores. Sue's reputation for long rides has put everyone off going with her. A two hour hack is plenty long enough for most people; few want to do six and a half hours like I did. Richard is amused by the show jumping, particularly the wall going up and up. I thank them for their hospitality and help, saying I plan to come back in eighteen months so that I am here for Timkat and the feast of Mariam, when it is the Gugse season. I am determined to see a game.

***

At Heathrow I notice my large rucksack has been opened. I am horrified to discover all my used films are missing. My unused ones, which were in the same bag, are untouched. Lying in the bag beside a long cut is an old-fashioned rusty razor blade. I can only think the invisible secret police took the films because of my association with Richard.

Return to Addis

The first night back in Addis I have supper with Richard and Carrie. He has recently returned from a trip to Eritrea for military advisers. He was horrified at the wanton destruction. One town had been razed to the ground, and an electricity substation completely destroyed. He asked an Ethiopian general why, and was told the victor has the right to destroy his enemy utterly; the same explanation I was given for the smashed combines near Awassa.

I ask about the famine reported on the BBC last year. He thinks it was over-hyped to distract the world's press from the Ethiopian advance in Eritrea. Certainly a lot of cattle died, but people died mostly because of bad communications. Relief grain stores had been set up throughout the region, but the store managers had no means of communication with their superiors. When someone asked for grain the manager had to check the situation before handing anything out.

Once assessed, grain was handed out. When the drought became severe, most of the support grain had already been distributed. Eventually replacement supplies were sent, but people starved while waiting. The government blamed the NGOs and they blamed the government.

Sue Kitson is away and Richard busy, so I try the Ethiopian Horse Association and other contacts, but nobody gets back to me. After three days I am wondering what to do, when an apologetic receptionist at my hotel hands me several messages. They had been given to someone else called Thompson who checked out this morning.

Sue is back; her husband broke his wrist, some ribs and bruised his kidneys paragliding. They didn't trust hospitals in Addis, so flew to Nairobi. She has found out there will be a game of Gugse in the village of Sululta during Timkat, in two days' time, and knows an old Oromo who will interpret for me. It is where she buys the hay for her horses, so the information is reliable. Unfortunately she will not be able to come.

I arrange transport with the hotel manager, but the car fails to appear. Leema, the interpreter, knows someone who drives for the Swiss Embassy and rings him. He gets to us by mid-morning.

Once outside the city, we career along a dirt track between large stubble fields. After half an hour we come across three riders on horses garlanded with brightly coloured woollen pom-poms. The men carry six foot staves and keep riding as Leema jumps out of the car and runs after them. They stop after a hundred yards. Leema looks frightened to go too close to them and can't understand their dialect, so calls to the driver for assistance. The driver gets directions, and we speed off again.

Leema explains that although he's an Oromo he's never lived in the countryside, and the locals distrust people who live in towns, or are not from their immediate area. We stop a young man with a herd of horses and the driver asks him the way. He points to a large eucalyptus wood some distance off the main track.

In a clearing we find a gathering of villagers round a tent where some priests, in full robes, carrying embroidered umbrellas, are chanting. The men don't look overjoyed at the arrival of strangers.

Knowing I would make things worse by photographing the ceremony, I ask Leema if it is OK for me to take pictures of the horses and their ornate saddlecloths. Without consulting any of the men he says it will be fine. I insist he asks first. In the end the driver asks and nods. I pick a bunch of horses grazing on the edge of the clearing. As I approach them I see there are others in the edge of the wood, about thirty in all. One of the horses stands out. It is a dark grey, taller than the others, with a beautifully embroidered Ethiopian lion on what looks like a silk saddlecloth. I get one of my cameras out.

While I'm focussing, the owner runs past me to his horse. He takes the bit, which is hanging on the pommel, puts it in the horse's mouth and undoes the hobble attaching the head-collar to the hind leg, and mounts.

I am impressed, under half a minute from passing me to getting into the saddle. Hopefully he will do some "heroic riding".

I raise the viewfinder to my eye and keep trying to focus as he comes towards me. Suddenly he is filling the whole lens, and I realise he is not "heroic riding", but riding me down. I dive out of the way as he brushes past me. When I get back to my feet he is chatting with his friends who are looking my way and laughing. Leema and the driver are standing to one side.

'I thought you got permission for me to take photographs of the horses?' I say angrily to Leema.

He nods. I think I know what that means – I'm too frightened to ask, but don't want to lose face by either asking and being turned down or being seen to back down.

'Ask him,' I point to the man who nearly rode me down, 'if it's all OK for me to take some pictures of the other horses.'

Leema and the driver have a short conference before the driver goes over to the horseman. He glances at me, nods, then says something.

'It is OK,' Leema says before the driver returns.

'Stay close behind me,' I tell him, 'I don't want any more nasty surprises.'

'It is OK. It is only horses you are photographing. I will be behind you.'

I set off across the clearing to the horses on the edge of the wood. There are several good saddlecloths, though not as fine as the other one. I can look at the bits and study the tack as well. I have my camera up to my eye when I am knocked flying as something hits me hard in the back. Looking up I see a horseman yank viciously on the reins so that his horse goes over backwards. Luckily it is still hobbled, and falls away from me. I scramble up as the horseman pulls his mount to its feet. I look round for Leema. He and the driver are a hundred and fifty yards away standing by the car. Damned cowards!

Shaken, I make my way towards them, but more horsemen have mounted and I run to a lone eucalyptus with a forked trunk. My camera is broken.

As the horsemen line up in two rows and jog slowly towards my tree, I take out my other camera. The line splits to go either side of my tree. No one even glances at me as I photograph them. They come past in formation twice more, their staves resting on their pommels, then head over to the rest of the villagers.

The chanting increases as young men with staves pick up a rhythmic dance stamping in unison, so that each step sounds like a drum-beat. They circle the tent before setting off for the village. Behind them come the priests, some carry their ark, which is draped in an ornate cloth, while others carry highly decorated umbrellas. Women and children follow them, with the horseman bringing up the rear. I stay where I am as the sound of the chanting is swallowed up by trees.

'They will play later in the afternoon,' says Leema.

'Where and what time?'

'They will play there,' he points to an open patch of ground. 'They will tell us.'

We sit by the roadside watching some cattle and sheep graze stalks of grass in the stubble. The boys herding them squat in the shade on the edge of the wood. In the distance we can hear drumming coming from the village; later some faint screaming. The bored driver says he will go to the village to find out what time the game starts.

When he returns Leema tells me there will be no Gugse today.

'Why not?'

'There has been a killing,' Leema looks at the driver who tells him what has happened. 'Two young men had a fight, they were drunk, and one killed the other with his stick. Now there is bad blood between families.'

'Will they play tomorrow?'

'No. The kabele and the priests have forbidden it. The young men get drunk, disobey the rules, and use their sticks for hitting instead of stabbing. Many players could be injured. I am sorry.'

Players pass close to the spot from which I was photographing them.

***

Riding with Sue Tilson the next morning, I relate the tale. She says I will get another chance in a few days' time at the feast of Mariam, when there is a big festival at the church of Mariam Entoto.

She has arranged to take Richard and Rita Pankhurst. He is the son of Silvia Pankhurst, who was a great supporter of Haile Selassie when he was exiled to the UK by the Italians.

Richard was the head of Ethiopian Studies at Addis Ababa University and is a well-known authority on the country. Sue is thrilled to be able to show him something Ethiopian he has never seen or heard of. Even she had no idea there was a horse game until I told her.

We call in at a village house, where Sue and her two grooms are regular visitors. We are offered coffee, and while it is being prepared I look round. The house is rectangular, with mud walls and a tin roof. The main room, in which we sit, besides having a table and bench, also acts as the grain store with sacks stacked along the far wall. At one end there is a door leading into the kitchen, and at the other, a curtained-off bedroom. There are a couple of beds against the sacks for the children.

Over coffee I ask about his horse.

'It is a good Gugse horse and he is treated specially,' Dereji translates. 'He is part of the family and a man may not sell a Gugse horse without the permission of his wife. Sometimes it eats better than my family.'

'How do you train them?'

'When they are two we put a child on their back and lead them round. For the next two years they are led round with a child on. When they are five we put a saddle on and a bit in their mouth. Only after that does the owner ride without a saddle. He runs alongside and jumps onto the horse's back. When it is fully trained we put the strong bit in its mouth.'

There is a shout from outside.

'He has to go,' says Sue.

We go into the farmyard where there are sheds of wood and tin, and a haystack with sheets of tin tied on top. One shed is the stable, and another has young cattle in. The door of that one is part of a wing of a Russian MIG fighter shot down during the war. The farmer's horse is ready saddled, and hung with red and blue wool pompoms, because he is going to a wedding. He is happy for me to photograph him and his horse.

He slips an Arab bit into his horse's mouth and, to my horror, blood gushes out.

Sue assures me there is nothing to worry about, and asks him to take the bit out. She opens the horse's mouth to show me a squashed leech. Horses regularly pick them up when drinking from waterholes. The underneath of its tongue has masses of lesions where ulcers have formed from previous encounters with leeches. I get a photograph of the farmer, but a second rider who joins him shakes his stave at me and shouts, making it quite clear he will not give me permission to photograph either him or his horse.

Late in the afternoon we come across some drovers with a large flock of sheep. The men, dressed in well-worn clothes, keep the sheep moving, while the donkeys with their belongings follow on behind. Some well-dressed men, waiting in the shade by the road, walk into the flock and start catching and feeling the sheep for fatness. Gebadi says the drovers are from Wollo, which is many days' walk to the north.

We watch as the buyers select smaller sheep, bargain for them, agree a deal, then, when the drover turns away, they mark a larger sheep.

It happens several times and Sue wants to go down and tell the drovers what is happening, but Gebadi says it would be wrong to

Men on their way to a wedding. The one in the foreground was happy for me to photograph him, but the one in the background got angry.

interfere. More buyers arrive and further slow the progress of the flock as the drovers try to keep them moving towards a set of pens erected close to the trail. In the morning the unmarked ones will be auctioned and taken to the abattoirs in Addis.

On the way back Sue swaps me onto the local pony Dereji was riding, so that I get a feeling for what they are like. As we descend a steep hill with some steps cut into the rock, I feel perfectly safe because my little mount is so sure-footed. I notice Prince, the half thoroughbred I was riding, is much more awkward on difficult going. My bruised back from my encounter with the horsemen at Sululta stiffens up while hacking back. After seven hours in the saddle, I again find it difficult to get off.

The feast of Mariam arrives, unlike the car which is booked to take me to Entoto. I manage to get a passing taxi, and the driver agrees to take me and wait for me. Despite passing a lot of people on their way back from the church, when we get there, there is a seething mass of humanity through which it is impossible to drive. I get out and make for a bunch of horses tied to some trees.

I ask if I can take photographs of the horses. The owners

misunderstand. One unties his horse and gives me a leg up. I am the only white person here, and being mounted attracts a lot of attention.

People crowd round me asking questions, the horse is scared by the crush and starts to play up. I sit still trying to calm it. Another horseman joins me and we push through the masses to a long gentle uphill slope, where he breaks into a canter scattering the outer ring of churchgoers. We pull up at a stick stuck in the ground with a woollen pompom tied to it.

'Gugse,' explains my companion pointing back down the six hundred yards we have come.

On the ride back I spot Sue's vehicle edging through the crowd. I wave but she doesn't see me as she tries not to run anyone over.

The crowds part for us and I hand over my horse to its grinning owner. I ask if I can take a photograph, and take out my camera. The mood changes and I hastily put it away. I thank the owner before pushing through the crowds in the direction I saw Sue go. It is hard work, most of the people are taller than me, and chat in tightly packed groups. Standing on some boulders to see over the heads, I spot her four-by-four.

She introduces me to the Pankhursts. Richard asks how Gugse is played, and I have just finished explaining it to him when Gebadi and Dereji arrive on horseback, leading Sue's best horse. The Pankhursts decide to watch from the four-by-four. I leave them and edge through to the front of the crowd, which is lining either side of the Gugse track. Dereji rides behind me, telling people to get out of the way, and says he will stay with me.

'Mister Bob, Missis Sue,' he points to the start of the course.

Despite people still being on the track, she and Gebadi are racing through them. Shouts precede them as the spectators scurry out of their way. Some cheer, urging them on, while others, who've nearly been run down, shout angrily. They pull up at the marker and, after a couple of minutes, do a return run down the now clear course. It is a close thing and impossible from where we are to see who wins.

I am facing into the sun and tell Dereji we will cross the course so that it is behind me for taking photographs. I am halfway across when a large man with a Kalashnikov slung over his shoulder and carrying a big stick bars my way. I try to go round him but he prods me hard in the stomach with the end of his stick.

'He says we must go back, Mister Bob,' Dereji says.

'But I will be photographing straight into the sun.'

'We must go back.' The man says something to Dereji; 'or he will arrest you. Please, Mister Bob.'

The man follows us to the edge of the course. He tells Dereji I am not to take any photos, but further down the track there is a man with a video, and near him a couple of people with cameras. I point to them and while he goes to have a word with them, I get my camera out. There is a brief argument before the man with the gun disappears into the crowd.

'Press,' says Dereji.

The first players come up the course. It is a non-event; the man with the shield is well in front and his horse is clearly much faster than his opponent's. (The shields are round, about three feet in diameter and used to be made of hippopotamus hide, but are now made of cow leather. The plain wooden staves are six feet long and held anywhere between half and three quarters of the way along the shaft.) On the return run, after swapping roles, the man with the shield does a brilliant job defending as the spear man on the quicker horse tries to hit him on the body. The crowd cheer the spear man on but, by the end, he has failed to score. More couples come, sometimes one after another, sometimes at ten minute intervals.

Dereji repeats that the team captains try to match the players equally to provide better sport. One of the teams is the local one from Entoto. All the riders wear western-style suits, open-necked shirts and sandals, so 'western' it is impossible for me to know to which team they belong. Occasionally, from the cheers when someone scores, I guess that a player is local.

Not everyone has a shield and some players have only their stick to defend themselves with. If the two are evenly matched there is a stick fight all the way up the course and the click-clack of the staves drowns out the drumming of the hooves on the hard ground.

As the afternoon wears on the riders and spectators consume more tej (local beer). The play gets fiercer and the crowd more vociferous. Looking round I see that Sue's vehicle has gone.

The next two horsemen are older and give a superb display of offensive and defensive play, putting all their energies into their roles, their well trained horses changing direction as they respond to the pressure of their riders' legs.

The start of a match.

The next pair has no shield, and one horse is much faster than the other. The attacker swoops in from the right, scores, drops back and attacks from the left. The other man can do little to protect himself, and by the end of the run the crowd are angry. The atmosphere has changed because it looks as if Entoto are losing.

'Mister Bob,' Dereji moves forward so that he is beside me. 'It is time to go now. We told Missis Sue we would look after you.'

Some of the judges are arguing and waving their arms.

The Ethiopian photographers have disappeared.

Some of the previously indifferent spectators glare at me. Could it be that they think this white man has brought bad luck to their team? Perhaps it appears that way to them after drinking tej.

I get on Sue's horse and ride to where the taxi is waiting, door open, engine running. Behind us the spectators roar as another pair gallop up the course.

The taxi driver accelerates away, and out of the back window I see Sue's horses cantering off, avoiding the crowds.

I have seen the elusive Faras Gugse!

***

As far as I know there is, these days, a 'demonstration' of Gugse for tourists at Janmeda every Christmas. There was increasing pressure from both the government and the Church to end it because it can lead to violence and killing, just as I experienced. So, whether there are any village games, like the one I saw, still being played, I'm not certain. Also, it being a game of the Oromo rather than the ruling tribes from the North, will mean it is not encouraged.

The origins of the game are obscure, but in the past Turkish soldiers were employed by the some of the Abyssinian Emperors and there is a strong possibility that Gugse is an offshoot of Çirit.

It is interesting that the game was used by the nomadic tribes as a way of stopping contested grazing rights turning into an excuse for wholesale slaughter.

The spears used by the contestants were single and double-headed and players were regularly killed or wounded. Today, despite the spears being rounded off at both ends, deaths still occur because the young men get drunk and use their staves as two-handed swords when they get close to an opponent.

CHAPTER SEVEN

Mongolia: Blue Wolf

'I would love to go to Venice at the end of September, to celebrate our 30th wedding anniversary,' Sue says.

I say nothing. After several years of not being able to get away, I am free to travel, but my itinerary does not include Venice.

'What?' she demands, giving me "the look".

'That's when I'll be in the Altai mountains in Mongolia looking at the horse games at the Hunting with Eagles Festival.'

I never tell Sue my plans until I'm sure of my leaving date. The Festival is at the beginning of October, but it will take several days to get there.

There is a long pause.

'I'll come with you,' she says. 'But I don't want to be away for too long, the dogs will get upset.'

For a moment panic seizes me. It will have to be an organised trip, no dashing off at a tangent when I hear of some different horsemen in a distant place. But it's the first time she's wanted to come with me.

'Great,' I say, wondering if it will be.

***

The setting sun is pinking the snow-capped mountains when we spot the Eagle Hunters' camp. It is amongst some scrub on the far side of a small river. Our minibus bumps down the bank, crawls in low ratio across the river and drives up the far side, stopping near their tent. Their golden eagles are tethered to some rocks close by, and their chunky ponies to some bushes.

Our camping stove, a metal box on legs with a short detachable chimney, is lit by our female cook, Kinjay. Bits of tyre and kindling get it going, then dried dung is added, and a stew-pot set on top. While the food is cooking, our guide, Bulbul, a girl in her twenties who speaks good English, helps us pitch our tent as night closes in. We eat the local

Me riding with an eagle.

dish of stewed mutton with dumplings, cabbage, onions and potatoes by the light of a lantern hanging from a stake.

After supper we are offered tea or coffee. Sue chooses hot water, but quietly tips it away when she sees the colour of it. Thousands of stars shine in the black sky as we walk a little way from camp to do our teeth and have a pee.

'If you need a pee in the middle of the night,' I say to Sue, 'stay in sight of the camp, or you'll get lost.'

To prove my point I shine the torch round. All we can see is four-foot high scrub. A short distance away a torch beam slashes through the dark, showing where the camp is. When we get back, the hunters, to whom we have not yet been introduced, are playing cards by candlelight. We retire to our tiny tent.

The early morning sun throws long shadows as it rises over the scrub in a cloudless sky. The breath of the eagle hunters comes in white puffs as they saddle the horses. The grass is stiff with frost and when we try to do our teeth, the water is frozen in the bottle. Kinjay comes to the rescue with some warm water left over from making tea. Breakfast is a cold omelette followed by piping hot wheat porridge with honey.

Aralbai the leader of the hunters allots us our ponies. My 13.2 hands coloured mare is slightly smaller than Sue's one-eyed bay, and my stirrup-leathers stop several holes shorter than I normally ride. This means either sitting on the large metal ring on the back of the saddle or bouncing on an equally large ring at the front. Luckily for Sue, her saddle is a good fit. We move off as soon as an extra pad has been found for my saddle.

The three hunters: Aralbai the leader; his son Arman; and Bakht, go at a steady trot, their golden eagles carried on their forearms. We follow with Bulbul. The hunters place their thickly gloved carrying-hands in the V of a Y shaped stick, the bottom of which rests on a pad on the front of the saddle. The hooded birds sit quietly, and turn their heads into the wind.

The low rolling hills are covered in what looks like a sea of brown grass, but once in it, the ground is stony with only intermittent grass stalks. The horses' hooves click metallically on the stones as we jog mile after mile. Despite the extra pad, the only way for me to get comfortable is to stand in the stirrups, holding on to the mane to keep my balance.

We are relieved to see the olive-green minibus waiting for us in the lee of a large rock-strewn hill. We dismount and stretch, before being given mugs of tea. At least Sue and I have been riding at home, but our guide, Bulbul, hasn't ridden for several years and she is quite sore. The hunters tie their eagles to large stones and allow the horses to graze. It is only when sheltering out of the wind beside the vehicle, we realise how hot the sun is. After a short break we are off again. The hunters suggest a steady canter, but we quickly realise Bulbul is not up to it. Luckily for me my pony doesn't pull, as I still need one hand on the mane to help me counter its short, choppy stride while standing in the stirrups.

After lunch we are introduced to the golden eagles which are all female. They are larger and more aggressive than males. Aralbai's is a twelve-year-old and was the overall winner at last year's Festival. It has a wingspan of over eight feet. Unlike the ponies which are named after their characteristics – Sue's is 'one eye' and mine 'the coloured mare' – the eagles are not named. Bakht's is six, just coming into her prime, but still needs to be more obedient when called. Arman's is just a year old and is coming to the Festival as part of its education. It has not yet flown.

To capture it, he and his father spotted an eagle's nest on a cliff-face and waited for the eggs to hatch. Then they climbed up and his father marked one of the female chicks by tying a piece of wool round its leg. Returning a couple of months later they removed it from the nest.

Aralbai and Bakht take turns getting their eagles to fly to them. They put them on a rock halfway up the hillside, walk back down and call them. Aralbai's opens its wings and swoops down onto his gloved hand to be rewarded with some hare meat kept in a bag attached to its owner's belt.

Bakht's sits through the calling looking round, seeming to enjoy the sunshine and the view. Eventually it lifts off, but flies to the vehicle where the remnants of lunch are being packed away.

To everyone's delight, Arman's makes its first flight. It is only airborne for 15 wobbly yards before crash landing. Aralbai gets to it first and offers it some hare. It pecks at it distractedly. Aralbai takes a sweet out of his bag, sucks it, then spits on the meat. The young eagle immediately tears at the flesh.

'Eagles have a sweet tooth,' Bulbul translates for us.

During the afternoon ride Aralbai asks if I would like to carry his

Aralbai with the young eagle after making its first flight.

eagle. We have to swap horses because eagles like a smooth ride, so he puts it on my arm while I am standing. It weighs more than I expected and I have to lean to counteract its weight. Once I'm mounted he hands the eagle up, telling me to keep a tight hold on the jesses. With my wrist resting in the Y stick, the weight of the bird disappears and it is easy to ride. I'm instructed to keep his head into the wind because they can then use their wings to keep balanced. The pony never even alters its stride when the eagle loses its balance and flaps wildly.

After an hour he asks if Sue wants a go, but she declines, preferring to take photographs.

Aralbai's pony is so much more comfortable than mine, and I am thoroughly enjoying the experience when I spot the minibus bumping across the plain towards us. There is a problem. Someone got the dates wrong. The Festival starts a day earlier than we were told – the day after tomorrow – so we need to ride on until we are well past our intended stopping place. With the gritty wind blowing in our faces, the last two hours are an endurance test.

That evening we eat in the back of the minibus, the only place it is possible to get out of the wind, unless you are an eagle, in which case there are crevices for them to perch.

The hunters in their huge coats and fox-skin hats hobble the horses and feed their birds before eating. Later a stranger arrives and the four of them play cards, crushed together in their little tent. Sue and I snuggle down in our tent as best we can. The grit, blown through holes in the fabric on a strengthening wind, covers us in a fine film. There are no stars tonight.

We are woken at dawn by the stranger shouting. He didn't bother to hobble his horse and, unlike ours, which are being led in by the hunters, his has disappeared; probably gone home.

Bulbul says when the man gets home his wife will be angry because he stayed out all night and lost money at cards. Clearly female emancipation has reached even the remotest parts of the world. Hardly the mythical hardy, competent nomad.

We breakfast in the minibus. It is bitterly cold and Sue just manages not to have a sense of humour failure. Used to being well-groomed, her hair is thick with grit and her riding clothes filthy. Her

Parade of eagle hunters at the Festival with their eagles.

178

comment, 'wet-wipes are a girl's best friend,' shows she hasn't lost her sense of humour.

Before we mount up Aralbai 'washes his eagle out'. He mixes sugar and water in a cup, puts a tube like a straw down the bird's gullet, takes a mouthful of water and gently blows it into the bird. He repeats the process two or three times, before doing the same with Bakht's. We are told it cleans the stomach, making the eagle hungry and keen to hunt.

We pass into an area of small flat valleys between steep, bare scree hills. We ride up a series of steep slopes, sometimes going up bare rock steps. Our ponies follow Aralbai, whose unhooded eagle turns its head constantly searching for prey. We ride along a ridge about a foot wide, while a couple of hundred feet below us, Arman on one side, and Bakht and Bulbul on the other, beat the grass for game.

I've just got the video out of its bag when there is a shout from below. Aralbai raises his arm and his eagle launches itself, wings outstretched. It quickly picks up speed as it skims down the mountainside. I can't see anything but the eagle changes direction. Aralbai turns his pony and rides down the scree, his horse sitting on its haunches at times as it half slides, half canters down the steep slope.

Sue follows, sitting well back. With the camera in one hand and the reins in the other I kick my feet free of my stirrups, so that I can sit deep, and not unbalance my sure-footed pony. As we do a long slide I can't help thinking there are no air-ambulances in the Altai.

Sue and I join Bulbul, who tells us it was a marmot which managed to escape into its hole. We start again, but this time we are beating and Bakht goes up. We spread out, but there is no more game. At the end of the hill Bakht dismounts and turns his horse down the steep side. Without any hesitation it comes straight down slipping and sliding, while his rider jettisons his eagle before descending. His eagle does short flights, catching up with him every time he pauses.

We try a couple more hills, then it is time to move on fast to get to Blue Wolf Tourism's headquarters in Ulgii for lunch. There we meet Canat, the boss, with whom I have exchanged several long emails organising the trip. He takes time to chat to us and says it is a long ride this afternoon, so we can go by minibus if we prefer.

Sue and I choose to ride. I am given Arman's pony. It's a great relief to ride on a larger saddle with longer leathers. However, it dislikes the sound of its shoes on the tarmac, and either tries to jump the side roads or gallops across onto the grass verge. Once in the country it settles down and we make good time. There are us two and Aralbai. Bulbul is going in the minibus to prepare our *ger* (Mongolian yurt).

At one point a vehicle comes up behind us and uses its horn because we don't get off the track quick enough. Sue's horse bolts. Luckily she sits tight and it slows up quickly after half a mile when we come to a rise. Aralbai congratulates her for sticking on. I hate to think what would have happened if she hadn't. The going is a mixture of stones and small rocks.

At one point we are stopped by an American photographer who insists on photographing Aralbai with his eagle. He resents her bossiness and laughs when she goes. He managed to keep the telephone wires behind him at all times so they will be in every one of her pictures. He then poses for Sue, without the wires. Halfway there the minibus appears; we are given a quick cup of tea and offered thick coats and fox-skin hats. Sue says she is fine, but I take advantage as it is getting colder.

The floodlit camp looks really welcoming as we ride down the long slope onto the plain in the dark. It is an old Russian army camp with gers pitched in the sports area. The ponies are taken from us and we find we are sharing with Anna, an English vet who qualified the same year as our daughter Caroline, and Anneka, a Dutch girl of about 30. Over supper in the large communal ger, Bulbul says we have covered 80 miles in the last two days. Our backsides agree! We need a shower, but there is only a thin trickle of hot water and no cold.

'I don't know if I can sleep with my hair full of sand,' Sue says, but she is asleep before the light goes out.

The Eagle Hunters' Festival

The sun has taken away the last of the frost by the time we set off for the Festival. It is only an hour's ride, but we are delayed because Bakht's eagle becomes ill after being given a sugar and water drench to clean it out before flying. All the competitors are milling about when we reach the cluster of gers, where the Festival is held on the edge of the plain.

They are waiting for the mayor of Ulgii, the provincial capital, who will officially start the games.

Half an hour later a fast-moving cloud of dust warns the Festival officials of the mayor's approach, and they call for the competitors to form up for the opening parade. The hunters, on horseback with their eagles on their arms, fall in behind the Mongolian flag, followed by the owners and riders of the racing ponies and dromedaries. As the mayor steps out of his car a tinny loudspeaker plays, 'The Beautiful Altai'. I try to photograph the parade from horseback; it gets me above the heads of the crowd, but my horse fidgets all the time, making focussing difficult.

After the parade there is an inspection of all the hunters. Besides checking the condition of the eagles, they look at the saddlery and turnout of the horse and rider. They even check the sharpness of the skinning knives and whether the meat carried in a decorated pouch is sufficient and not rotten. While the last hunters are being looked over, the first ones are starting the 'Calling the Eagle' competition.

The hunter leaves his eagle on a rock high on the hillside above the plain, then canters down to the bottom and rides along calling it. Most wave a piece of meat as encouragement, as they give a high-pitched cry to attract their bird's attention. None of the first competitors manage to get their eagles to leave their perches. When one finally does, a cry of excitement goes up from the crowd, but the eagle rises on a thermal and glides high above the spectators before landing in the horse and dromedary park. The spectators laugh as the owner gallops round behind the gers and the stalls of saddlery and carpets to retrieve his bird.

The last hunters to go are the most experienced and they put on a great display. Their eagles are highly trained and all of them fly to their owners. Those who choose to dismount are ruled out and the winner is a hunter whose bird leaves the rock at his first call, swoops down the hillside at a height of four feet, and then rises to feather back so that it lands lightly on the outstretched arm. It is a magnificent display, and the crowd cheer wildly.

'Catching the Lure' follows. The rider has to ride along the far side of a line of stones about a quarter of a mile from the bottom of the hill, dragging a lure, which is either a fox pelt or a dead hare. After the first competitors fail to get their eagles to move, we retire for lunch in the VIP ger. We are served fried meat with rice and cabbage. Sue says the meat is the best she has had in Mongolia, then is horrified to learn it is horse.

The tail end of the competition is more ragged with several eagles flying to the lure but failing to secure an instant hold. The judges watch from their table nodding and pointing as they discuss each successful flight. It is late afternoon before the winner is announced.

Before, 'Catching a Live Fox', there is a dromedary race. The racing camels are soon spread out with one opening up a clear lead. At the end of the first circuit it gives a bellow and sits down, despite the liberal use of its rider's whip. It is only once most of the other competitors have passed, and the prodding of several spectators, that it gets to its feet. Once going again, it overtakes all but the winner, making it an exciting race. The speed of that one camel is quite amazing.

The top dozen hunters, including Aralbai line up on their horses, their eagles unhooded on their arms. This is the race to catch a live fox. The poor animal has been dragged round on a rope lead all day. As it is being taken to where it will be released, an eagle breaks free and dives onto the fox while it is still on the lead. The officials rush to prise the eagle off, and berate the owner who has galloped forward to collect his charge. Once freed from the eagle's talons, the petrified fox is taken further away and then let go. It breaks into a hobbling run before another eagle swoops onto it, bringing an unsporting end to the first day of the festival.

When we arrive the following morning, the judges are sorting the running order for the 'Pick up a Coin' competition for riders. Instead of a coin they have to pick up four well-spaced plastic flowers to be scooped up from the ground at full gallop. All the young men compete, some slow to a standstill before leaning down to pick up the flower and one of the early competitors falls off at a trot.

The happy crowd delights in the misfortunes of the lesser players, but cheers wildly when two or three flowers are picked up at a canter. One skilful rider gallops flat out, picks up the first flower with his left hand, the second with his right, but as he leans over to the left again his horse veers away slightly. He reaches out too far and unbalances his horse, which falls on its side scattering the closest spectators.

The American female photographer who took pictures of Aralbai is here. Unlike the rest of us, who stay on the side lines, she insists on taking pictures on the course, despite the polite requests from officials for her to get out of the way. A couple of riders swerve to avoid her, but then one doesn't and she is knocked flying. She goes one way and her camera the other. The crowd cheers, but whether it is because the rider picked up the last flower, isn't clear. The play continues as she is helped into a jeep and driven away.

The winner makes it look easy, dropping down alternate sides to scoop up the flowers, with his horse barely altering its stride. Despite the exuberant atmosphere, I was slightly disappointed by the standard of horsemanship; many of the competitors in the Pony Club Games would have shown greater skill.

There is a carnival air, with everyone laughing and joking, while jostling to get the best view of 'Kiss the Girl on the Horse'. A man and woman race over a distance of about 400 yards; they start level and if the man gets ahead and stays there to the finish line he gets a kiss. But, if he fails to get far enough in front of the girl, she can whip him with her riding crop. The spectators cheer every time a girl lands a blow; the loudest cheer is for a girl who misses with her last strike, overbalances and falls off. The brightly coloured dresses of the women riders add a touch of glamour to the arid surroundings.

Kiss the girl on the horse. A game remembering the time when brides were often kidnapped to stop small households from inbreeding.

Tug of war: the most seriously-contested of the games, requiring strength and cunning.

It is the only time I have seen women taking an active part in any of the games I have watched. This particular game has its genesis in a time when men often used to kidnap their brides, because the people in the small communities were all too closely related to one another. Kazakhs were only allowed to marry someone who was at least five times removed, so even marriage between distant cousins was not allowed.

'The Tug of War' is the most seriously contested of the games. It is a test of strength and cunning between two individuals. The judges pair off the contestants. The first of a pair is called out to pick up a buz, the carcass of a dead goat, from the ground. As soon as he has lifted it, his opponent can get hold of whatever part of the goat he can. Generally it is the back legs, because the first person will have grabbed the horns.

Mongolian 'Tug of War' has to be the forerunner of Buzkashi. The Afghans told me the game started to be played on the northern plains after the Mongol invasion in the thirteenth century. It is easy to see how Buzkashi evolved, with friends helping each other, it went from the Mongolian game to the Afghan one. In both games, at the end of each bout the buz is returned to the pick-up point, once the player has wrested it from his opponent. In Buzkashi the scorer has to drop the buz in the scoring circle.

The more skilled players keep their horse turning to fend off their opponent until they have secured a decent grip on the buz. Only then will he allow his opponent to grab the back legs.

Occasionally a horse won't go near the buz, because it is frightened by the smell of blood and death. It shows the contestant has not practised with a dead goat, or at least a skin. In these cases the other player gets a walk-over. Some contests are over in seconds, while others last several minutes with the horses weaving in and out of the spectators.

A couple of players break through the encircling crowd, some of whom are mounted and race away across the plain, each leaning out almost parallel to the ground, trying to pull the buz away from each other. For a couple of minutes the pair disappear behind some vehicles, then the winner canters back alone, the buz bouncing against his horse's shoulder.

The bouts get longer and more skilled as the afternoon progresses. Some of the young men cling on to the buz until they are dragged from their horses. Arman is one of these.

The horses join in, either with their legs braced against the opponent's pull, or leaning over to one side to give their rider more leverage. The best horses remain unflinching as their rider twists and turns in the saddle.

At one point a nasty scene develops when a mounted spectator, trying to help a player into a stronger position by turning his horse, hits the hand of a past champion by mistake, making him let go. The officials have to keep the two men apart while the triumphant young winner deposits the buz in the centre of the ring for the next pair.

Before the semi-finals we all go to the far side of the plain to see the finish of the thirty kilometre bareback horse race. While we wait for the horses to arrive the last pairs battle it out with the buz, but with the disappearance of half the spectators the atmosphere is lost.

A shout from someone on top of a nearby hill announces the leaders have come into view. Officials force the crowds back as they threaten to swamp the final hundred yards to the winning post in their efforts to see.

The winner is a boy of about twelve, driving his pony on with the spare end of his reins, his legs flapping against the bare flanks. After

Picking up the buz.

the first three have finished, relatives of some of the remaining riders gallop alongside, beating their worn out mounts into one last effort. The exhausted riders, between nine and thirteen years old, go to sit in the vehicles while their older siblings lead the horses round to cool off. The young jockeys start at eight or nine years old, as soon as they are strong enough, but by the age of thirteen most are considered to be too heavy.

Dusk is falling as we motor back to our camp, where a Festival meal has been prepared in the big dining ger. We are entertained with the unique music of a troupe of Mongolian throat singers, who produce a vocal range from a deep growl to the whine of a violin. They are amazingly tuneful. They sing until the cooks come round with steaming plates of mutton and rice. Halfway through the meal, Canat, the head of our Blue Wolf travel company and organiser of the Festival, comes over to our table with a Russian General, who delivers a long flowery speech. Canat tells us that the General congratulates Sue and me on thirty years of marriage and he would like to give us a bottle of vodka, and also a bottle of 'Brown Bear' aphrodisiac, 'to help with the next thirty'. The toasting goes on well into the night before anyone decides to retire.

And the aphrodisiac? Before we go to bed Sue and I try some 'Brown Bear'. It is disgusting and within minutes we are throwing up outside the ger.

***

The following evening we photograph what we are assured are Bronze Age petroglyphs in the mountains. The clarity of the drawings makes it easy to distinguish not only animals, but hunting scenes. One shows dogs baying at a deer and a horseman with a bow and arrow close by. There are Bactrian camels, people hunting on foot, deer, a snow leopard and several horsemen, all armed, but they appear to be hunting rather than fighting. From the size of the men in relation to the horses, they appear to be Mongolian ponies and from the drawings it is possible to discern reins.

The light is fading as we reach a river we have to cross to get to the farm where we are supposed to stay the night. The driver enters the water too fast, brakes and stalls. He curses before rolling up his trousers, taking off his socks and shoes, and stepping into the icy water which is nearly up to his knees. Kinjay hands him the crank handle because there is no push-button starter. By the third swing I am getting worried, but then the engine catches and he jumps back in and guns the accelerator. We drive up to the farm, but it is deserted.

There is a light about half a mile away, so we wind our way there along a narrow track. It is a ger belonging to a young couple who kindly say we can stay with them for the night. We have to wait to use their

Refusing to let go of the buz despite being pulled off.

cooker because the wife is boiling yak's milk. She keeps scooping the boiling liquid up and pouring it from shoulder height. Kinjay says the process thickens it, and in the morning the bowl will be full of cream. It works! Next morning we have thick layers of cream with our bread and jam. We watch the wife milk the yaks. First she gets the calf to suckle, then her husband drags it away while she milks. Once she has finished milking the house yaks, the rest of the herd are freed from their overnight enclosure. They walk down the hill and cross the ford, breaking the ice as they go. The husband has breakfast, before riding after the cattle to herd them for the day. As we leave, the wife is collecting dung from where the cattle were overnight, patting it into cakes and laying them out in the sun.

In the late afternoon we arrive at another farm where we will stay for the next couple of days. The house is a single-storey rectangular mud-brick with a flat roof on which is piled the wooden framework of two gers. It is in the middle of a saucer-shaped valley surrounded by barren hills. Either side of the house are low farm buildings, the elder son's house and animal pens.

We recognise our host, Intan, from the Eagle Festival. He has a white beard and a pair of bottle-bottom glasses, and was the only hunter to wear a sheepskin coat and trousers, rather than the thick black woollen coats worn by the rest of the competitors. We thought he must have been roasted in it.

We pass his eagle, hooded and tied to a large block of wood, before entering the back room, where we leave our boots. We are offered some water in a flower-patterned enamel bowl to wash our hands. The open-plan interior is divided into two by a large pillar and the cooker – the same as Kinjay's, only larger. There is a television on a stand in the kitchen area and two bare electric light bulbs hang from the ceiling, one in the living room, and the other in the kitchen. The electricity comes from batteries, which are charged by the omnipresent Chinese-made solar panel. Bright carpets and a stuffed owl, with wings outspread, hang on the walls.

I enquire about the loo. It is pointed out to me. It is a hundred yards from the house and consists of a pit with two nine-inch-wide boards to balance on and three pieces of two foot six high corrugated iron to provide some privacy. The entrance side is open. The wind whistles underneath the walls, quickly chilling my exposed nether regions.

Our host from the farm where we stayed in his sheepskin hunting outfit.

In the gathering dusk we watch as the sheep and goats are penned, young cattle tethered to a long rope near the house, and the daughter does the last milking of the mares for the day. Her brother unties a foal and it is allowed to suck its mother for a short time before it is pulled away and held at the mare's head. The sister then milks the mare, having used the foal to get her to let down the milk.

They go from mare to mare. Once she has finished, the mares and foals are turned loose together for the night. During the day the foals are tied up to stop them sucking, and allow the mares to replenish their milk.

After supper Intan tells us about his eagle. Rather than taking her from a nest he trapped her. He thinks she was about two years old, and for six months she was hooded and fed only by him. When she got to trust him he removed the hood. First he got her used to being carried on his arm, then when he was mounted. He started on an old pony, which wouldn't take fright when she flapped her wings trying to keep her balance. He says only special ponies are used for hunting. They have to have a smooth gait and a calm nature. It can take as long to train a horse as it does an eagle. Some never accept their rider carrying a bird.

His eagle is nine years old and didn't really become good until it was six years old. He says that in the summer the eagles are not hooded because they are too full and lazy to fly. It is only in the winter when they are fed less and are fit for hunting that they need the hood lest they escape. When it is twelve or thirteen he will set it free. He will take it to a place where it has often hunted, and leave it with a couple of dead rabbits, or sometimes part of a dead sheep. Setting the eagles free means they have a chance to breed and so the stock of golden eagles is preserved.

After a final drink of tea (with butter and salt mixed in) we lay out our sleeping bags on the living room floor. Intan's daughter and son sleep on the two beds against the far wall, while he and his wife go to their curtained off bedroom next to the kitchen. We are woken before first light by Intan's wife cooking her breakfast. It is Ramadan, but she is the only member of the family to observe it.

There is a change of plan. Intan has to go to a funeral, so instead of going hunting with him, we go for a ride round the valley floor. Everywhere there are fat-tailed sheep, goats, cattle and yaks, as well as horses, all tugging at the long coarse brown grass. Streams meander through the valley floor forming natural boundaries for the livestock. Intal's son knows where all the fords are, and shows us the way we will go tomorrow. It looks as if it will take a good two hours to reach the hills before we start hunting.

We pass an ancient Russian lorry bringing the women of a family back from the summer grazing. The men, who are droving their animals, will arrive in a couple of days. Bulbul says men herd and tend the livestock, while the women milk the yaks, cattle, sheep, goats and horses, clean the house, make cheese, keep the fire going and make felt.

Dromedaries used to do the carrying, but have largely been replaced by lorries. The lorries are often jointly owned and can move several families in the time it used to take to move one. Sue points to a scarecrow, but Bulbul says it is to deter the wolves which come down from the hills in the winter.

Hunting is cancelled the next day as well. The wind is directly from Siberia and too strong for the eagle to fly safely. It brings a cold which penetrates our clothing, even the thick coats which go over all

Players go into the spectators.

our own modern cold weather clothes. We go in the minibus with Intal, who is in his sheepskin suit and fox-fur hat, to the hills on the edge of the plain.

Both of us are relieved not to have ridden there. In a sheltered valley we watch Intal work his eagle, getting it to fly to him and following a lure. When he nearly gets knocked over by the eagle, which is caught by a large gust as it lands on his outstretched arm, he says it is time to return to the farm.

In the afternoon, like farmers everywhere, we discuss farming. We sit on the floor round a low table. Intan says he has 150 sheep and goats, 50 yaks and cows and 20 horses. Some of the horses are for riding and the rest are for meat, but when a man dies his best riding horse is killed and fed to all the guests as a mark of respect.

At the beginning of November he kills ten sheep, a cow and a horse to keep them in meat through the winter. Because it is so cold the naturally frozen carcasses are kept in a larder at the end of the entrance lobby.

The farmers go up to the mountain pastures at the end of May before the rains and mosquitoes start, and the plain turns into a marsh.

Charms and owl feathers plaited into a racehorse's tail.

They return in late September to get settled in before the cold weather. The young men come back to cut the hay at the end of August when the rains stop. It is cut with a scythe and takes three days to make. It is moved to the farm on sledges pulled by horses.

I ask about the horses. There is a pause while our tea is replenished and a plate of curds and cheeses are offered. The cream cheese is strongly salted, some of the curds are good, but one is so hard that it is impossible to bite into it.

Intan tells me he has two herds: riding horses and eating horses. The riding horses and mares and foals will stay at the homestead for the winter, but the eating horses will be turned into the hills to fend for themselves. Hay is too precious to use on them. After the snow has gone they will be rounded up and sorted. Only the old or injured succumb to the wolves.

When they are two years old, the young riding horses are led round with a child on their back. They are four or five before an adult rides them. The males not wanted for breeding are gelded at four or five. All the mares are used for breeding and milk. There are races every year where the fastest are selected and they are put to a racing stallion.

Intan gets up and goes out through the kitchen. He returns and hands me a horseshoe. He says they shoe four times a year, changing the shoes with each season. They have a different number of holes for different times of the year, with more nails for the winter to stop them slipping on the ice. The heads of the nails are over half an inch long and the metal round the toe is ridged. He makes all his shoes himself.

He starts to tell me about how much grain they feed when his wife says he must get ready because they are going to break their fast with some relations on a nearby farm. He gives me a grin, he has been nibbling all afternoon. He shrugs on a thick coat and departs with his family.

Over supper we swap superstitions with Bulbul and Kinjay. They say owls ward off the evil eye that is why there is an owl in most houses, and why the eagles and horses have owl feathers attached to them. Bulbul says if a fox crosses the road in front of you it is bad luck. I say with us it is a black cat. Sue mentions a single magpie flying across your path. Bulbul says you must wear a scarf over your head at night because the devils will be attracted to your hair.

'We say, visitors are like fish, both are past their best after three days,' I tell them and they both laugh.

'It is bad luck in Mongolia to do your washing on Tuesday or Friday,' Bulbul says. 'Also for visitors to arrive on those days.'

We are already in our sleeping bags when Intan gets back. He says it will be a very cold night and piles more dung cakes on the fire. I have noticed they get through several buckets of fuel a day.

The early morning sun glows on the snow-covered hills. The snow has nearly reached the valley floor. The driver slams the minibus door having finished putting in the oil and water. The sharp metallic clang is lost in the still freezing air. All around, the breath of the animals comes out in white puffs. The son and daughter walk across to the mares, which are already waiting for feed before being milked. The daughter wears a mask to protect her red cheeks from chapping. After the ordeal of shaving in the open air, I go back inside for my wheat porridge.

***

In Ulgii we meet up with Alan, an American who rode back with Aralbai from the Festival. He was on Sue's horse and enjoyed the ride. When they arrived at Aralbai's house a sheep was killed in his honour. He watched it being cut up, and eagerly awaited the evening meal. Aralbai's wife brought in a large platter on which was the sheep's head – minus the lower jaw – with the entrails encircling it. He was presented with the knife to have the first cut. He sliced off some cheek, part of a lip and some entrails. He waited for the inevitable tea to wash it down, but none came. Some soup was brought but it was so salty he nearly spat it out. It was only when the meal was finished that the tea arrived.

'Let me tell you,' he says in his American drawl, 'don't ever eat lip. Ten minutes after you start chewing, you've made no impact at all.' He laughs.

'I think I would have burst into tears,' Sue says.

Tomorrow we fly to Ulan Bator. I'm relieved it has gone so well, and look forward to north-east India next spring, but I will have to come back again. There is still so much for me to learn.

CHAPTER EIGHT

Manipur: At Last

I had first enquired about going to Manipur to see Sagol Kanjei in 1972, then again in 1983, but both times I was told it wasn't possible because of civil unrest. This time, despite the travel agents in the U.K. and India telling me it is impossible to go there as a single traveller, I feel certain that if I can just meet the person who runs Purvi Travel in Dibrugarh, in Northern Assam, everything will fall into place.

Based on this belief, and having promised Sue I'll be back for lambing, I pack my backpack and fly to Calcutta.

***

'Do you know the telephone number for Purvi Travel?' I ask the receptionist at the hotel in Dibrugarh.

'They have gone out of business,' he says.

That accounts for them not answering any of my e-mails and telephone calls.

'But,' he glances round furtively, 'I will telephone Mr Singh. He is much better than the travel agent the hotel tells us to recommend.' (I suspect this means he pays more baksheesh.)

Mr Singh arrives within ten minutes. He speaks hardly any English, but is accompanied by a thin young man who does. I tell them I want to go to Manipur to see Sagol+ Kangjei and any other horse related games. He says he knows a horseman who might be able to help, but Manipur will require a special permit, which takes many weeks to obtain.

While we wait in his office for the horse person, Mr Singh offers me a selection of vehicles to explore the local area. I choose the cheapest, a small car with a driver who speaks almost no English. We are working out an itinerary when an Asiatic looking young man enters, and talks briefly to Mr. Singh.

'My name is Doljit. Why do you want to go to Manipur?' The newcomer's English is excellent, and his manner direct.

'To see Sagol Kangjei and Arambai Hunba.'

Doljit stares at me.

'Arambai?'

'Yes, Arambai.'

Doljit

A slow smile spreads across his face until it is one huge grin.

'How did you find out about Arambai?'

'I saw on the internet it was a Manipuri martial art on horseback. The Pitt-Rivers museum in the UK has a quiver of darts, but don't know much about them.'

'I will get you into Manipur to see Arambai Hunba and Sagol Kangjei,' Doljit says still grinning. 'You are the first person I know from outside Manipur who has heard of Arambai. It will take two weeks to get the necessary permits; what are your plans?'

I tell him I am going to Nagaland for a week, then a couple of days in the game park at Kaziranga before going to Manas wildlife park for three days. He says that will be long enough.

Conch shell blowers. They blow at the beginning and end of each half, and also when a goal is scored.

He is in a rush because at lunchtime he is taking a group to Arunachal Pradesh, so we dash to find a photographer to get some passport photographs. Back at the office I pay him £200 in advance for the permits and he says he will meet me at my hotel, the Nova in Guwahati (the capital of Assam) in two weeks. Then he is gone, leaving me wondering what I have done. The whole trip is going to cost about £700, more than I had planned, but everything is included. Will he really come to the Nova? Am I mad to have handed so much to a complete stranger? Will my efforts to get to Manipur for over 30 years finally succeed, or will it fail like all my other attempts?

***

I look at my watch again, nearly eight thirty and no sign of Doljit. With deep disappointment I have to accept he isn't coming. Let down again! Time to have something to eat and make new plans.

Doljit arrives at Reception as I come down the stairs. I can hardly believe it. We shake hands like long-lost friends while he apologises for being late. He tells me the permits have yet to be signed, but his friend in the permit office is certain his boss, whose signature is needed, will be in tomorrow. Rather than hang about waiting for the telephone call confirming the papers have been signed, he will, in the morning, take me to the Umananda Temple on an island in the Brahmaputra. Now, he shakes my hand again. He must get back to the final evening of the tour he has been guiding.

The ferry to the island docks at a floating jetty. This is now some 20 feet below the landing stage used during the monsoon. We walk slowly round the island before visiting the colourful temple. It is packed with foreign and local tourists, as well as worshippers. Doljit joins a queue, and shuffles forward to get a blessing from a priest.

Outside the temple we sit on a bench in the shade watching the monkeys, which are everywhere. They check anything dropped by the visitors in case it is edible. One shins down a tree, runs across the path and rips the bottom of an unsuspecting tourist's plastic bag in search of food. We laugh. Anything to take our minds off the signing of the permits is a welcome distraction.

About two o'clock we go to a smart hotel which has a fax machine. Doljit checks, but there is no message for him. Over lunch he tells me

An Arambai player in traditional dress.

we will have to fly to Imphal, because it is unsafe to travel by road. There are 26 different guerrilla bands who dominate large parts of the countryside. Although they are all dedicated to Manipuri independence, their agendas vary widely, with some being little more than bandits. Also there is a medical conference in Imphal starting in two days' time so, as soon as we receive confirmation, we must purchase tickets for tomorrow's flight. They are fully booked after that.

A waiter comes over to tell Doljit he has a telephone call. It is now three o'clock. I try to eat, but my stomach is churning. Apparently his friend's boss has only been in the office once in the last week. Time goes slowly, the food grows cold and it is a quarter-past. Doljit comes back all smiles. They are sending copies of the permits by fax. We must go as soon as they come through. He will wait by the machine while I pay for lunch.

For the actual trip Doljit wants to be paid partly in US dollars and partly in rupees. The first ATM is out of action, the second doesn't seem to work either. Doljit comes into the cubicle with me and shows me how to work it, but my cards are blocked. We have to find a money-changer for my British pounds before we can book flights. We are still sorting the money at half past four.

However we make it, and on the flight Doljit admits he wasn't at all sure we would actually get the permits through on time. His friend said his boss called in briefly to sign a stack of urgent papers. Ours were tucked in the middle, in the hope he wouldn't notice them. Luckily he didn't, and he signed them along with the others.

At Imphal airport we are met by Philip, an ex-polo player friend of Doljit's, in his forties, and Basanta, a top polo player and show jumper. We will travel in Philip's car while we are here.

There are Indian soldiers everywhere in the city, either in vehicles with mounted machine guns, or patrolling the streets on foot. They wear flak jackets and tin hats and carry rifles. Many have black scarves over their mouths and noses. It feels like an occupied city. We drive to a backstreet room where I am to stay. All the hotels are full for the conference.

Before going to the market to buy some essentials, Doljit tells me to lock the door behind him, and only open it to him, no one else. He will knock four times. I hang my mosquito net, lay out my sleeping bag and spread out my belongings. I open the door on hearing Doljit's four knocks. He and Basanta enter, quickly locking the door after them.

'We are leaving, Mister Bob,' Doljit says as he swiftly jams all my things back in my pack.

'Is there a problem?'

'No,' he says, cutting the string holding up the mosquito net rather than untying it. 'You will be staying at Philip's sister's house.'

He and Basanta pack up my luggage, check round and start down the stairs. I follow. Outside, Philip has the engine running. They throw my packs onto the back seat and squash in on top of them. Before I have the car door shut Philip guns the engine and we hare up the narrow side street before slowing as we join the main road. Nobody offers an explanation.

Philip's sister's house is a modern two-storey building set in a large garden on the outskirts of Imphal. Their eldest son is away, so I am given his room. There is a television, music system, computer with printer and scanner, and trainers piled in a corner – only the posters proclaim a different culture from home.

Doljit urges me to hurry, we are late for a horse show. He says I can unpack and meet Philip's sister later.

Manipuri Kangjei

It is difficult to find anywhere to park outside the Imphal Polo ground, because of all the army vehicles. We are questioned briefly and then allowed in, but I notice army snipers on several of the surrounding flat roofs. There are only a few spectators in the tiered seats of the grandstand, except in the VIP area, where there are a lot of army officers and men in suits. It is a long concrete building taking up over half the length of one side of the pitch. There is another much smaller open stand opposite, and walls or high wire netting surround the rest of the ground.

In the grandstand we are too far from the show jumping, which is in the middle of the pitch, to take good photographs, so we go over to the ring. Although the riders vary in age and size, the horses are all about 13 hands high. The riders are smartly dressed in black jackets, long riding boots and breeches. Basanta joins us, leading his mount. He leans on his lance as his pony nibbles the short brown grass, while waiting for the start of the tent-pegging, which follows the jumping. He points to the marked lanes in which the ponies will run and the row of wooden pegs at the end.

Doljit says tent-pegging originated from soldiers practising to take the war-elephants toenails out during a battle. If they succeeded, the injured animals would turn, causing havoc as they ran back through their own lines. A discussion follows because I say it has always been exactly what it says – getting skilled at pulling tent-pegs out of the ground. The objective, I argue, was to gallop into an encampment, pull up the tent-pegs so that the tents collapsed thereby disabling those underneath. This gave the attackers time to take what they wanted, or spear the trapped enemy inside the tent with minimum risk. Doljit sticks to his theory, but Basanta agrees with me, saying you would never be able to get close enough to an elephant because it would swipe away the lance with its trunk. In the end Doljit appears to agree and we walk over to get some close-ups of the tent-pegging.

'Why the hurried change of my accommodation?' I ask Doljit.

He looks round to see no one is close before answering.

'While we were in the market Basanta heard someone saying that there was an Englishman staying in a flat in a side street, and how long before he was taken hostage?' He looks down and scuffs his feet.

A Konyak farmer from Nagaland. The brass heads on the necklace show how many men he has killed and whose heads he has presented to his chief.

'There are a lot of different guerrilla armies in Manipur all trying to get the upper hand as well as fight the Indian government. A foreign hostage would be a powerful weapon.'

'Thanks for moving me,' I say, not unduly surprised. I always pictured guerrilla armies as hiding out in the jungle, not being in towns. Stupid of me; the IRA lived in the towns as well as in the countryside. I am relieved they are going out of their way to keep me safe.

'Here come the first team.'

Doljit points to the start of the marked lanes where four horsemen are urging their mounts into a gallop. All lower the tips of their lances as they approach the tent-pegs. Some crouch lower over their ponies' necks, while one leans out to the side. They shout as they flash by. Spear arms follow through, in an arc. One man's peg flies off his lance point while two others hold their lances erect having firmly impaled their targets. The other player, who was leaning out, misses completely.

I turn to watch the next four gallop towards us. Basanta is on the right. It is easier to follow the horsemen with my video camera, than shoot single pictures with my ancient Pentax. Unfortunately I have only 90 shots left on Sue's small digital camera; my spare memory cards, along with some ordinary film, disappeared after handing my valuables to the hotel receptionist in Calcutta for safe keeping.

The team are galloping flat out, their ponies' hooves drum on the hard ground. Beside me Doljit is whirring away with his new big digital. He was given it by a photographer for whom he was a guide.

Bokhtar, my guide in Nagaland, remarked on how quickly I take photographs. I said I had to, horse games tend to be speedy and most incidents are never repeated. He told me that one photographer he was guiding took so long to set up a picture of a lady crossing a rope bridge, that the sun had gone by the time he was ready. It took three more days for the sun to be in the right position with no clouds.

Basanta lowers his point and spears the tent-peg. Two of the others miss and the other rider's lance grazes the peg, knocking it over.

'I think I got some good photographs,' says Doljit turning his camera to look at the viewing screen.

I look over his shoulder. I can just make out the shape of the horses and riders in the blurred images.

'I am still not used to the camera,' he says. 'I was only given a short explanation and no instruction booklet.'

'What are all these dials and buttons for?' I point to the top of the camera. There are more down the side.

'Telephoto, wide angle, playback,' he points them out, 'but many

Sagol Kanjei players in traditional dress.

of the others I'm not sure. I am experimenting every time.' Doljit looks at his watch as another tent-pegging team thunders past. 'It is time for us to go to the Palace Polo Ground to see them practising Sagol Kangjei. It is not like polo in the rest of India.'

How true! The polo ground looks like an overused park. The patchy uneven grass is strewn with litter. There is a football game going on at one end, just past the polo goal line, and some other boys are having a kick about on the polo pitch itself, while the horses are warmed up. A young man canters down the pitch practising his swing, while his pony's foal canters behind. All the riders wear jeans or slacks and T-shirts, and their footwear varies from flip-flops to army boots. One rider is riding barefoot with a toe stirrup.

The horse tack is equally varied. Everyone has rope reins, but some head-pieces are made of leather (a couple held together with string), and others of rope. A few ponies have woollen pom-poms to protect sensitive parts of the face. Most of the saddles are from the army, but several are the old Manipuri style with a high rounded pommel, raised cantle and large hide side panels which cover the whole of the pony's flanks. The stirrup-leathers are generally string, and one girth is a piece of rope inside a length of plastic pipe.

Throwing a single arambai using a throwing stick.

'The ponies are expensive to keep,' Doljit says. 'Often there are two or three owners. They all want to play, so they take it in turn with each owner playing half a game. Instead of chukkas there are two halves of twenty minutes with a ten minute break in the middle.'

He explains the game as more ponies arrive. There are no goal posts. A goal is scored whenever the ball is hit over the lines marking each end of the pitch. As soon as a goal is scored another ball is thrown in at the centre line, so play is continuous. In the past, the length of a game was determined by the number of goals set, with half time being when the first team reached half that number. Because of the ease of scoring it was not uncommon to have a game with 50 or 60 goals.

'The game will start soon.' Doljit points to a bunch of horsemen trotting towards us. 'They are from the tent-pegging.'

'But most of the ponies were show jumping as well as tent-pegging...'

'And now most of them will take part in two full practice games. Not long ago they rode to Loktak Lake, 35 kilometres away, played a demonstration match and then rode back again, all in one day. The Manipuri ponies are tough.'

'With all they do, they must get a lot of injuries?'

'That is a problem, but it isn't just from being ridden a lot. For instance,' he points to the foal now feeding from its mother as her rider, still astride, waits for the warm-up to end. 'Tonight after the practice matches, she and a lot of others will be ridden back through the town to their grazing grounds five kilometres away. They will have to ride through the traffic while it is getting dark. There are often accidents, especially if a foal is separated from its mother and goes out into the middle of the road.'

'Is there nowhere nearer?'

'Everywhere has been built on. Sometimes ponies are left here for the night, but there is nothing for them to eat, and because it isn't fully enclosed they wander into town. They eat from the piles of rubbish, and every year some die from colic after swallowing plastic bags.'

Somebody gives a shout. The two teams form up. A ball is thrown amongst the 14 players (two teams of seven) gathered at the halfway line.

I'm surprised to see a player trying to catch the ball. Doljit says it can be caught and carried, but must be dropped and hit over the line to score a goal.

Several players swipe at the ball as it hits the ground. One connects, and everyone gallops up the pitch after it. Some of those at the back of the bunch rein in their ponies and return to the centre line, ready to receive the next ball. At the end of the pitch there is a flurry of sticks and a cheer as the first goal is scored. At the centre line another ball is thrown in, and the play recommences. The goal-scorers and defenders gallop back to join in the fray.

A horseman not taking part rides into the football game to retrieve the first ball. When the next goal is scored, the riders battle right up to the goal line and scatter the footballers while turning their mounts. The footballers retreat to watch from the side line. There is no let-up in the play. Both sides are evenly matched and the goal tally steadily increases.

At half time the players jump off and lead their ponies round. Two young children, with huge grins, are held in the saddle by their elder brothers. At the far end the football game resumes.

There are some substitutions when the game starts again – a change of riders rather than ponies. Sometimes the dust obscures the play. One time they emerge from it in a roughly fought chase after the ball, and a player cuts sharply across an opponent bringing him and his pony down. The game keeps going as the fallen player limps off, leading his pony. A substitute gallops from the side line to join the game. We go to look at the pony. It is uninjured, if a bit dusty. Doljit has a word with the rider, who says it is owned by three people and will take part in the next game. No wonder so many ponies are worn out by the time they reach their teens.

There are no falls in the second game, which finishes as it is getting dark. The bridles and saddles are removed, head-collars put on, and the ponies begin the journey back to their grazing. Most of the ponies are ridden bareback, and each rider leads three or four ponies. I hope they all reach their destination without incident.

Back at Philip's sister's house I chat to the second son, who explains how difficult it is to get a job. In Manipur the best jobs are in the government, but a big bribe is needed before the officials will consider an applicant, and even then there is a fair chance of not getting employment.

It is disappointing to hear how difficult it is for the young from the North East because of their Asiatic looks. Many Indians regard Manipuris as foreigners and discriminate against them. Also if one of the separatist guerrilla groups injures someone from another state, the local people will take it out on the Manipuris. Most jobs are thousands of miles away in Delhi, Bangalore, Mumbai and other big cities. Living there is expensive, so there is no spare money to send home to support elderly relatives, as has always been the case up until the last few years. Although he has a 'First' in mathematics, he hasn't had a job offer and is not sure what he will do.

***

Next morning we visit the secretary of the Polo Club who is an authority on Arambai Hunba (and also, intriguingly, the professor of Anthropology, who in the next few days will be examining Doljit's sister for her MA). Arambai Hunba, he tells me, is throwing a dart (an arambai) while on horseback. The dart has a four inch metal point that was once dipped in poison, so that even a scratch would kill. It is flighted with peacock tail feathers. The darts are mainly thrown in bunches. If a single one is used, a throwing stick was inserted to support the feathers so that they didn't break under the weight of the metal point. The

Tent-pegging. The peg has to be cleanly speared and pulled out of the ground.

throwing stick, which is about two foot six inches long, also increases the length and accuracy of the throw. In the past a good thrower, at full gallop, could hit a man 100 yards away. Often horsemen would ambush an enemy, galloping out of the jungle on their little ponies, throw two or three bunches and retire back into the trees before the enemy could react.

The professor says that the throwers came from selected families who trained solely in this martial art, and were answerable only to the king, not the generals. Their job was to harry the enemy on the march, in camp or when forming up into battle line. He says that during the Burmese occupation in the 1800s, it is said the Burmese soldiers marched looking up at the sky watching for "arambai rain". Today there is a group of horsemen who prastice the old art, giving demonstrations with the Manipuri secret weapon that once helped them to overrun a large part of northern Burma. I am thrilled to hear that he has arranged for the arambai throwers to give me a demonstration this afternoon.

On the way to the stables where the ponies are being got ready, Doljit says I will need to give today's riders some money, and also those taking part in the Sagol Kangjei match, which is being specially organised for me in a couple of days' time. After a bit of discussion we settle on £80 for both.

When we get there the ponies are saddled with four quivers of twelve to fifteen arambai attached to each saddle – one on each side at the front of the saddle and the same at the back. Those at the front have throwing sticks inserted into the feathers.

The riders have tightly wound black turbans held on with red scarves tied under their chins, which makes them look like the washerwoman from *Wind in the Willows*. Their uniform is a black tunic with red and gold fringed neck and short sleeves, black baggy trousers and long red shin-pads that reach well above the knee, and are tied on with string. They carry a hide whip to make the ponies go faster, because there is no way they can use their legs with the protective saddle side-panels covering their ponies' sides.

At the Palace Polo Ground, after brief demonstrations of throwing with a throwing stick and casting arambai in bunches, they ask me to have a go. One of the riders gets off, slips the thong of his whip onto my left wrist, and hands me the rope reins. He is at least six inches shorter than me, and one glance tells me the stirrup-leathers won't adjust. I perch on the saddle, almost jockey-like. I'm given an arambai with a stick inserted. I have to grip the very ends of the feathers against the stick with my thumb and forefinger, while my other three fingers wrap round the end of the stick.

'You have to stand up to throw,' Doljit says helpfully.

I wobble up as I straighten my legs. The large pommel curves back towards me, and digs into the front of my thighs. Without warning the pony ambles into a choppy little trot, not the long-stride I am used to

Learning to follow mum. The Palace Polo Ground is several miles from the grazing so the foals accompany their mothers. Every year several are killed or badly injured when going through heavy traffic.

on my thoroughbreds. I overbalance and hit myself on the side of the head with the arambai as I sit down heavily. I hear chuckles. Luckily the pony slows to a walk, and I manage to stand up again and throw. It goes under ten metres. Pathetic!

'Now Mister Bob you must throw a bunch at the gallop. You go with him', Doljit points to a rider who threw a bunch 40 to 50 metres in the demonstration. 'First time watch, next you do like him.'

We ride to the end of the pitch. He turns to me and nods. He hits his horse and we gallop forward. While I try to keep in the saddle he reaches behind him, pulls out a bunch and at the halfway line throws. As the darts fly high both ponies turn to run at 90 degrees to the target area, which is suddenly showered with arambai, the peacock feathers quivering. Nobody warned me about the turn and I only stay in the saddle by clinging to the mane.

The rider whose horse I am riding hands me half a dozen darts, but I shake my head.

'Please tell him I need a lot of practice before I can throw a bunch while galloping,' I instruct Doljit. 'Say I am frightened of not turning fast enough and the pony getting injured.'

When I dismount I can see how relieved the pony's owner is. Clearly I wasn't the only one to have no confidence in me.

Loktak Lake

On a day out to Loktak Lake in Philip's car we call in at the history department of Imphal University to see Basanta's uncle, who runs it. Hearing of my interest in military history, the uncle has arranged a special viewing of a film made up from footage, shot at the time, about the halting, and then defeat, of the Japanese invasion of India via Imphal, where their objective was the railway and the vast ordnance depot that supplied the British army throughout the area. It shows the appalling conditions both sides fought in, and how the Japanese helped bring about their own destruction. They had enough food and supplies for three weeks, after which, General Mutaguchi believed they would have captured Imphal and its supply depot.

However , the British, Indians and Gurkhas hung on and refused to budge in hand-to-hand fighting and so the Japanese didn't break through. Instead, they had to rely on pack animals using narrow tracks through mountainous jungle to carry all their supplies. While thousands of Japanese soldiers were killed in suicidal attacks, many more died of dysentery and malaria. Without food or ammunition the remainder were eventually forced to withdraw, but most of them died of exhaustion and malnutrition.

Soon after leaving the university with its modern buildings, paved roads and neatly mown lawns, we see a farmer fishing in a flooded paddy. He carries a bell-shaped wicker basket which he keeps dipping into the water. Doljit explains the bottom end of the basket is open, and each time he pauses, he is feeling for any slight vibration against the side of the basket. This means there is something there, so he reaches into the basket through a hole in the top and feels round until he catches whatever is there – sometimes a small fish, sometimes a shrimp. His pregnant wife stands at one end with a bag, while a large cat sits patiently at the other.

'That cat reminds me, you said you saw a tigress at Kasziranga Game Park,' Doljit says. 'Was it luck, or had someone seen her and passed on the message?'

'Bit of both. We pulled in at a viewing tower, and were told we had just missed a large tigress. We climbed up to get a view of the area and relax in the shade, when a warden whispered she had returned. She came past us, 50 yards away, difficult to spot in the long grass, and behind her were two three-quarter grown cubs.'

'You were very lucky,' Doljit says. 'I have only seen a tiger twice there and I have been many times. You are a lucky man I think, Mister Bob.'

'Yes, I was thrilled. Bokhta, my guide, said it was the first time he had seen one in Kaziranga, and that was his tenth visit.'

We stop in a village to watch a different type of fishing. Every village has several fishponds which filled every year during the monsoon. Here a lot of the villagers are gathered on the banks of a half-full pond. Triangular nets attached to wooden frames are lowered into the water by ropes. Several men walk round in the waist-deep muddy water driving fish towards the nets. At a signal all the nets are pulled out of the water by their ropes.

An anguished cry rings out, and a half-raised net falls back into the water. All heads turn. A woman's sarong has fallen off and the poor thing is naked from the waist down. There are peals of laughter as she re-wraps herself, then grabs the rope to pull her net out. There is nothing in it, and only a meagre catch of tiny fish in the rest. At another command the nets are lowered again, and the men resume their walking.

'They crush all the little fish and make them into a paste to go with rice, their main diet,' Doljit explains.

Further on we come to a causeway, with a metalled road, that takes us to an island in Loktak Lake. On one side of the causeway the water laps against the embankment, but on the other, thick weed has taken over. Doljit points to a decrepit fishing hut with a board pathway across the weed; a few years ago it was on the edge of the lake, now it is over 50 yards from it.

As we pull into a car park on the edge of the island two army jeeps flash past us, horns blaring. Both have mounted machine guns and four armed soldiers in the back. They each appear to be to be carrying half of a short extendable ladder. Doljit grins and Philip shrugs as we cross the road to a drinks stall, where half a dozen soldiers are taking their ease under an awning of split bamboo. The jeeps throw up a dust cloud as they leave the tarmac, entering the gates of a well-fenced army camp.

'We go that way,' Doljit says, pointing to a tree-shaded hill leading away from the camp. 'It is a favourite place for picnics. A lot of people come here from Imphal on holidays.'

On the way to the hill I see a brightly coloured lizard scuttling round the base of a tree. I get out my video camera and follow it. I follow it in and out of the roots as it circumnavigates the tree twice. On the start of the third circuit Doljit interrupts me.

'Mister Bob, you must stop filming. Now!' His usual calm has vanished. Standing next to him is a soldier with an SLR (self-loading rifle) pointed in my direction.

'Why?'

'Because this soldier says you are filming in a restricted area, and he will arrest you.'

'You're serious?'

'Yes Mister Bob, and so is he. He says you could be filming the camp.'

I sigh, not surprised.

Throwing a bunch of arambai at the gallop. The horses are taught to turn as soon as the darts leave the thrower's hand.

I look down, the lizard has gone. Not wanting to be accused of spying, I put my video camera away before walking up the hill. The view is well worth the climb. To our left the open waters of the lake stretch to some distant hills, but to the right the lake is divided into circles of open water bordered by weed. Each circle belongs to a fisherman. We watch a man with a large Chinese-style hat, paddle his flat-bottomed boat over to his circle, the gentle ripples of the wake wrinkling the smooth blue surface. We sit and watch as he checks round his fish-field before moving on to another one. The silhouetted hills and the fisherman remind me of the "willow pattern" plates my parents had. I ask about the tin shed with a verandah perched on a patch of weed between us and the camp. It was a restaurant, but is now closed because of its proximity to the camp.

On the way back we stop briefly at the Japanese War Memorial. It consists of a paved area and a shrine surrounded by metal railings. It marks the nearest point the Japanese got to Imphal.

Back in the city we visit the beautifully kept British and Indian Cemetery. There are long lines of small white gravestones with the name, rank, number, regiment and dates. Trees cast long shadows as the blood-red sun begins to drop beyond the horizon. It is now a place of tranquillity and peace. Some of the epitaphs requested by the dead men's families, such as, "He loved the dawn chorus", or "We think of you every day" bring tears to our eyes.

Sagol Kangjei

Before the start the players line up down the pitch. Kneeling between the two teams are the ball thrower and, either side of him, two young men with conch shells. The shells are blown to mark the beginning and end of the halves and announce the scoring of each goal. The teams stand, heads bowed, holding their horses.

'What are they doing?' I ask Doljit.

'They are praying to give the watchers a good game, also to bow to the dignitary,' he points to a man in a suit sitting on a camp chair a few feet back from the line marking the side of the pitch. 'If there is a problem the ball thrower cannot solve, the dignitary will make the final decision.'

The run of play is similar to the practice games, except now it is easy to distinguish the teams, one in yellow shirts and the other in white. All the players have white dhotis and turbans tied under their chins with a white cloth. The ball thrower and conch blowers are completely in white. Within a minute of blowing the start, the conches sound again for the first goal. In a sudden spate of goals just before half time their hooting is almost continuous.

'What do you think, Mister Bob?' Doljit asks as the horsemen come off the pitch.

'They need those small ponies with seven in a team. Big horses would never do the tight turns or be as agile; they would get into each other's way.'

'The ponies enjoy playing, I think.'

'They seem to, there is no need for the riders to use their whips. They follow the ball flat out on their own. They work well for their riders. Have you ever played here?'

'No. Basanta said I should try, but I'm not a good enough rider. I would get in the way or get knocked over.'

I've started to change the film in my old camera, but it's stuck. For some reason it won't wind back. I put the video camera on the ground and work at it. Suddenly the blockage gives and I crank the handle to rewind. As soon as the indicator says zero I open the back and the exposed film bursts out. I groan. It's ruined and I had some super shots on it.

'Hurry up, Mister Bob, they're starting again,' Doljit urges.

The conch shells announce the start as I bundle the film into my bag and load a new one. It is hard to follow the intricacies of the game as well as taking photographs and videoing at the same time. Doljit keeps up a running commentary, though I still miss some of the action. It is an exciting climax, with the yellows winning by three goals. As they ride off the pitch, I note the similarity of many of the ponies.

'Do they have organised breeding?' I ask Doljit.

'You will see tomorrow at the stud farm.'

***

It is a dull overcast day as we drive past the fenced paddocks of the stud. We are met by the manager who first shows me some 16 hand horses imported from India for show jumping. They are hoping to cross them with the Manipuri ponies to breed a larger polo pony which retains their hardiness, temperament and intelligence. I ask about the ever-decreasing numbers of Manipuri ponies. The government is supposed to support the stud, but little money filters through.

We walk to two paddocks where all the mares, stallions, foals, yearlings and some two-year-olds have congregated, waiting to be let out over a narrow bridge onto the common. There is no grass in the paddocks, just weeds. A fortnight-old bay foal bursts into a gallop. He goes twice round his paddock flat out, through the open gateway, weaves between the waiting ponies, before racing back to his mother. It's a miracle he wasn't kicked.

A Manipuri stallion, which has just finished his breakfast of soaked chick peas after a practice polo session, is released into the herd. Immediately a couple of other stallions approach him and there is some squealing and flashing of hooves as the horses rear up, before the pecking order is re-established. He goes to a mare which is suckling a young foal. He nudges the foal away, and tries to mount the mare.

'He is a good polo stallion,' Basanta says.

'Yes, but how many foals a year do you lose through injury?'

'About 20 to 25 percent die through illness and injury. We can only afford to worm twice a year and that isn't enough. The grazing on the common is shared with cattle and there is very little grass. In the monsoon season some of the horses have to be tied up and fed hay, because most of the grazing is flooded. Also.' he points to a row of newly-built houses. 'It is easier to build on the common than on the jungle-clad hills behind.'

'We will go to the marsh,' Philip says. 'It is where most of the ponies live and I want to see my mare and foal, and show you my milking cows.'

'How many cows do you have?' I ask surprised, he has never mentioned them before.

'Ten.'

'How much do you get for your milk?'

He tells me and I quickly work it out. 25 pence per litre compared to 14 pence in the UK. I tell him and he is astounded.

'How can they make a living?' he asks.

'Our small herds are over 100 cows.'

'I prefer to live here,' he says with a grin.

Out on the marsh, ponies and cattle are scattered over a large area of coarse grass, intermingling as they search for the best pasture. One horse catches my attention. She has a broken leg! Each time she walks her off-hind, from six inches below the hock, flaps like a paper bag in the wind.

'Mine,' says Philip. 'She broke her leg in a cattle-grid two years ago. We nursed her, but it never mended. She formed a thick layer of skin round the injury so the bone didn't come through the skin,' he pauses as she hobbles a couple of paces. 'She was a brilliant polo pony and that is her foal beside her. She went to the stallion earlier this year, so hopefully she is in foal again.'

'Keeping the ponies fed during the monsoon is a big problem,' Doljit explains. 'Only a few people can afford to tie their ponies up because hay is expensive. Most ponies have to scavenge on the sides of the roads or in people's gardens. Every year there is more housing, so less grazing.'

'What about the hills?'

'No grazing, just trees. I think,' Doljit says sadly, 'in a few years there will be no place in Manipur for the Manipuri pony. Arambai Hunba and Sagol Kangjei will disappear with it, unless somebody does something like buying enough land to keep the ponies and the games going.'

***

At the last minute a threatened 'bund' (strike) over the treatment of some villagers by soldiers of the Assam Rifles is called off, and the final of the show jumping and tent-pegging can take place.

Just a few weeks earlier I had seen demonstrators taking part in a bund in Tripura and again in Nagaland. Both times I had to stay in the hotel, while heavily armed police and soldiers controlled certain key crossroads, in case things turned violent.

Sadly I get little chance to watch the show jumping and tent-pegging – because I am interviewed by the local television, then by Chang Li, the Reuters correspondent, and finally am constantly harassed by a man making a film about the Manipuri pony.

Once the cups and rosettes have been given out Chang Li insists we accompany him to the outskirts of Imphal where his brother lives. He is a professor of English at the university and would like to discuss the finer points of the English language. Doljit is doubtful, saying the area is known to be heavily infiltrated by local freedom fighters, but Chang Li assures us we will be safe with him. He knows the local commanders through his job. I hope he is right.

The professor's house is surrounded by a high wall and has large sheeted metal gates, which are opened as soon as we turn off the dirt street onto his concrete drive. When we get out of the car the professor says it isn't safe, and that we should go back immediately. Chang calms him and we go inside for tea. The professor turns out to be less interested in English than the political situation.

Manipur only came fully under British/Indian control during the Second World War, and was promised autonomy when it ended. Indian Independence was brought forward a year and, in the rush, the guarantees to the North Eastern states were forgotten. Up to 26 different groups have been fighting for 'Home Rule' ever since, and the Assam Rifles are seen as an army of occupation, rather than a force to promote a peaceful way forwards.

Inserting throwing sticks amongst the peacock feathers. Besides aiding the distance thrown, the stick gives the feathers support so that they don't bend and scratch the thrower, because in the past the darts were poisoned.

While we are talking, music starts up from a marquee across the street. Chang insists we go over and have a look, even though Doljit and the professor say there is a chance I will be grabbed by a motorcyclist and taken hostage. Persuaded by Chang we join the party. There is a band in the centre lit by some spotlights and flickering electric lights round the walls. It is like a line dance, with women, children and a few men dancing round the band holding hands.

Chang Li parts two women and puts my hands in theirs. It is a simple dance. Two small steps to the right, kick the right leg forward and a larger step to the right. Doljit and the professor, still looking worried, watch from the tent entrance. After four dances Chang says it is time to go and several women and children come with us to the house gates to say goodbye. The professor, lit up by the headlights, looks relieved as he waves us off.

'You see! No problems!' Chang says. 'Tomorrow night you must come to me for the evening meal.'

His house is smaller and older than I expected. It is built on stilts with the kitchen and dining area, once the garage, underneath, and the bedrooms and sitting room above. We sit on the sitting room floor, resting against pillows, a lantern and candles provide the light – yet another power-cut. We get onto the subject of children grinding their teeth at night.

'It is caused by a worm in the blood,' Chang Li affirms.

'But there have been countless negative blood tests,' says Doljit.

I am too fascinated to comment.

'Because they test at the wrong time,' says Chang Li. 'They never test when the child is grinding its teeth – that is when the worm moves. If you keep waking the child as soon as it starts grinding, the worm will eventually die.'

Am I really hearing this from an educated man?

'It is very infectious,' he continues. 'If a child sleeps with another child or with an adult the worm can get into them. It is essential you wake the child every time.'

'So I have heard,' Doljit says, looking sceptical, but not wanting to argue with our host.

'Also you should only sleep on your right-hand side so you don't squash your heart or other essential organs.'

Before we can discuss this point we are called to dinner. It is laid for the three of us. He says his wife and children will eat in the kitchen. It is a feast, with boiled bamboo slivers, several different curries, heaps of rice, another dish I'm not quite sure about, and some deep-fried insects. The conversation dwells mainly on the political situation and how the British betrayed Manipur. I'm glad they don't think of me as being responsible simply because I'm British.

It is after midnight when I am dropped off at my hotel. The night-watchman is slow coming to let me in, and Chang frets, saying that it's not safe to sit around in a car in a deserted street late at night.

The following morning I fly to Calcutta, after saying a sad goodbye to Doljit who has been such a wonderful companion and brilliant guide. I wish him well with his project to breed Manipuri ponies on his farm on the banks of the Brahmaputra. He says when he has enough ponies he will introduce foreign tourists to Sagol Kangjei and Arambai Hunba.

CHAPTER NINE

Cameroon: Going North

'Cameroon couldn't be safer,' I tell Sue as I arrange my flights. 'Anne [a neighbouring farmer's wife] was there in the late Sixties and was able to travel round the whole country in her Volkswagen Beetle. I'll be fine.'

'It is not like it used to be,' says the grey-haired Greek sitting next to me on the plane. He has been dealing in timber in West Africa for over forty years. 'Now you must be very careful. A white man is a target for muggers. In Douala you must never walk on your own, always take a hotel taxi, and make sure it will wait for you. There are no second chances and the police will not help, just demand money. I will help you through Customs.'

The hotel courtesy car fails to appear, and halfway into Douala my taxi driver demands a doubling of the fee. At one in the morning I pay up rather than get left on the side of the road.

In the morning I resolve to go up-country as soon as possible, but find I have brought Sue's bank card instead of my own. During a frantic phone call she gives me her pin number, and agrees to telephone her bank to say she is in Cameroon.

***

The train creaks as it slowly passes through a mud-hut village straddling the line. Despite some villagers hacking at the jungle, it is already reclaiming several houses on the edge of the clearing. Children run alongside shouting for plastic bottles, or offering fruit to the passengers standing in the open doorways. At the edge of the clearing the train puts on speed, and soon we are rattling along with the jungle once again brushing the carriage sides.

I am on the train from Yaoundé, the capital of Cameroon, to Ngaoundere in the north to see the household cavalry of the Lamido (king and religious head of the local Muslims) of Rey Bouba. I was informed by an old anthropologist the cavalry still wear chain mail. It is a flying visit, because my main goal is to see horses racing in the streets of Kumbo, which is in the North West. I am planning to meet the owners and discover what game or games they play, but so far have been unable to find out when the races are. All I know for certain is they are always run in November.

Before I leave Douala my taxi driver, Mr. Thales, introduces me to an attractive middle-aged European lady who runs a small travel company tucked away at the back of a guarded courtyard. She says she will telephone me as soon as she knows about the races. Mr. Thales tells me she is well connected, having been the mistress of a cabinet minister.

The three Spaniards in my couchette crowd the window as the train slows, coming into a station. Hawkers selling fruit, cooked fish and anything edible, close in on the train as it comes to a stop. Passengers leaving the train carry their belongings over to some minibuses, and pass the luggage up to the bus boys perched on the roofs stacking suitcases and bedding. One is loaded so high that the boy can't stretch enough to put the last item on. In a corner, away from the crowds, a large lady reaches under her dress and pulls her white knickers down before squatting. She is very discreet, but when she stands again she gets in a muddle, exposing her enormous backside. A woman fish-seller stops below the open window and asks if I want one of the dried fish from the basket balanced on her head.

'Non, merci,' I say as we jerk forward.

In the late evening we slow down to pass a stationary train in a siding. There are a large number of slatted box-cars full of cattle. Herdsmen walk alongside, checking that all the beasts are standing, while others on the roof of the cars poke sticks through open hatches to get the cattle to move round, so the men on the ground can see more easily. We watch in the gathering gloom as the men spot a fallen steer and frantically try to get the other cattle to give it room to get up, but no luck. It is impossible for the men to go into the truck because of the long, sharp horns, so in the end they leave it.

Despite the heat we shut the window – the mosquitoes seem to be sucked in as we gather speed. The waiter who handed out our supper comes to collect the trays. The Spaniards offer him money, but he explains we pay after breakfast. They don't understand, until I use a mixture of French, English and sign language. They only speak Spanish, so it takes some time. With my money belt and my cameras under my pillow, and well-plastered with insect repellent, I soon fall asleep.

A noble, note the long ornate boots and the toe-stirrup.

Nobles waiting for the Fantasia. Chiefs' horses all have four white socks and a blaze.

In the morning we stop at a village in a large clearing. Looking each way out of the window, the train is so long I can't see the front or back. There is one train up and one down every day. In Yaoundé there was a board with the departure time, and another with a list of stations we stop at, but no times for when we get to them.

The Spanish girl gives a horrified cry as a man appears at the window holding the lower half of a monkey by its tail. He moves on, and meets brisk trade at the open doorway. One passenger jumps off to chase a man carrying the hind leg of a small deer, then returns grinning and holding up the haunch.

As I am packing, the business card of the well-dressed woman I sat next to on the bus from Douala to Yaoundé falls from my pocket onto my couchette. She never spoke a word the whole journey, but handed the card to me as we got off. I had forgotten all about it in the rush for the station. I pick it up. In raised type it says, "Mlle Marguerite Echandou, Sex," and a telephone number. She seemed so demure!

The Ngaoundere tourist office suggests I visit Le Ranch Gnaoudaba, about 40 kilometres away, because they have horses, and might know about horse culture in the region. They also say the Lamido of Rey Bouba disbanded his household cavalry at least ten years ago and, in any event, no foreigner can visit without first obtaining his permission in writing. I decide to go to Le Ranch for a few days. I try to telephone Jaqueline from the travel company, but the line to Douala is down.

A Dutch entomologist, Yse and his son Idsert, whom I met on the train, are interested in coming with me, so we share a taxi. It is an ancient Toyota, which slithers about on the wet mud road, until the driver says he's not going any further. After some haggling, we agree an outrageous price for him to drop us at the end of the drive to the house. A rutted track takes us through the scrub for a mile to a stone hunting lodge. Stuffed heads of antelope and other animals decorate the entrance hall.

I ask about riding, and learn that the horses have gone to Ngaoundere to be vaccinated against flies. The owner and grooms have gone with them, and won't be back for at least ten days. In the evening I chat to one of the staff who is armed with a small hunting bow, three arrows and a torch. He looks as if he is going "lamping" (shooting at night with the aid of a spotlight), and I ask if I can join him. He looks perplexed when I ask what he is intending to shoot, and says he is the night guard. The bow and arrow are to frighten off intruders.

Next morning, once the torrential rain stops, our guide takes us down the steep path from the garden to the volcanic lake the lodge overlooks. He asks if any of us want to go out in a little tin rowing boat, just big enough for one person. It is half-full of greenish water, the same colour as the lake, which suggests there is a leak. The guide says he used to fish from it, but now he fishes from the bank. His invitation is declined.

We, like the surrounding vegetation, are soon steaming under the hot sun as we walk through the scrub to the cattle dipping bath, where the ranch's cattle are having a bi-weekly dip against flies. The cattle are far less reluctant to enter the mud-coloured water than my sheep at home. They gallop in and come out shining, the sun reflecting off their sleek coats.

At my insistence the guide takes us to a village to ask about horses, but nobody knows anything. Back at the lodge I'm shown some bronze figurines of horsemen from different parts of Cameroon. Each is quite different and shows riders with their weapons, some with short swords others with broad-bladed spears. Each saddle is styled to the area they come from, as are the clearly defined breeds of horse, ranging from the solid Adamowa with its blocky head, to the much finer Barb Arab. If they are accurate, they give me an idea of the horse culture from the past.

Fantasia

Moussa, our guide, is taking us round the Lamido of Ngaoundere's palace when he picks up a spear. It has the same type of blade as the Adamowa horse-riding figurine. He shows me other pieces of a horse-warrior's equipment; a long sword with a cross guard like that of an ancient Crusader; an oval hide shield, a saddle with a high pommel and cantle and an Arab bit attached to some broken leather straps. He says we must see the Fantasia this evening. Many of the Lamido's notables (nobles) will be riding their best horses. It is a great spectacle. He will meet us at the palace entrance at four o'clock, and make certain we have good seats.

Yse and Idsert need to go back to the hotel, which is some distance away, so I/we set off in search of a taxi. Moussa tells me that the Fantasia is in honour of the Minister of Transport, who is visiting Ngaoundere. Normally Moussa shows people round the palace, which consists of a series of huge round huts, until six o'clock, but is finishing early today. The huts are about twenty-five feet high, thatched with fine, pale grass which comes down to about four feet from the ground and looks like a badly cut fringe.

Tomorrow the Lamido will hold a picnic for the Minister on the bank of a volcanic lake ten kilometres away. The Minister will travel by car, but the Lamido will be part of a mounted procession. I ask if the horses are used in any kind of game. He says that once they were used for war, but now just the rich people have them, and bring them to the palace two or three times a year to take part in a fantasia.

Long trumpet announcing the arrival of the Lamido at the start of the Fantasia .

There is no sign of Yse and Idsert as Moussa shows me to a seat at the back of the officials' area under an archway. One of the first horsemen to arrive is a tall, slim noble on a chunky, roan Adamowa horse – again the likeness to the figurine is amazing.

He carries a spear with an eighteen inch point and has a sword on his hip, but what stands out are his bright pink, long soft leather boots. Not only do they disappear under his yellow jalaba, but they are specially cut, with the big toe separated from the other toes, so that he can ride with just his big toe in the stirrup. I saw paintings of toe-stirrups in Ethiopia, but never expected to find horsemen using that style of riding on the west coast.

Colourfully dressed horsemen continue to arrive on Barb-like mounts. I leave my seat to get a closer look. Most of the horses are tightly constrained by their bridles. All have severely curbed bits with long shanks and broad metal nose-bands attached to the bit and held up by a strap going to the head-piece. They ride on a loose rein, except when they want to show off their skills. Then, as soon as they take tighter hold, the horse starts to prance. Some of the horses canter with their front legs and trot with their hind. I ask Pink Boots about their peculiar gait, and he says it is the most comfortable pace, but it takes a lot of time to train them to do it.

A man arrives with huge speakers on the back of his motorbike. Moussa says I should go back to my place because the entertainment is starting. A drummer and a man in a beanie hat, striped floral jalaba and white shoes starts singing into the newly erected microphone. He is joined by four ladies whom, Moussa informs me, are the Lamido's junior wives. They move with the music. Then, when it gets faster, the women turn and jiggle their backsides to the great enjoyment of the spectators.

The combination of sitting under the arch and cloudy evening mean I have move to get enough light for any decent photographs. Just as I am leaving the stand the Dutchmen arrive, rather out of breath. They had difficulty getting a taxi and, on their return, found the road closed. The wailing of sirens announces the arrival of the Minister. He is escorted to a chair in front of where I was sitting. The Lamido appears several minutes later to a throbbing of drums, fanfare of trumpets and the low notes from a seven-foot long silver horn.

Once he is seated the first group of five horsemen burst into the square in front of the palace at full gallop, going straight towards the dais. At the last second they rein in, their mounts almost sitting on their quarters as they come to a halt. As they turn away a foursome waving spears gallop past them. Moussa tells me that the best horsemen are those who pull up closest to the Lamido. The Fantasia shows the loyalty of the nobles and the trust the king has in them.

The show goes on for half an hour with the riders getting closer to the Lamido and the crowds urging them on. All the time I try to get photographs, but the failing light and the speed of the horses are against me. I try to get nearer the action, but sometimes the horsemen turn towards me instead of going the other way. Luckily Moussa grabs me when it looks as if I might be ridden down. Finally, in the gathering gloom all the horsemen enter the square in a long line, with Pink Boots out ahead on his own. Once they are all in, he gives a shout and they spur forward before pulling up with a final flourish.

Walking amongst the horsemen after their last charge, I notice Pink Boots' horse's muzzle is blood-stained, as are most of the other horses. It is undoubtedly from over-use of their fearsome bits. The blood is even more clearly visible because most of the horses have white noses; Fulbe nobles prefer horses with a large white blaze and four white socks. Moussa says many chiefs think colouring is more important than performance.

The decoration of horse and rider depends on their tribe and finances. A bay horse from the north is heavily garlanded with white woollen pompoms hanging from his brow-band and layers of green, yellow, blue and red hanging from his neck-strap. Some of the riders wear long boots decorated with patterns, while others are barefoot, their big toes wrapped round the slim stirrup-sides. As long as a noble has a horse, he can take part.

The following day the Lamido's 'progress' is greeted by hundreds of cheering subjects whenever he passes near a village. The only part of him you can see are his eyes; his head swathed in a white turban, his body in a gold jalaba. His grey horse is surrounded by drummers and

Fantasia. Horsemen gallop flat out waving spears before reining in at the last moment. The nearer the dais, the better the horsemanship.

footmen with spears, while alongside him walks a man with a long-handled, brightly coloured golfing umbrella, keeping the sun off him. At either end of the escort there are horsemen armed with spears and swords. It takes two and a half hours to get to the crater with a lake. The Dutchmen and I are kept well away from the Lamido's and Minister's picnic. I am constantly accosted by the 'Notables de Lamido' demanding 'cadeaux'. Luckily I meet a young noble who wants to study in the UK and, as long as he stays with us, the monetary demands cease. He is an engineer but, unfortunately for me, knows nothing about horses or equine traditions.

Bamenda

'I'm afraid the news from Kumbo about the racing is neither good nor bad,' says Jaqueline at the travel agency when I return to Douala. 'No one knows anything. The rumour is it will not happen this year, because when the race committee went to the cave to consult the ancestors, the signs were not good. Probably they are short of sponsorship money, but disapproval of the ancestors is something everyone here understands.'

'Could the races still go ahead?'

'Yes, perhaps. Anyway I have booked two seats on the bus to Bamenda for tomorrow. You will be able to find out more from there.'

'Two seats?'

'It's the only way to travel by bus in this country. The seats are narrow and many of the ladies...' she pauses, 'are, er... a little large.' She smiles.

Back at my hotel I walk up and down 100 stairs ten times carrying my pack. There is no air conditioning in the stairwell, but it is the only place I can exercise because it is unsafe to go for a walk, even a jog around the block. Also, one gets accosted by the girls hanging round outside, waiting to be invited in. Most are not in the first flush of youth and their broad shoulders would sit well on a rugby player. I book a provisional date for my return from Bamenda and they agree to store my extra baggage.

The bus station for Armour Mezzam, the company the travel agent said is the best, is in a shanty town on the far side of the river. It stinks compared to the air conditioned waiting room for the Yaound bus; the smell of the latrines overpowering that of the close-packed humanity in the waiting room.

The bus is supposed to leave at 07.30, but ticket sales are slow, and it is not until 10.30 that it is full. As we pull out there is a fight in the back. Not everyone has paid and those who have are claiming their seats. It takes another 20 minutes to sort it out.

We stop for lunch at some tin-roofed food stalls on the outskirts of Melong. Everyone goes down a convenient side road for a much needed pee; men nearest the bus, women a little further on. For lunch I choose some thin slices of meat cooked over some coals – the highly spiced meat takes a lot of chewing. I am only halfway through when the driver honks the horn.

Soon we are weaving our way up the steep road which climbs from plains to the fertile plateau that is the start of the highlands. Instead of bush meat, there are now piles of vegetables for sale by the sides of the road. The vendors give the driver a tip whenever he stops for the passengers to buy their produce.

Cantering back after their charge.

The few taxis at the Bamenda bus station are quickly taken by locals, and I end up pillion on a motorcycle. After a journey of limited steering, due to my backpack being balanced on the handlebars; numerous large potholes, round which all vehicles swerve in all directions, and a wet slippery surface, I am very relieved to reach my 'seen better days' hotel.

The Tourist office contacts a local guide, Mnango Joseph, who meets me at the hotel. He is slim, about five-foot six, has greying hair, wears a dark suit, and speaks English. He confirms there is no racing at Kumbo this year because the ancestors have said it shouldn't take place, but he knows two places where there are a lot of horses. He says there is no point in going to Kumbo because the horsemen only go there for the races. Tomorrow he is booked, but after that he available, as is a friend who has a taxi. He says I was lucky with the 'moto' taxi because several tourists have been taken to a bad area, instead of their hotel, and robbed. He tells me it is safe to explore round the town in the day, but to stay in the confines of the hotel at night.

I have a long chat with two Presbyterian missionaries, Frank, who emigrated to Canada three years ago from Suffolk, and Eugenie, who is of Ukrainian extraction. They are here to award grants and loans to individuals setting themselves up in business. They have whittled the claimants down to the last few and invite me to join them as they do some final interviews at a café in town.

The first is a young man who wants to start a pig farm on a cliff-like piece of land he bought cheap. He says he will terrace it, but they deem it unsuitable because, in the heavy rains, the run-off will pour down the hillside onto the houses and stream at the bottom. Next up is a young man who wants to expand his computer café from one to eight computers. After a finely put case about how the use of them will help local businesses as well as individuals, they agree to subsidise six. There is an engineer, a person interested in fabric printing, a potter and a girl who wants to set up a hairdressing salon.

She is 25, a qualified hairdresser and manicurist, with an eight-year-old child. Many women have their nails done once a week, and their hair washed and wig changed every three weeks. Most women wear wigs – a hairnet stuffed with hair, which is woven into their own hair so it doesn't slip. School children are not allowed wigs at school and they come to the hairdresser to keep their hair at the regulation length. It is clearly a good business to go into, and she is given a loan.

'What about chickens?' The would-be pig farmer accosts us as we are getting ready to leave.

Everyone looks bemused.

'If I did chickens? Instead of pigs?'

'That's a possibility,' says Frank, 'but we would need to see some figures and we have finished for today.'

The pig farmer pulls a piece of paper out of his pocket with something scribbled in pencil.

'It has to be a proper application,' Eugenie says, frowning.

'But you leave tomorrow.'

'Not until mid-day.'

'I will have it all done by eight o'clock.'

'Nine will do,' Frank tells him. After his departure, Frank comments, 'That is one I'm not worried about. He is bound to succeed with all that energy.'

Walking round the market Eugenie points out that we are a target for a group of young men. Apparently they have been tracking us for a

The Lamido on a "progress" on his way to a picnic.

while, all the time edging closer. Suddenly Eugenie turns to confront them. The shoppers at the stalls near us look up as she raises her voice.

The young men stop, not sure what to do now they have been noticed. A large lady swipes one of them with her bag and others follow her lead. The young men scatter under the onslaught.

'You OK, Reverend?' asks the lady who led the assault.

'Yes, thank you,' says Frank. 'You were in church on Sunday, in the choir.'

She beams and nods her head.

'Thank you everyone,' Eugenie says.

'May Jesus keep you safe,' says another lady.

While Eugenie inspects the stalls for presents to take home to her nieces, Frank tells me about the Christianity practised here. It is more spiritual than in the West, with a lot of casting out of evil spirits and praying for healing. Some of the rituals closely resemble old pagan chanting and dancing. There is even an African Bible, which allows a man to have more than one wife - though he has yet to actually see one of these bibles. Most of the schooling in Bamenda is at church schools and on certain days all the pupils from all the denominational schools walk in a long line through the town singing hymns. He says the enthusiasm of the worshippers is something that can only be dreamt of in an English church.

Next morning Joseph arrives with his friend Jacob the taxi driver and we are off on the Kumbo road in an ancient yellow Toyota with a badly cracked windscreen to see some horses. First stop is a crater-lake surrounded by trees, where the spirits of the ancestors are said to live. Every year the locals come here, sacrifice and cook goats, sheep and chickens at a religious ceremony, then throw the meat into the lake to feed the ancestors. They believe that if the ancestors are not fed they will come from the lake to steal food from the houses, and bring either a cattle plague or crop failure. The grey water reflects the low clouds above us, and the wind ruffles the surface.

There are some rotting boats half in, half out of the water. They were made for a fishing project run by a foreign aid programme, but all the fish died. Joseph tells me it was because the ancestors were angry, but it is a stagnant volcanic lake. It fills during the rains, then slowly subsides when the dry weather comes.

The car creeps along a badly rutted track until the driver says we can go no further. He says he will join us when he has managed to turn round and park. We walk down a hill covered in lush grass to a tin-roofed farmhouse, where several half-naked children run indoors screaming. A slim man with a greying goatee stoops out through the low doorway. As soon as he recognises Joseph his face lights up and he insists we have tea. We sit on blocks of wood in the farmyard waiting. The farmer and Joseph talk pigeon English. I pick out the odd word and occasional phrase, but I'm no wiser what they are talking about. A pretty girl of about sixteen brings the tea. In the background two older women hover, but are waved away.

'She is his new wife,' Joseph says with a grin. 'He is very pleased with her.'

'She is pretty. How many wives does he have?'

Joseph has a word with the farmer.

'It is difficult,' Joseph says. 'Depending on who is counting them, four, more or less.'

'Is he Muslim?'

A bit. The arched piece goes in the mouth.

'He is Fulbe, so of course. Drink up. He is keen to show you his horses.'

The tea is still really hot, and takes time to drink. They get tired of waiting for me and go through a gap in the hedge beside the house. He shouts and two teenage boys run past me. I am just in time to see half a dozen horses and a couple of foals galloping away from us with the boys giving chase. Luckily one of the foals goes off at an angle and gets trapped in a fenced corner. The mare goes back for it and is caught, while the rest scatter some sheep a quarter of a mile away on the far side of the field.

The 15 hand mare is a classic Fulani chief's, with four white socks and a blaze. The farmer is pleased because she is his best dancing horse; apparently there are horse dancing competitions at the end of Ramadan and also at other festivals. Most of the local farmers like to compete. Until the new big chief of the tea plantation at Ndawara arrived all the locals stood a chance of winning, but now he has so many good horses and grooms, they seldom get a prize.

Head groom of Ndawara.

When the farmer mounts, her back dips slightly as he swings his leg over the high cantle. He seems not to notice, and rides her away from us over a small ditch before turning. Pulling back on the reins and squeezing with his legs he gets her back onto her hocks. She balances briefly on her hind legs before dropping down. He tries again, but I can see that she is weak on her off-hind and is obviously uncomfortable. He says something to Joseph, who tells me the mare hurt the muscles in her quarters a few days ago and the farmer doesn't want to do any more with her. She is lame when she scrambles back over the ditch. There is no chance of seeing any of the others, they are bunched, tails in the air, a good 500 yards from us. I thank him, and Joseph says something to him. It sounds like, 'we no go not now'.

'What did you say?' I ask.

'I tell him we are leaving.'

Obviously two negatives make a positive in their strange pigeon. We walk back to the car, then slowly bump our way back to the main dirt road. We are weaving along, avoiding a deep rut caused by the rain, when we meet the Kumbo minibus. It too is avoiding the deep gutter, but is going much faster than us, and on our side of the road. Jacob slams on his brakes as he drives into the soft ground on the edge. The minibus hits the rut, takes off and lands hard before veering into the bushes on the other side. The passengers get out, push it back onto the road and collect the luggage which has come off the roof-rack. One suitcase has burst. Its scattered contents are picked up by the women while the men push. Jacob has a word with the driver and once the minibus is back on firm ground, the men come over to help get us back onto the track. I suspect the minibus has broken a spring because it is listing heavily on the near-side rear.

We follow a steep well-worn track up to the Ndawara tea plantation where Joseph says there are over 2,000 horses, as well as 12,000 cattle and over 2,500 hectares of tea. The owner, Baba Ahmadou Danpullo, has built up the estate over the years, providing work for many of the nomadic cattle herders who lived in the hills. He is also reviving traditional Fulani horsemanship. He is not in residence, but after a lot of negotiating Joseph arranges with the estate office that, in two days' time, we will get a guided tour with the head horseman and see the style of riding used in competitions.

Ndawara

With a day to spare we go to Bafut to see the Fon's (local king) palace. It isn't a glorious building like an Indian palace, but a brick-walled compound with firing holes cut in the walls. It was built by the Germans when they colonised the area in the early 1900s. Inside there is a large dilapidated house, a series of brick huts where the Fon's wives lived, and a tall, carved wooden temple, said to be the oldest building in West Africa, which only the Fon and selected nobles are allowed to enter.

Outside the compound there are two large stones (one for men, one for women) on which criminals, including adulterers, were executed. Despite the Fon having as many wives as he wanted, sex outside marriage for his subjects was punishable by death. The last Fon had over 400 children, and the succession was agreed with his nobles well before his death. The custom is to say he has gone away on a hunting trip and install the new ruler before anyone knows of the death. When it is announced three weeks later, the successor has already been crowned.

Joseph takes me to the law court. There are three high-walled enclosures – one where the judging nobles sit, the second for the speaker and the third for the defendant. The speaker relays all communication between both parties, saying exactly what has been said. It was supposed to make a fairer trial because there can be no prejudice as neither party can see or hear the other. Until recently, regardless of whether they were Christian or Muslim, when a man accused his neighbour of something they both had to swear on a grotesque wooden idol that they were telling the truth. If the accused didn't die within seven days, the accuser was punished.

In the museum there is a wonderful collection of masks used in dances, and both German and local weaponry used in the war to subdue the area. Oddly out of place was a glass cabinet with two Toby jugs, a large china fruit bowl and an ornate old-fashioned coffee pot, which had been swapped with Arab traders for slaves who were prisoners of war. There is nothing related to horses. Joseph tells me that is because the surrounding countryside used to be covered in thick jungle, unlike the open hills near Bamenda.

The oldest building in West Africa, according to my guide

On the way back we stop at the Sagoda botanical gardens, halfway between Bamenda and Bafut. There were several little gardens from different Cameroonian cultures and some conservation plots. Quite a lot of work now goes into discovering the medicinal properties of local plants. Joseph points to a plaque on a small arched brick wall in front of some purple flowers. "Environmentalists Sasakawa Sarawiwa, Prince Philip, Prince Charles, Mother Theresa, Ngwache Nthenda".

***

Back at Ndawara we wait to meet up with the horse-master. Rather than sit in an office like last time, we wait at the central crossroads, by the hairdresser's, sitting on a felled tree-trunk. Opposite us is a chattering group of women in brightly coloured clothes, their babies strapped to their backs. Three pick-ups arrive and the women clamber in before being driven off in a cloud of red dust.

On the verandah of the hairdresser's, a young woman in a yellow and white striped dress is having her hair done. She spots us and looks

Ndawara, clinging on, just. The head groom is seen here practising for a horse dancing display.

at us embarrassed as her long back-combed tresses stand on end. The hairdresser takes no notice until the girl says something, and they go inside.

After an hour and a half a man from the office arrives. The horse-master isn't answering his mobile, so this man will show us round instead, though he is sorry that he knows nothing about the horses.

We walk to a walled corral with a concrete manger built into the wall. In the field beyond he says there are 90 stallions, some of which are the best dancing horses, but he is not sure which they are. There was a big dancing festival at the end of Ramadan, and since then the horses have not been ridden much, because the next competition isn't for a couple of months.

Jacob, the driver, shouts as an ostrich tries to grab his baseball cap. We all laugh, but keep a safe distance from the pen the bird is in.

Baba Ahmado Danpullo the owner of the estate is keen on birds and is planning to get several more ostriches. In a paddock nearby three huge Brahmin bulls, imported from the US, are grazing quietly, grey backed birds with yellow beaks search for insects on their backs. The man from the office suggests we skirt round the field, though he hasn't heard of the bulls being aggressive.

There are so many mares and foals in the next paddock it is not possible to count them. Quite a few are sheltering from the sun in a large barn, while others keep away from the main herd, their young foals close to their sides. The colour ranges from bays, chestnuts and greys, to one with a white head, white legs and quarters and, the rest of it, a mottled chestnut. There are several chief's horses as well as a good number of Barb and Barb crosses. Most are 14 to 15 hands, though those with thoroughbred blood are nearer 16 hands and have finer heads.

The views are stunning in contrast to brown scenery round Ngaoundere: here there are different shades of green as far as I can see. Stretching along the more rounded ridges are the tea plantations, while some of the flatter ground and the hillsides are covered in grass. Tree-lined fences keep the cattle out of the tea. It looks wonderful riding country.

On the way back to the crossroads we have to wait for a mounted cowboy gently herding some cattle to a new pasture. Later we see a boy of eight or nine riding bareback, leading three stallions. Threads from his baler-twine reins shimmer in the wind.

We wait in the new hotel/restaurant, which is having the finishing touches done to it. The estate is expecting bus-loads of tourists to start coming in six weeks to have a 'tea experience' on the largest tea plantation in the country. In fact it is already bigger than the rest of the plantations in the country combined. While we are sipping our complimentary tea, the office man returns to say we can meet the horse-master if we are here by nine tomorrow.

The journey back is slow. We have to pass a line of school children about half a mile long, all in blue shirts and dark shorts or skirts. They walk three or four deep, and every time a car comes the other way we have to pull in amongst them. Entering a village near Bamenda the locals pull a thick rope across the road. As soon as we stop, the car is surrounded by women carrying baskets, and we are not allowed to go on until we have each bought some fruit.

At the last crossroads we are stopped by the militia-police. A drunken soldier demands my passport. I only hand it to him after consulting Joseph. He flicks through it and throws it back at me.

'D'argent!' he demands.

I hand him the passport again.

'D'argent,' he slurs. 'Cadeau.'

Suddenly I'm pissed off. It has been a long, mainly fruitless day. Despite Joseph's cry, I get out of the taxi. The law says a tourist must not be asked for money. I hand him my passport. He takes it and looks at it upside down, settling on the page with the Mongolian visa.

'D'argent!'

'Votre nombre?' I ask taking out my pad and pencil. 'Aussi votre nomme?'

He looks bewildered, but his mate realises they could be in trouble. He gives Joseph back his identity card, comes round the car, takes my passport from the drunk, hands it back to me and holds the door open for me to get in. Finally, he salutes as we drive off.

Next morning the horse-master, tall, slim, in his thirties and his assistant, a foot shorter and ten years younger, are waiting for us. Before we go anywhere, they tell me they must telephone their boss, Baba Ahmadou Danpullo, who is in either Nigeria or South Africa. I am not clear which. Unlike some of the UK countryside, the reception here in the mountainous highlands is good, and the horse-master gets through straight away. After a brief conversation the horse-master hands me the telephone.

'Mister Thompson, what is it you want and why?' asks Baba Ahmadou.

His English is good and the line is clear.

'I would like to see your horses and find out about any games played on them. Also I would like to know any equine traditions.'

'Why?'

'Because I am writing a book on horsemanship in Africa and Asia.'

'I wish you luck. Hand me back.'

'Thank you,' I say before returning the mobile to the horse-master.

Joseph looks enquiringly at me, I shrug and we wait for the telephone conversation to finish. Eventually the horse-master hangs up, and sets off, talking to Joseph as he strides along. Baba Ahmadou has said to show us everything.

Joseph relays to me that we will look at a young stallion that is being trained for dancing competitions. They use stallions because they are stronger. Horse dancing has long been associated with Fulani riding. It originated to make a horse responsive, well-balanced and agile in battle. It has been revived by Baba Ahmadou for competitions and entertaining people.

The horse-master vaults onto a horse; there is just a blanket to sit on, and his feet hang down to just above its knees. After a short trot round, he gathers the rope reins and the horse crouches on its hocks, so that its front hooves hardly touch the ground as it moves sideways towards me. The horse-master has one hand on the rope reins and the other holds the mane, while his legs are constantly squeezing the flanks. It is like something from the Spanish Riding School. When he gets near to us he relaxes his hold on the reins and dismounts.

Without waiting for any comment he leads us past Baba Ahmadou's mansion (a huge white, chateau-style house, with a turret in one corner, arched windows and a steep slate roof), to the corral we saw yesterday. Now it is full of horses – all stallions – milling round as several men single out the ones they want. The horse-master points to a distinctive bay with four white socks, a white blaze and large white patch on its jaw. His assistant catches it and slips on a rope bridle and throws a rug on its back, which he secures with a surcingle. He rides it over into a corner while the rest of the horses are let out of the corral through the high wooden gates.

After a short warm-up, the assistant canters the horse round the corral before trying to get it to stand on its hind legs. The ground is too soft and muddy for it to balance, so they take it into a field beside the mansion. He canters down to the far end, where he tries again. The horse keeps giving a half-rear, then cantering forward a few strides. The horse-master shouts to bring the horse to him, so that he can ride it.

The horse-master rides to the bottom of the field where he gets the horse back on its hocks, making it turn left and right, before facing up towards us. I have my video trained on him as he gives a shout. The horse rears up on its hind legs, jumps forward landing on its hind legs, then takes a cantering stride before repeating the movement.

It comes all the way up the field jumping on its hind legs and taking one stride between each jump. The horse-master clings to the mane with one hand and controls the reins with the other. His knees come up with each jump and go back down on the cantering stride. It is an amazing piece of horsemanship. We can see the 150 yards the horse has come have taken a lot out of it because it is breathing heavily and starting to sweat.

He calls for us to follow and we go to an area about the size of two football pitches, marked out with tyres and two grandstands. He tries to get another horse to perform some move, but nothing specific happens and he jumps off, saying the horse is tired and unfit. This one, like a lot of the other stallions, is having a rest before coming back into training for the next competition.

A groom takes the horse as the horse-master leads us off round the farm. He points out a field where there are two hundred mares with foals, but it is so big that they look quite scattered. I ask about the breeding policy, but he strides on, and instead tells Joseph how the Fulani cavalry led several jihads in the Sahel region, and what wonderful horsemen they were. He says they train through kindness and the use of ropes rather than using sticks.

We get in the taxi to go to a couple of outlying fields where there are more horses, but the ruts are too deep. I ask about other traditions.

He says he doesn't know of any, then says he must leave us.

On the way back to Bamenda I spot some hobbled horses in a village and get out to look at them. They are in good condition and have obviously been well handled. A group of male villagers keep a wary eye on us, but move away when we approach. Joseph tries to talk to them, but they continue to edge away. A shout makes us turn round. Several soldiers with rifles, led by an officer, run towards us. Behind them, Jacob is sitting very still, with a soldier pointing a rifle at him through the open driver's window.

'Just stand still,' says Joseph quietly.

'What are you doing here? Why are you talking to these men?' asks the officer in English.

Joseph answers for me, and there follows a swift interrogation.

'You're writing a book?' the officer asks me.

'Yes, that is why I stopped here, to look at them,' I point to the horses grazing close by.

'A book about horses?'

'Yes. I was going to ask the men who they belonged to, and what traditions they have.'

'Those men are not allowed to talk to foreigners. You must leave, right now!'

Joseph and I walk through the line of soldiers back to the Toyota. Jacob guns the engine and we speed off.

'I'm sorry, Mister Bob, I should not have let you stop there. The people there elected their Fon, but the government in Yaound appointed a different person. There has been a lot of trouble, and the army have been sent to keep order. There have been a lot of arrests and some shooting.'

The evening before I leave I telephone Mister Thales (my driver in Douala) to arrange for him to meet me at the Armour Mezzam bus station. I have heard too many tales of whites taking taxis and getting robbed, or having to pay extra once the taxi is in a bad area. Joseph insists on seeing me off. In the end he has to go to work, because the 07.00 bus eventually leaves at 10.30. I am glad I booked two seats – the large lady next to me takes up hers and half the spare seat. She fidgets. At every stop she opens the window and takes her cardigan off then, as soon as we move on, the reverse.

We are well entertained. First there is an ex-priest selling ginseng. With a bible in one hand and a packet of powder in the other, he extols the virtues of the plant saying it will cure bad stomachs, impotence, even malaria.

His final exhortation is, 'Without it, your bones will turn to butter, but with it, you can break rocks with your bones.' He sells all his stock. After him comes someone selling Chinese medicine, then Mister Super Soap. He has a cleaner that will scour your loo, get rid of stains on any piece of clothing, is good for washing floors and dishes, and will even clean any jewellery dipped in it. He sells a good number of bottles filled with his yellow liquid.

After the lunch-stop a pregnant lady gets on, carrying a large bag. First she liberally dabs everyone with a foul-smelling perfume that will clear headaches, sinuses and breathing problems, while keeping mosquitoes away.

I can well believe it.

Then she produces 'Wormit 100', something to get rid of everyone's worms. She holds up placards of all the different types of infestation to emphasise her point, and most of the passengers buy at least one packet. Now she comes to 'man and woman talk'. Antibiotics for after sex. They will cure anything a man might catch, and keep a woman healthy after menstruation. The male passengers buy the lot.

The bus is six hours late getting to Douala, partly because of setting off late, but also having to wait while the road is cleared after a crash. An overloaded taxi tried to overtake a tanker and ran straight into an oncoming lorry. When we pass what is left of the taxi I can see why no one survived. Luckily I manage to borrow a mobile phone so that I can ask Mister Thales to wait for me.

I'm relieved to see his smiling face. The shanty town is no place for a white man to be at night. We have to take a different route back, because after dark every taxi going through the dock area is stopped by local gangs, and everyone has to pay a 'toll' or is robbed.

At teatime on my last afternoon, while waiting for the airport minibus, I go into the hotel garden to watch the evening flight of thousands of fruit bats making their way across the city. Above them eagles circle, then swoop, but never seem to catch one. It is a sight I will always remember. Equally memorable is the number of prostitutes flowing through the lobby on their way to client's rooms. It is difficult to understand why so many apparently intelligent businessmen will risk so much just to scrum down with a local girl built like a rugby player.

CHAPTER TEN

Mali: 'I know where the horsemen are'

The ancient driver twiddles the wires together until the equally ancient taxi fires, then we are away, out of the airport and onto a new dual-carriageway. Low black clouds seem to hang just above the scrub. As we approach Bamako a few large raindrops explode on the windscreen, causing runnels in the film of dust. We weave from one lane to the other as the driver steers with his knees, while connecting the wires that operate the wipers. Even when they are going, the badly perished blades make little difference. Luckily we are able to follow the hazard lights of a four-by-four.

Once, when it stops, we slide gently into his bumper and I pray we never have to do an emergency stop. We go over the new bridge, the Niger river invisible through the rain. By the time we get to the hotel the sun is out, the ground steaming and the dirt side road one big puddle.

'I know where the horsemen are,' says Bocary, a cocky, square-set man in his thirties who works as a guide for several hotels. He speaks passable French, but no English, and comes from the Dogon country, which he assures me is the home of the horsemen of Mali. I don't take to him, justifiably as it turns out, but none of the other guides know anything about horses, so in the end I book him to take me to the Dogon. As a precaution I say I will pay a quarter of the fee now, a second quarter when we set off and the remainder when we get to our destination.

In the early dawn the bus compound is crowded, there are queues everywhere. Sellers of pastries and bread, last minute ticket sellers, and taxi drivers demanding payment from those they have just brought, eddy round the passengers trying to stow their luggage or jostling to get on the buses to secure a seat. Above the noise of blaring hooters announcing imminent departures, arguments over seating and frenzied goodbyes, is the smell of exhaust fumes and overflowing lavatories.

Bocary guides me through the press to our surprisingly smart bus. He has told me it is 'top of the range air conditioned – the best transport in the country'. Once my backpack is secured in the hold, and I have tipped the bus-boy to make sure nobody takes it, we climb into the warm interior. Bocary assures me that as soon as we move off, the air conditioning will come on. I am not used to something so luxurious, and recline my seat, fully intending to enjoy the journey to Djenne.

The air conditioning does come on as we pull out from the depot, but dies after ten minutes. The driver and bus-boy fiddle with knobs, but after a couple of coughs of cold air it gives up completely. After half an hour the door is opened. It is the only way to let fresh air in, because all the windows are sealed for the proper functioning of the air conditioning. The two stops before lunch are a brief respite from what has become a garlic-breathed, mobile sauna.

Bocary points out a place for lunch then, to my surprise, says he is off to see his brother. I join several other passengers at a rickety table. A dollop of rice is spooned onto a plate someone has just finished using and a piece of chicken with some sauce is slopped on top. The unwashed spoon is placed on the side of the plate, which is handed to me. I wipe the spoon with my handkerchief and dig in. My mouth is on fire – the sauce must be pure chilli. I grab the water jug and have

Boy on stallion in Dogon country.

several fills from the communal tin mug, much to the amusement of my fellow diners.

It is then a short journey until we get off the bus at a crossroads in a small village to wait for transport to Djenne. Bocary talks to the villagers while I get out of the sun in a flimsy open-fronted shelter with grass-matting sides. Everywhere shimmers in the afternoon heat. An eagle hovers, wings motionless, as the thermal from the road pushes it up in the dazzling blue sky. The odd puff of wind finds its way through the matting, but it isn't enough to make any difference. A goat saunters by, its chewed rope trailing in the dust. It stops to eat a watermelon skin, then moves on. A black plastic bag wafts towards the mud-brick houses, before joining the other refuse on the side of the road as the gust dies. The faint rhythmic drumming of women pounding millet comes from behind the houses.

Bocary comes running to me, pointing at an ancient Peugot 504 estate with no glass in the windows. My backpack is thrown into the back and Bocary and I join the other three passengers on the rear seat.

The air rushing through the speeding car soon cools us. We are just about settled, when the driver swerves to avoid some camels which walk out from behind some tall bushes. By the time we have settled ourselves again I look out to find the scrub has given way to green rice paddy stretching away on either side. The air becomes more and more humid and, by the time we get to the ferry across the Bani River, our back-seat pile of humanity is soaked in sweat.

We drive onto the ferry, a low flat vessel with ramps at either end, and clamber out to join other passengers in the wonderful fresh river breeze, which quickly dries our sodden clothes.

Djenne

Entering Djenne, the road winds through ancient streets with mud-brick houses and open drains on either side. After a few hundred yards we come into the town market square, which is dominated by the largest mud-brick mosque in the world. Every year, after the rains, 10,000 volunteers help re-plaster it with mud. At first sight it looks slightly like a hedgehog with beams sticking out the sides.

Bocary says the beams support the planks on which the plasterers stand. Our driver weaves his way up a street on the far side of the square trying to keep his wheels out of the grey, evil-smelling, open drain that twists round the lumps in the road.

Le Campement, where Bocary has booked, was once an ancient caravanserai and little has been added to the room I am allocated, except for a bed with a mosquito net and a fan on a stand. To get rid of the dank smell I leave the door open, but the bare electric light bulb attracts insects in the growing twilight.

In the open-sided bar I chat with a couple from the Dutch Embassy I met on the ferry coming here. They are still having trouble with their guide/driver, who sulked during the whole journey from Bamako, because they told him off for being late. Now they can't find

A visitor among the village granaries. Nowadays most people use motorbikes, but his village is too far from the nearest fuel station, so he still uses his horse. He had ridden 20 km to offer his condolences at the death of his uncle.

him anywhere and need to plan where they are going tomorrow. While I am talking to them Bocary interrupts to say our meal is ready, and escorts me to our table. Over the first course he suggests visiting the museum early tomorrow, because it is about half an hour's walk, then looking round the town and visiting some horsemen in the afternoon.

On the way back from the museum Bocary points out a mud-brick hotel just before the causeway into the almost moated town. It looks no different from any other large house, with an ornamental entrance, and has a rutted mud track leading to it, with two rows of sandbags to keep out the flood-water. Two donkeys harnessed to a flat cart stand patiently by the water, while a couple of naked boys dive off the causeway and swim between the long pinnaces moored nearby. He suggests we call in for a drink. It's cool sitting amongst large square pillars in the covered bar area. I order iced coffee and Bocary, as soon as his beer arrives, disappears.

I am thankful to relax on my own. All morning he has either been hurrying me when it suits him, or on a 'go slow', if he is talking to someone he knows. Annoyingly, I have to put up with it because he has made all the arrangements. I take a wander round and go up some steps to the sitting area on the roof. From here I look back across the water to the old city, the mosque and its spiky minarets topping all the other buildings.

On my way down I see a white woman in a large hat and flowing dress walk past the bottom of the stairs. She turns and introduces herself. She is Sophie Sarin, the beautiful Swedish owner of the hotel. When she hears why I am in Djenne, she insists I join her in another iced coffee.

No sooner are we sitting down than Bocary appears and says we have to go. I tell him to have another beer and wait till I am ready, and ask Sophie about herself. It is wonderful to speak in English.

Always keen to own a hotel, she came to Djenne, loved it and in 2006 started building one here, using traditional methods. She is adding two more rooms because the hotel was full during the last tourist season. The difficult thing is getting everywhere repaired after the rains, before the first guests arrive. The heavy downpours wash away some of the mud plaster and soak into the bricks underneath. Also the river rises and this year they had to use sandbags to stop it washing away the base of the surrounding walls.

She has two horses, Napoleon, a 13.2 hands high Barb and another younger horse. She takes me out to the shelter where they are stabled. It is on a raised patch of ground beside the water, next to the hotel vegetable patch. She explains that Napoleon is quite thin because he has had malaria – at least that is the diagnosis of Hydra, a local horseman. Certainly there are plenty of mosquito bites on him despite being plastered with the mud that is supposed to keep them away.

She bought a horse from some travelling singers from the Dogon country who dealt in horses. Unfortunately it threw her and Hydra swapped him for Napoleon, whom she loves riding. She asks if I would like to go for a ride the following evening and I eagerly accept. She says she will try to persuade Hydra, the last of the old horsemen in Djenne, to join us. There used to be 150 horsemen taking part in displays in front of the mosque at festivals, but now there is just him. We agree to meet up in the early evening when it is a bit cooler. She apologises for not being on top form, she has a touch of malaria herself.

After lunch, during which Bocary irritatingly talked into first one then the other of his mobile phones, we go to the house of a retired horseman. We pick our way along the narrow street carefully avoiding the gutter with its semi-liquid ooze. I am amazed at how agile the loaded donkeys are, hopping from side to side, keeping their hooves clean. A boy standing in a doorway says something to Bocary.

'Nous sommes ici,' Bocary says, mopping his face.

It takes a minute for my eyes to adjust to the gloom. The only light comes from a shuttered window and the doorway we have just come through. Sitting on a small stool is an old man with grey hair. He says something to the boy, who opens the shutter. All along the far wall are saddles in various states of dilapidation, and above them bridles hang from hooks. He offers me a stool, leaving Bocary and the boy to stand or squat.

The old man apologises for having no horse in his stable. It is much cheaper to keep one out of town on grass, especially as he has

Loading millet into a granary.

nothing to ride with, his saddles and bridles all need mending. Once he had a new bit for each horse he purchased, but now, I am saddened to hear, there are no craftsmen who can repair, let alone make new tack.

The only horseman left with the full regalia of tack and horses to put it on, is Hydra. A man, with whom this old man's family are not friendly, has tack but no horse, and there is no way either would lend to the other. Much of what he tells me confirms what Sophie said. I ask about how they train the horses, but all he says is 'a lot of patience'; perhaps one of the Dogon will show me.

The boy says something to Bocary; he stands up saying it is time to leave.

Back at Le Campement a bus load of British tourists from Explore have arrived. They are hot and tired and soon there are complaints about the lack of water for showers. Jane, the Explore rep, does what she can, then retires to the bar where I buy her a drink.

Djenne, the largest mud-mosque in the world. Every year 10,000 pilgrims re-plaster it after the rains. The wooden spines sticking out are to put planks on when re-plastering.

I am surprised to discover that she has been in the country under a week, and this is her first time in Mali. Tonight she will escort her charges to a concert being held on the bank of the Bani River, with a band which recently was meant to play in the Albert Hall, but failed to get there. Two members of the Explore group joined specifically to see tonight's concert. The poor girl has a stinking cold and is finding it quite a strain because it is the first time she has met any of the guides or been to any of the places. Bocary comes over and inserts himself between us. Do I want to go to the concert? I decline but say of course he can go, but he must remember we have a 6am start to go round the big market.

Next morning I go in search of Bocary - it is five to six, and time we were moving. I find him snoring on a camp bed on the hotel roof. I lift his mosquito net and try to rouse him, but he just grunts. He stinks of beer. Not wanting to miss the start of the market, I set off without him.

In the mosque square the first stallholders are digging holes to plant the supports for their shelters, while buses and pick-ups arrive full of goods and people. On the water, pinnaces, weighed down with passengers, sacks of grain and other produce including sheep, glide to the landing stages. On the far side of the water, horse and bullock carts arrive, many carrying sheep and goats as well as people. Women in bright dresses with their babies strapped to their backs walk over the causeway balancing huge bundles on their heads.

I ask about the horse market? There isn't one! How could bloody Bocary have got it so wrong? I begin to doubt if he really does know where the Dogon horsemen are. At least I know, through Sophie, there are horses there – I just need to find them.

Back at breakfast I meet Jane who is gathering her flock for a walk round the market. She looks completely done in. Last night's concert had to be moved because the original site had no electricity. It was meant to start at 8.30pm, but didn't get going until 10.30. By which time her clients were not feeling very jolly. Also, only half the band turned up. To make the night a complete disaster for her, she discovered a hairy caterpillar wriggling its way up her arm, leaving a trail of nasty blisters.

Today, after looking round the market, her tour will embark in motorised pinnaces for the two-day journey north to Mopti, before going on to Timbuktu. I wish her luck, as several of her charges are very overweight.

Bocary is still asleep.

I don't need him, so I leave him.

Back in the square more latecomers try to find a space to pitch their stalls, while the earlier arrivals are doing a brisk trade. In the food area, besides spices and grains, there are piles of dried or smoked fish. The butchers not only sell meat, but cook it on corrugated iron on top of mud-brick ovens. The ovens have one large log which sticks out at the bottom and is periodically pushed in as it burns. When they have finished cooking, the log is pulled out and the burning end extinguished.

The only livestock trading is in sheep and goats. The horses and cattle appear to be all draught animals and are tethered to or near their carts. The horses are mainly Barb crosses and in good condition. They are washed off in the river as soon as they arrive, then tied up with a bucket of water and some hay.

Bocary is full of indignation when he finds me eating lunch. Why did I go without him? Why didn't I wake him? Do I know how it looks for a guide to be left and his client go off on his own?

I say he shouldn't have drunk so much.

He sits down opposite me and his phone rings. He talks on it while I eat; when I ask what he has lined up for me this afternoon, the other phone goes. I finish my meal while he continues talking.

'What time is the bus tomorrow?' I ask getting up from the table.

He points to his phone. I walk away and am going out of the entrance when he grabs my shoulder.

'Where are you going?'

'For a walk.'

'I will come with you,' he gives an ingratiating grin. 'But first I must have something to eat.'

'The bus, what time tomorrow morning?'

'Six thirty.'

'Where does it go from?' He points across the road. 'Tell the hotel I want breakfast at six.'

'You give me the rest of the money, now.'

'When we arrive in Dogon country.'

'No, now!'

I turn and walk towards the market.

'I will come with you,' he wheedles.

'Don't be late in the morning!' I tell him and walk away.

I arrive at the Djenne Djenno Hotel after the heat of the day has gone. I have a cup of tea with Sophie, who is feeling better, and then we go to mount up, but neither horse is saddled. The barman was meant to tell the groom, but he never quite got round to it. Sophie explains that if someone is told to do something they feel it isn't part of their job, they won't do it. Yesterday evening she was so poorly she went to bed before the guests arrived. Her manager failed to check the rooms, so a blown light bulb wasn't replaced, towels hadn't been put out and a waste-paper basket hadn't been emptied. Little things, but important if you want to run a good hotel.

Hydra arrives while we are saddling up. He is in full festival clothes and tack. He is wearing a voluminous gold boubou which covers him and most of the horse. He says this used to be worn into battle. The flowing robe protects the wearer because the loose material absorbs sword cuts and spear thrusts. The metal on the horse's bridle stops it being cut and protects the nose and cheeks. The large padded breastplate stops cuts and the spearing of the horse's chest. The drapes down either side protect the flanks. Also the high cantle and pommel

Hydra in his best riding dress.

255

guard the rider's lower abdomen. There is also a second rein in case the first is cut. It is a display of colourful practicality.

Once I have photographed him, he moves away to show me some of the moves he has taught his young horse. He does some static turns, canters away, then back towards me and, after some patient coaxing, it prances as if it is dancing to music. However when he tries to get it to stand on its hind legs, it only picks its front hooves about a foot off the ground.

'He says he will show you on Napoleon,' Sophie tells me.

I remember she bought him off Hydra, and told me how the first time she rode him he stood straight up when she squeezed with her legs to get him to go forwards.

Hydra rides Napoleon up and down the track to warm him up, then says to watch how it is done. But either he is pressing the wrong buttons, or Napoleon has forgotten his training, because the most he does is a brief half-rear. As the twilight darkens it is clear the horse will not do his party trick.

Hydra's bridle. It is all military: protective metal plate headpiece, two sets of reins, large breastplate, a lot of loose clothing to absorb any spear or sword thrusts.

Eventually Hydra gives up and remounts his own horse. I ask how he trains his horses, but he tells Sophie he can't stop to explain because he doesn't want to ride home in the dark. I thank him for making so much time for me, but it is clear that he feels he has performed badly and canters off along the track into the gathering gloom.

Sophie offers me a drink and we sit on the roof watching the sky redden, briefly outlining the spiky minarets, before the curtain of the encroaching night blackens all about us. We chat softly as the hotel staff go about their final preparations for the guests. We are both a long way from home, yet each is fulfilling their own dream. She has ideas for helping the local women earn money from weaving cloth and making clothes, also of finding a scholar to copy the ancient manuscripts from the library in the mosque. She is just telling me about her last visit to see her mother in Sweden and staying with friends in London, when three four-by-fours drive in through the archway.

It is time for her to welcome everyone, and me to go back to my not so tangible quest; but for just a few minutes, in the gathering darkness with the gentle breeze rising off the river it was fantastic to bond with someone who is also fulfilling their dream.

Cavaliers de Bankass

We get out to push the car through the soft sand. As soon as we are on harder ground, I jump in the front, and the locals who helped us climb in the back with Bocary. We agreed to give them a lift to Teli, the village where we will be staying, for helping us. The track meanders along the bottom of the Falaise de Bandigara, the high escarpment that runs northeast for 200kms across southern Mali. On either side are fields of recently cut millet. Twice we have to edge past donkey-carts piled high with the cobs on their way to the granary huts.

We turn up a road barely wide enough for the car, and stop beside some large wooden doors in a high mud-plastered wall. Inside there is a large courtyard with an open-sided shelter thatched with millet stalk. Round the edge are cell-like rooms built into the outside wall. The loo is a 'long-drop' in one of the rooms, and the shower – water is carried to a plastic tank on a roof – is in a small walled area with a concrete floor. The trouble is there is no lock, and the staff walk in to pee in the hole in the corner while I am showering.

When I clamber down from making my bed on a flat roof – so much cooler than indoors – Bocary introduces me to his half-brother, Sussenni, who speaks some English. He explains that the reason so many people are related is because there is a lot of divorce and remarriage. He and Bocary have the same father. Susseni's mother has remarried someone in Bandigara, while Bocary's mother now lives with her new husband in Burkina Faso.

Bocary suggests we eat our evening meal before it gets dark, because insects are attracted to the lanterns. As darkness falls the noise from the village subsides. Sussenni and I talk quietly, while Bocary goes in search of beer.

At nine o'clock I retire to the roof. Only the occasional bark of a dog and whine of a mosquito breaks the warm silence. Most of the village is in darkness, but the occasional lantern-light shines out of the odd window. Insects flicker round my torch which I leave on outside my mosquito net. Once I am comfortable I switch it off. The night is black except for the myriad of stars I can see above me through the fine netting.

I am woken by the bright, rising half-moon. A cockerel crows. A dog barks and others join in as the moon clears the escarpment. A donkey brays soulfully, and others answer. Woken children wail and the whole cacophony echoes off the cliff. As the noise abates I realise I need a pee. I go over to the parapet, as instructed earlier. Everywhere is silent, except for my urine splashing onto a leafy bush in the garden below.

It is cooler now, I am glad of my sleeping bag. A few hours later dawn comes with a rush. There is a brief lightening of the sky, before a large red ball appears round the corner of the cliffs. It changes to gold as it climbs higher, dispelling the remaining cool of the night.

Bocary is nowhere to be seen. After breakfast of fried millet cakes with jam, Sussenni, who appears to have taken over from Bocary, leads me up to the old village, built into the face of the cliff underneath the overhang. It is worth being out of breath for the fantastic view. The modern village is huddled below us. Beyond it the trees grow sparser

One of the Cavaliers de Bankass, the only person willing to perform again so that I can video him.

until they die out at the base of a sandy ridge. Either side of us are high cliffs with shrubs and grass growing in the crevices. The mud houses of the ancient village are no longer occupied, but grain is still stored in the granaries.

Sussenni tells me that the Tellem (red-skinned pygmies) lived first in the caves and then in the cliff-village, until the Dogon drove them out. However many of their beliefs were taken up by the invaders, so that today there are as many animists as Muslims or Christians.

Most of the doors have crocodiles and tortoises carved on them. Crocodiles are sacred because they led the Dogon people to water during the 'Great Drought' (rather like the 'Flood' in the Bible), and tortoises because they will not eat poisonous food. The hogons (witch doctors) often use them as food tasters, eating only what the tortoise has nibbled at. Sussenni shows me some monkey heads nailed to a wall, saying people used to eat them and they have been there for hundreds of years.

It reminds me of visiting a temple in Aswan. The guide said a shallow pool with steps was where the priests fed the baby crocodiles. When he was on his own I commented that it looked just like an Orthodox Christian baptismal pool.

'It is,' he said, 'but the tourists prefer the story about the crocodiles.'

On the way back Sussenni stops to talk to some village elders who are lounging in the shade of a toguna, a men's talking house about four feet high. He asks them about horses. The old men say the culture of dancing horses has died out, as has much of the horse racing. The young aren't interested in horses – motorbikes need less looking after and are quicker.

'Do you know about togunas?' Sussenni asks, as we walk down the street.

'Tell me.'

'They are where the men of the village hold their meetings. They are low so that everything must be discussed sitting, this stops people getting violent during an argument. If a man gets angry and stands up he will bang his head,' he pauses as we turn down a narrow side street. 'It is for men only. If a woman enters it has to be burnt down and rebuilt. Every year, at a special ceremony, more millet stalks are added to the thatch. After ten or more years it is rebuilt.'

He opens a door off the street, announcing, 'My brother has a horse.'

Balancing – part of a dancing competition.

There is a 14 hands high bay in the courtyard. Its off-hind leg is tied to a stake and another rope runs from the near-fore to the near-hind.

'That is so it learns to move those two legs at the same time.'

'Why?'

'I don't know, and my brother is away.'

'When will he be back?'

Sussenni disappears through an open doorway. The horse, a Barb, takes no notice as I walk round it. There are some sliced millet cobs in the hollowed-out wooden manger but it is more interested in a small pile of dried grasses.

'He is away for a few days.'

'What about other people with horses?'

'They are harvesting; you've come at a bad time. Tomorrow Bocary will take you to Ende to meet some horsemen.'

***

Before we set out for Ende I give Bocary the rest of the money. Despite the talk about local horsemen and a Frenchman called Thierry from Burkina Faso, who brings riding tours here, there are no actual horsemen or horses. I spend part of the day watching an artist painting scenes on T-shirts, which he sells to the walking tours passing through. Tomorrow, I am assured, we will visit a farmer who breeds horses.

Once we are a couple of kilometres into our walk back, Bocary stops.

'Cadeau!' he demands turning to face me.

'What? I've just paid you.'

'Cadeau!' he says again.

I glance round. The harvesters in the fields have all gone home. The path is deserted.

'How much?' I ask as casually as I can, putting my hand in my pocket for my cosh – a bunch of coins tied in the end of my handkerchief.

'Grand cadeau!' he gloats. '100 English pounds.'

I am aghast. The bloody effrontery of the man.

'For what? You were a bloody awful guide.'

'I am good guide,' he glares at me angrily. 'Cadeau, now.'

'Fuck off!'

I slowly start to ease my handkerchief out of my pocket. We lock eyes. Suddenly the thought goes through my mind we are like two gunfighters in a film. I almost giggle. Then the faint noise of voices comes from beyond the corner a hundred yards away.

Bocary suddenly smiles and slaps me on the shoulder as some locals appear with a donkey and cart. He sets off at a brisk pace, and when I ask him to slow down, breaks into a jog and before long disappears.

On my way back I plan what I am going to say to him, but when I get there, Sussenni tells me he has gone off on a motorbike. What about tomorrow? I am pleased to hear Sussenni has already been asked to do it. He is far more helpful and understanding than Bocary. We will leave early because the farm we are visiting is over ten kilometres away.

As it turns out, the only horses we see are a surprisingly youthful 27-year-old and a young unbroken mare, the rest are away with the men in the fields. On the walk I mention the 'cadeau' incident, and Sussenni is shocked. He doubts I will hear from Bocary again. He laughs when I mention the two phones. Apparently Bocary keeps ringing himself to appear in demand.

With no more horses to see in the area around Teli, Sussenni organises for a horse and cart to take us to Bankass, the local town about 15 kilometres away. Luckily it is cloudy with a breeze, because we have to get off and push whenever we hit soft sand. At least I am not carrying my backpack.

Late morning we get to the Hotel des Arbres, a modern-looking hotel set amongst tall trees. We shout, but nobody comes, so we have a look round. In the first bedroom there is sand on the floor, a bed-frame with no mattress, a table with a missing leg and the light switch hanging on bare wires. The second room has a heavily stained mattress and...

'Where else?' I ask.

'There is a new hotel the other end of the town, my uncle is the guide there.'

'We'll try it.'

It is a concrete block two-storey construction, clean and comfortable, with electricity from the town's generator, so I get a fan and a light from six till eleven every evening – luxury. Issa, Sussenni's uncle, arrives as I sign in. He says most of the horses are out in the villages to the south, so will arrange a vehicle for tomorrow morning.

***

Whenever I get out of the four-wheel drive in a village, children circle me shouting 'le blanc, le blanc'. It always follows the same pattern. A brave one will tentatively hold my hand, then they all want to. Issa explains they have never seen a white man, and probably neither have their parents. He says it is quite possible no Westerner has been here since independence in 1960.

In one village an old man insists we have lunch. He holds up a scrawny chicken which he kills and plucks in front of us, before giving it to his wife to cook. While it is being cooked he takes us round the village. In the centre there is an open area with a toguna, a big mosque with lots of beams sticking out of the walls and a large pool surrounded by trees.

'It is a crocodile pool,' Issa says. 'Although most of the people here are Muslim, if they have a problem they go to the hogon, who will get them to sacrifice to the crocodiles.'

Part of a dancing competition. The rider must make his horse lie down with him on top.

'Isn't it dangerous to have crocodiles in the centre of the village?' I ask, watching some children playing in the shallows.

Issa asks the old man.

'Two years ago a goat kid was taken, but there are so many sacrifices that they are never hungry,' Issa translates for me. 'If a person is ill or can't have a baby, they will go to the hogon. He will tell them to make a sacrifice – normally a white chicken – and the only person to breed these is the hogon. If the person gets what they want, the hogon tells them to sacrifice a sheep or goat. It has gone on for hundreds of years.'

On the way back to lunch we meet a man who has ridden half a day to come to a funeral. He says he prefers to travel by horse; motorbikes break down, but you can still ride a lame horse. Also fuel is expensive and it is difficult to get it in the district where he lives.

Each day we try a new area, stopping in villages to ask the way; often pushing along overgrown tracks, the branches squeaking as they scratch the sides. One day we give a lift to a teacher and her daughter who have been waiting five days for transport to a new job near Bankass.

We see a lot of villages, any number of harvested millet fields, and huge herds of cattle being looked after by Fulani, but only a few horses.

One place we stop, we see a lovely 13.2 hands high stallion, ridden bareback by a barefoot boy in shorts and a holey T-shirt. Another place a man keeps hitting his horse trying to make the confused animal dance. I ask Issa to take the stick away and am bundled into the vehicle when the rider jumps off and threatens to hit me. In the fields there are several hobbled horses, but the owners are harvesting and too busy to talk.

Back in Bankass I again ask Issa if he is sure there is not some sort of horse organisation in the area.

'L'Association des Cavaliers de Bankass,' he says, pleased with himself for remembering.

'But we have just spent three days driving...' I let it go. 'Is there any chance of meeting them and seeing them riding?'

'I will ask,' he says and departs.

After an hour of haggling it is all arranged.

The next morning, having supplied breakfast for about a dozen riders and their horses, we go to the local football pitch. The horsemen in their flowing robes circle round me on their beautifully decorated horses. A man on the side-line starts drumming and a couple of horses

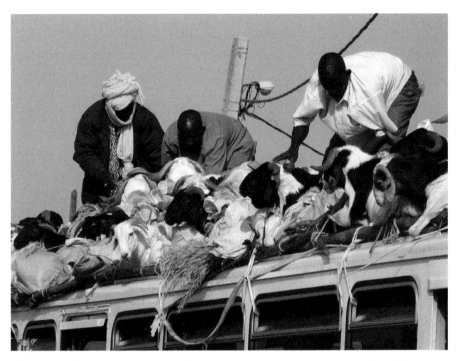

Sheep on the bus luggage rack for the long journey to Bamako. The back-ends are all put in plastic bags so that the muck is contained and does not run down the sides of the bus.

are encouraged to prance in time to the beat. A young rider carrying his own drum tries to get his horse to dance, but is too encumbered, and the horse takes off across the pitch.

Suddenly the drumbeat quickens as a rider forces his horse to its knees, and then it lies down with him still in the saddle. Several women spectators do a type of yodel while others cheer. After a couple of minutes the horseman pulls on the reins and the horse gets up again. Another man gets his horse to stand balanced on its hind legs, neither animal nor rider moving for over ten seconds.

'This is all part of military training,' Issa tells me. 'Lying down is one of the most important moves. When scouting, a soldier gets his horse to lie down, so that he isn't seen by the enemy. When ambushed a man shelters behind the body of his horse. The other movements are either to help the rider to use his spear or sword, or protect the horse.'

A turbaned rider with thick glasses and a piece of straw sticking out of his mouth gently encourages his horse to go down. As it lies

Playing tag. Note the briefcase attached to the saddle.

down he goes forward to sit on its neck to keep it pinned down. I notice blood trickling from its open mouth: the ferocious Arab bit must have snagged it. I am intrigued at how they get the horses to take the Arab bits so easily, when in the UK some horses won't even take a snaffle without a fight. The rider moves back onto the saddle and sits quietly, holding onto the high pommel as his mount gets up. More riders try to get their horses to stand on their hind legs, but are too rough or unbalanced, and all they manage are half-rears. One horseman has his laptop case strapped to his saddle.

The tempo of the drum changes and a pipe joins in as the horsemen go to the far end of the pitch, and split into pairs. They come galloping back, two at a time, sometimes holding onto each other, sometimes racing, but always stopping in a flurry of dust, their horses' nostrils flared and their open mouths dripping blood.

Issa says this is to show off their control. When they have finished the first horseman asks if I would like to see his horse lie down again.

'Certainly, please.'

He shortens his reins, takes his right foot out of the stirrup and applies his spurred heel in front of the shoulder. Twice the horse bends its knees, fights him and staggers up. The third time it sinks to the ground. All the time I am videoing with my left hand and photographing with my right, something I have now got used to. I thank him profusely, as he gets the horse to rise. It takes its time, then treads on itself and pulls a muscle, so that when it follows the others it is lame. I feel guilty. This is the first time in all my travels that someone has willingly repeated a move for me.

Outside the football ground the riders disperse, mingling with the people coming into the market. There are camel carts as well as horse. The big pads of the camels hardly stir the dust, while the smaller hooves of the horses churn the sand to powder. Like Djenne, the horses are washed off at the well area before being tied to their carts and given some hay. I ask about a horse market, but they don't have one.

By mid-morning, women with babies strapped to their backs, Fulani in their conical hats and flowing robes, and men in western clothes all jostle in the market street. They pick through the brightly dyed cotton clothes, check the piles of 'flied' rice – sometimes there seem to be more flies than grains of rice.

 Issa and I stop beside the stall of an ancient hogon with an age-creased face wearing a monkey-skin hat. He sells cures for everything from infertility to headaches. There are unrecognisable dried parts of animals, roots, herbs and several monkey skins. Issa says for a price a curse or love charm can be purchased, or a curse lifted. The skins attract a myriad of flies, which the hogon keeps airborne with a horse-tail fly switch.

At lunchtime I organise my onward journey, I've only two days left on my visa. Then we go back to the market. On the main road a line of minibuses are piling their roofs with all manner of goods. Sheep with their back-ends wrapped in plastic bags are passed up to men on the roof of the big bus going to Bamako. They are tied to the roof-rack for the 18 hour journey. Issa says the wrapping stops the faeces and urine running down the side of the bus.

Issa drops me off in Koro to catch the minibus to Burkina Faso. The previous one left twenty minutes ago.

The next one will go when it is full.

I buy a ticket and organise for the bus-boy to call me when it is ready to go, then I relax in the shade at an unkempt modern hotel.

By teatime there still are only four passengers, so it looks as if I will have to stay the night. I ask to see the rooms. They are hot, dark, stink of unwashed bodies and have filthy bedding. A girl in a short skirt and thin blouse asks if I am interested in going to a room with her. I decline and enquire if there is another hotel. She says there is, but it is a series of mud huts.

I collect my backpack and make my way there.

'Are you going to Burkina Faso?' asks the owner.

'Yes.'

'There is a French lady leaving tomorrow morning looking for someone to share fuel costs.'

Fantastic!

CHAPTER ELEVEN

Burkina Faso: Bobo Dioulasso

'It's still there!' says Michelle, the middle-aged French lady as we pass the minibus. 'Eight passengers.'

'Another eight to go.'

'It won't be leaving before mid-day.'

I agree with her. I'm so glad I'm in her jeep. She knows this route well, because she comes four or five times a year to check on the school she founded in a village near the Falaise de Bandigara. She goes regularly to help improve conditions and to find out if the children are attending. It is a constant battle because some of the parents prefer their children to beg from the tourists rather than go to school. Michelle has also installed a well and written a book, 'Une École au Mali'.

The border police know her and her driver, so the passport formalities don't take long. But, because she trades in Malian jewellery, customs make us hang on for over an hour. While we are waiting a donkey cart with a whole family and three goats comes trotting past. As it disappears down the road, armed police charge out of their barracks. Two squad cars and two motorbikes with pillions roar away, sirens blaring. Ten minutes later they are back, a grinning pillion carries a goat across his lap.

'Their lunch,' Michelle explains disgustedly.

That evening in Ouahigouya she takes me to supper with a plump Swiss financier who spends six months here every year, helping set up projects. Another guest is athletic-looking Philippe, who runs a quad-bike safari business. He knows Thiery whom I heard about in Ende. He runs Cheval Mandique, a riding school in the capital Ougadougou and is keen to do riding tours. Philippe suggests visiting the Oasis du Cheval, also in the capital, about which he has heard good reports. However there is nothing horsey round here.

On our way to Ouagadougou (the capital) we run over a three foot crocodile scuttling across the road to another pond. For a short distance after the collision the driver has a job keeping the four-by-four on the road, he is upset because crocodiles are sacred here as well, so he mumbles something to protect him from being cursed, and keeps going.

I am dropped off at the Hotel Belle Vue, a solid square commercial travellers hotel set amongst the jumbled architecture of Avenue Nkrumah. The old part of the city was flattened some years ago, to make way for new buildings sporting everything from porthole windows to plate glass, high-rise to single storey, and painted all the colours of the rainbow. It is a place of donkey carts, the latest four-by-fours and thousands of Chinese motorbikes puffing out black exhaust smoke.

Cheval Mandique is not what I expected. It looks as if a tornado has hit it. Several stables have lost their roofs and others have been flattened by a fallen tree. Thiery, slim and well-weathered with a ponytail of greying hair, is teaching a girl in a manège, which has several broken rails round it. I look at the horses; some are in good condition but others are too thin. At the end of the lesson the girl hands the reins and riding hat to a groom, and jumps onto the back of a motorbike.

'I would never do that,' Thiery says coming over to me, 'let one of my children go pillion, even if I was driving. There are too many accidents.'

He gets me a Coke from the dilapidated clubhouse and says they have had an extra-long rainy season – not good for him or the horses.

He expresses regret for the state of some of the older horses. He says once a horse loses weight here it is hard to put it on again, because of the heat and the lack of good forage.

'Where do they come from?' I ask, pointing to three fine dark brown horses which stand out from the others.

'Niger. Like my wife,' he laughs. 'It has the best women and the best horses.'

He confirms what I was told in Mali about the battle purposes of the tack. The style of riding was much influenced by the Moors, who introduced Islam and some of the architecture seen on old buildings. He is interested in doing riding tours, but privately I think British customers would be greatly perturbed at the state some of the horses. He suggests I go to Bobo Dioulasso, some 250 kilometres away, and see Yakouba, a great horseman and one of the country's top stuntmen.

A village mosque with a taguna, a male meeting house. The roof is low so that no one can get angry and stand up during a debate. It is rethatched with an extra layer of millet straw every year. If a woman enters it, it is burnt down and a new one built.

***

Lucien, my guide in Bobo Dioulasso, takes me to Yakouba's scrapyard in our attempt to meet up with him. One end is piled with rusting lorries, smashed cars and bits of metal, the other is his poultry farm. Besides chickens, he has geese, guineafowl, which are considered a great delicacy, and some pet tortoises. It seems to be an unfathomable jumble of chicken netting pens, but the boy showing us round knows what feed is needed. He says Yakouba is at home, but busy, and suggests we go to see what, in his and Yakouba's opinion, is one of the best horses in Bobo.

We enter a courtyard, and there under a tree is a fine-looking grey lying stretched out on its side. As we shake hands with the owner, the horse's hooves scrape the torn ground as another colic spasm takes hold. The owner apologises for the sight, but says it will be dead soon. We sit and have tea within yards of the poor animal. It's clear it has been there some time; flies feast on its lolling tongue and on the urine soaked dust. I feel useless, but the owner says it is the will of Allah.

When we leave we catch Yakouba on his way out to a meeting. He

Mare and foal in a freshly cut millet field.

is sad to hear about the grey; he rode it a lot for the owner and it was a good dancer. He says he will meet us tomorrow morning at my hotel.

Lucien suggests that, as a farmer, I would be interested in visiting an experimental farm.

There is a smart drive between fir trees, ending at a small uncared-for house. We get out and walk round. The machinery is modern, as is the Massey Ferguson tractor with flat tyres. A tree is growing out of the bed of the forage wagon, the seed drill, half-hidden by long grass and the rusty mower wouldn't look out of place at Yakouba's scrapyard. It is not just the tractor, nearly every tyre is flat. The huge empty cattle barn is big enough for 150 animals. One of the two men left to look after the farm shows us to an enormous piggery. Parts of the roof are missing. In one pen there is a sow and two young pigs. All three have sores on their bodies and one piglet has a badly infected back leg. The farm worker says he has been waiting over a week for the person who bought them to pick them up. When he waters them, they slurp it straight away, but it runs out of a hole in the bottom of the trough faster than they can drink. I get Lucien to make the man get another bucketful.

Out in the unkempt fields there is a waterbutt with US AID written on the side, and near it, solar panels completely shaded by bushes. The other worker is cutting millet by hand.

'What has happened?' I ask Lucien.

'The authorities lost interest, and there was nobody able to mend the machinery.'

The man with us says something.

'He says the aid money has stopped.'

What a waste!

***

Yakouba insists we have tea before he shows me his favourite horse. He tells me he has loved horses all his life and, because Burkina Faso is a centre of films in this part of Africa, he takes part in a lot of films. His favourite horse is over 20 years old and he has had it since it was three. The horse whinnies as soon as it sees him. He opens the stable door, slips on a bridle, then vaults on as it goes past him. He rides it round the garden a couple of times to stretch its legs. The horse is a Barb, no more than 14 hands.

'Now watch,' he says as I desperately grab my video and camera from my daysack.

He squeezes with his legs and the old horse rears up. Instead of holding on to the mane, Yakouba leans forward sliding his hands along either side of the neck, leaving the rein slack. He does this several times, then moves his feet back to the horse's stifle, getting it to buck. By shifting his legs he gets it to see-saw, bucking and rearing alternately. After this he slides off and stands in front of the horse. He says something and the horse half rears and places his hoof in Yakouba's outstretched hand.

'Shaking hands,' says Yakouba with a grin.

He then walks alongside the horse, bends down, puts his head and shoulders underneath its stifle and lifts its quarters. Yakouba sidesteps and the horse takes a couple of steps forward. Finally Yakouba walks in front, turns his back and shouts. The horse rears up. Yakouba gets between its forelegs, taking the weight on his shoulders. Together they walk towards the stable. It is one of the most thrilling displays of complete trust and balance I have ever seen. He takes the bridle off and gives the old horse the run of the garden while we have more tea.

Later Yakouba says he will take us to Brasso. At first I think we are going to a village, but Brasso is the mayor. When we arrive Yakouba bends down and touches Brasso's foot with his hand. Brasso is a big man with a booming voice. A well-known singer, he has sung in Europe and America as well as being involved in films here.

He is putting henna on the mane and tail of a pale grey horse in an attempt to ward off alopecia. Greys here start to lose their hair when they are five or six, first on their noses and then on the rest of them. Without the protection of their coat they get sunburn and often have to be shot. He says henna will help, though he can't say how.

Brasso invites us in for tea. As is the custom in this part of West Africa, each of his four wives has her own hut, while he has a larger one with several rooms. Each wife has a cooking fire by her hut. The wives range from ancient to his latest, who is sixteen.

For me it is a relaxing time because Brasso's French is easier to understand than Lucien's lisping and Yakouba's more African accent. He tells me local horse dancing has died out, and there are no other horse games.

'They still have hundreds of horses at the festival in Barani,' says Yakouba.

Yakouba walking his horse into its stable.

'But it is in February,' says Brasso. 'So you will have to come back next year.'

The next day Lucien insists on taking me to the spectacular waterfalls at Banfora and then going hippo spotting on the nearby lake, without success. Sitting in a small boat gently paddled by an old boatman is a wonderful interlude before returning to the bustle of Ouagadougou.

Gorum Gorum

Back in Ouagadougou I go to the 'Oasis du Cheval'. Moyenga, a tall slim French-speaking African who runs the riding club, shows me round. The stables are all heavily thatched to keep them cool. They have solid wall partitions and proper stable doors, rather than the railed

A chain noseband rather than a bit.

pens with slip-rail entrances at Thiery's, which Moyenga describes as 'fatigué'. Some horses are in the stables, while others are tied to trees. Their coats gleam and everything looks in good shape.

Over a drink in the immaculate clubhouse he is telling me about the festival at Barani, when his French wife insists I look at the photographs of it on their computer. Instead of the hundreds of horses I was told about, there are only twenty to thirty. They explain that ten years ago there were many more horses, but each year there have been fewer young men willing to learn the ancient riding skills. It is still an exciting two days of horse-dancing competitions and racing. Horsemen from Mali and Burkina Faso take part. He and his wife go by jeep with people from the club. However, it would take too long to ride there and back.

I ask about training the horses to dance, but he only knows they do it very patiently using ropes. Each village has, or had, a slightly different way of doing things and the elders will only pass on the knowledge to their young men. He has never found anyone who will tell him. Many of the more intelligent young men aren't interested. They go away to school and university and don't want to return to the restrictions of village life. Few of those who remain want to train horses or learn how to make and mend tack.

Over lunch he tells me about his horses. The larger, finer horses come from Niger, while the thicker-set ones are from Benin and Togo. Also he has one from northern Ghana, from where the Mossi tribe originally came. He says the Mossi go for the 'cinq points', four white legs and a blaze, while the Fulani go for the best horse they can afford rather than its looks.

While local people, over the last couple of decades, have got bigger through a better diet, here and in Mali the horses have got smaller. This is because much of the grazing land has been taken over for cultivation, leaving less for the mares and foals. He suggests I visit the market at Gorum Gorum in the north east. It is a camel area, but there are still some horses. He gives me the telephone number of a horse breeder.

He tells me the man is away a lot, but interesting to meet – a horseman among camel men.

The bus goes as far as Dori, from where it is bush taxi. I am lucky, there are four places left on the open-backed lorry to Gorum Gorum. The luggage is piled in the centre, with bicycles and a small motorbike on top. The twenty passengers have to sit, stand, or squat where they can. The metal supports for a tarpaulin would give some form of stability, if they weren't too hot to touch. After the first half-mile I take off my hat and wrap it round a support. Better to have a burnt head than badly bruised ribs. The children sitting on the luggage bounce with every bump, while their parents cling on with one hand steadying them with the other.

There is a bang. The lorry swerves erratically as the driver jams on the brakes. All of us in the back are thrown together.

Everyone gets off to look at the blow-out. Six inches of the tyre wall has split. The luggage is unloaded to get to the spare tyre. Several passengers relieve themselves, women on one side of the road, men on the other. Some take off their winter coats – it was 34 degrees in the shade in Dori, and there is no shade here.

The driver and his mate wedge the wheels with rocks before using the jack. It won't lift high enough, so they make a pile of stones, put the jack on top and try again. The new (completely bald) tyre is put on and we are off. Within a minute there is a clanking from the wheel and we stop again. Two wheelnuts have come off and the remainder are loose.

A box of at least fifty nuts is pulled from under the driver's seat, and there follows the long process of finding some that fit. The thread seems irrelevant, if the driver's mate can force it tight, it will do.

While we are waiting I ask if anyone knows the 'Encampement Rissa' in Gorum Gorum, where I'll be staying. Someone suggests there is one on the road to Niger. I check my Lonely Planet guide and ask the driver, who is watching his sweating mate replace the last nut.

'I will stop,' he says. 'Vite, vite, we are going'.

The light is beginning to fade as he pulls up in what appears to be the middle of nowhere. I am helped off, while my bags are thrown at my feet and the lorry departs in a cloud of dust. I look round. There are several distant huts. The nearest two have a tumbled-down pole shed with a rotting palm roof next to them. The long table, on which some of the support poles are leaning suggests it could once have been a communal eating place. I go over to two young men sitting by one of the huts.

'Encampement Rissa?'

'Oui, ici.' The young man points to the two huts. 'You can stay there,' he points to the larger hut, or there,' he indicates a bed in the open.

Apparently there used to be several huts, but the rains were so heavy that they all collapsed. Earth mounds show where they had been. The piles of mud-bricks stacked the far side of the site are for new huts. One man goes off on a bicycle to get two buckets of water while the other starts a fire for supper. By the time the goat stew and couscous is ready, I have had a "shower" (a small jug dipped in a bucket to pour over yourself), and erected the mosquito net on the outside bed.

Once the sun goes down the night air cools quickly. The two men hurriedly swill the cooking pots, hand me a lantern and depart. I suddenly feel very vulnerable in the middle of nowhere just off the main road with no night guard. I bring my backpack and camera bag inside the mosquito net, before watching the moon rise.

At dawn I am woken by a flock of sheep coming through the camp. The shepherd beats the branches of an acacia tree with a long stick and his sheep scour the ground for the pods and fallen seeds. I get up once he has moved on. I am shaved and packed by the time breakfast arrives – tea, three slices of bread and a token dot of honey.

I ask about somewhere else to stay and am told there is nowhere. However, when I walk into town, there is a concrete block hotel. I

Horse and cart carrying people and sheep to market.

return for my backpack and after some bitter haggling (I refuse to pay Ougadougou rates), I stroll to my new base, where everyone is most helpful.

The horse breeder lives 25 kilometres away and the only way I can get there is pillion on a motorbike taxi or by camel. I try telephoning the breeder's mobile, but can't get through, and keep trying throughout the day. Tomorrow I will go, even if I can't contact him.

Lasso, my motorcycle driver, is about 16 and is driving for his brother who has taken someone to Dori. Despite my complaints he drives as if he was on a speedway, and my nerves are slowly shredded. He tries to keep on the hard edge of the track, but goes too fast into the corners. Twice we end up stalling in the soft sand in the centre. I ask him to slow but he goes even faster so that he can drive through the soft sand and keep going to the hard on the other side. The fourth time we skid through the sand and leap into a field of cut millet, I lose my nerve and make him stop.

I ring the horse breeder and get his son. We have difficulty understanding each other, but eventually I establish that his father is in Ouahigouya, en route to the capital. With more than a little relief I tell Lasso we are returning to Gorum Gorum.

On the way back he drives much slower and I get a chance to look at the countryside rather than cling on tightly, staring straight ahead. It is poorer than anywhere I have yet been. The grain stores are made of matting, rather than thatched mud-brick huts; thin cattle pick at shrivelled patchy uncut millet, while goats browse leafless bushes. Everywhere dust swirls in even the slightest breeze. I get him to stop at a small market. Each stall is under an acacia tree. Some have a few clothes, but most are selling millet, donkey and camel equipment, or kitchen utensils.

Market day in Gorum Gorum is the only one with a direct bus to Ouagadougou, and it leaves around midday. Daweed, Lasso's brother, collects me to go to the animal market. No horses needless to say, but there are some impressive Niger cattle standing about five feet at the shoulder with four foot long horns. I am so busy trying to get photographs that Daweed has to drag me out of the way of a frightened cow, which nearly mows me down.

There are no livestock pens. The farmers keep their stock, which are used to being herded, in tight groups. The buyers move among the stock marking the ones they want with paint. There is no auction; bargains are sealed with a slap of the hand and the money is paid straight away.

I am intrigued to see the sheep's ears are notched the same way that farmers do on the Welsh hills.

On the way back into town I watch a boy fill water buckets from a pond where cattle have stirred the water to a grey soup. Two camel herders lean against the sides of their reclining mounts waiting for tourists, of whom there seem to be none. Under a single acacia a family with a donkey cart set out their few wares.

The new market in the centre of town is crowded with shoppers. There are women in brightly coloured dresses, men in trousers and others in boubous, some with turbans, and Fulani in their conical hats. On the side of the main street there are bales of 'jumble' – western scarves, sweaters, shirts, jackets and winter coats – being sorted and sold. Articulated lorries are parked alongside donkey carts. Tyres and engine parts are sold alongside cart shafts and bridles, but again there

All these people squeezed onto the bus from Gorom Gorom to Ouagodougou in which I was travelling – well over one hundred of us, some sitting, some standing.

are no horses. Walking back, Daweed points to some goats scavenging next to a television dish on the millet-thatched roof of a house.

The bus to Ougadougou is already full when I get there, but the old man who sold me my ticket pushes through the throng and pulls someone out of my seat. Everyone, except me and the smartly dressed lady next to me, whom I discover is the bus compound owner's wife, is ordered off. All those with seating tickets are then allowed on, followed by those with standing tickets – well over a hundred of us in all. Luggage, including two motorcycles, sacks of grain and a spare tyre are hauled onto the roof with ropes. The bus has extra home-made roof props all the way down the central aisle. Outside, the sun blazes down. Inside, we sweat for a further half hour before the bus moves off.

To start with the speed is so slow the air hardly circulates, and when we get held up at a police checkpoint because of a bald spare tyre, everyone demands to be let out to get some fresh air. We are kept waiting for an hour and seek whatever shade there is. The new tyre has the canvas showing through, but the police are happy. No doubt they pocketed the fine. Once more we enter the bus's fetid interior.

The lady tells me she is returning to Ouagadougou University to complete her geography degree, then never speaks to me again. As soon as the sun goes down she puts on a thick jumper and, after the dinner stop, covers herself in a thick blanket. When she takes it off at the end of the journey a waft of her superheated air hits me. It is eleven o'clock at night and I am still sweating in shirt sleeves.

If we were in Mali, she would have talked the whole way, and I would have known all about her and her family, but here people are much less outgoing. A Belgian professor, who has taught at the University for 18 months, still does not know if his driver is married or whether his fellow teachers have families. No-one has ever asked him round for a meal.

Over the next couple of days Moyenga tries to contact the Gorum Gorum horse breeder, but no luck. With my visa close to expiry, I feel I have learnt what I can about the remnants of equine culture here and it is time to start the long journey home.

***

The old equine world is steadily being replaced by the new. Traditional games, which were often training for war, are giving way to modern games such as show jumping. Those who can afford them, buy imported competition and race horses. These are often crossed with the indigenous horses to 'improve' them. Whereas the progeny might be larger or faster, they often lose their resistance to local diseases and parasites, and only thrive if given a much improved diet.

It is wonderful that there are people like Doljit who are not only trying keep the traditional games alive, but also the ancient breeds on which the games are played. Whether they are wealthy like Baba Ahamado Danpullo in Cameroon and do it on a grand scale, or less well-off like the eagle hunters of the Altai, it is the enthusiasm of these horsemen which will preserve the history and spirit of tribal horse games, even if they are watered down to attract tourists.

As for me, I believe there are still undocumented equine cultures to be recorded and I need to find them before they disappear, so my search will continue…

Other equestrian titles published by Merlin Unwin Books

www.merlinunwin.co.uk

The Byerley Turk Jeremy James

Saddletramp Jeremy James

Vagabond Jeremy James

The Tack Room Paula Sells

Horse Racing Terms Rosemary Coates

The Ride of my Life Michael Clayton

The Racingman's Bedside Book BB

Right Royal John Masefield